A ROMANY

by

GIPSY PETULENGRO

With four illustrations

Gipsy Petulengro

TO
MY MOTHER
ANYETA

CONTENTS

A ROMANY LIFE

ILLUSTRATIONS

The sketches are drawn by the Author

I

To be asked where I was born or how I spent the first few years of my life would be more than I could answer. A Romany mother has no time to waste telling her child of birthdays, even did she know them. My mother and father did not know their ages, let alone the dates on which they were born. Each day to a Romany is the same, red-lettered here and there by the big fêtes and fiestas.

I have a dim memory of a river and a great assembly of *tans*, the tents which were the homes of the people to whom I belong. Old men with lean, spindly legs; old women with faces the colour of mud and wrinkled like the outer shell of a walnut; some with hooked noses and piercing black eyes, making them look like birds of prey. These were the *choovahanees* of the tribe, the witches or fortune-tellers, the kind of old women who, in spite of, or perhaps because of, their ugliness, are preferred by the ladies and gentlemen for the reading of hands and the laying out of the *Tarots*. There were young girls, lithe, strong, with skins like an olive, and pretending to be shy, especially when the *boro-ryes* were near. The *chals* ever on the alert for begging, and countless mud-stained *chavis*, bare-legged, bare-footed, tousled-headed. Such a one as these last was your humble servant, who, at that distant time, rejoiced in the simple name of Tarno Siani (Little Brilliant One), later to become Petulengro.

I have been told since that the river was the Danube and the town which we were near was Galatz in Roumania. The

I

Blue Danube they call it, but what little I remember of it is that the only blue thing about it was its smell. I can remember being one of the children who used to go down to the ships that lay in the river, and remember also how surprised we always were at the ignorance of the men we found there because they could not speak to us in any language we could understand. We used to wonder among ourselves where these ships went to. We had never heard of anything being beyond the horizon, so we supposed that they went to the brim and then came back again. It seemed a foolish thing to do. I write of the days when windjammers were still much in evidence and steamboats were not what they are to-day. We were often scolded and sometimes *coored* for wasting so much of our time watching the sailors repairing the canvases and repainting their ships.

One day a big, strange ship came into port. On this *beren* was what to my round new eyes looked the most beautiful and most gracious lady it was possible to imagine. She invited three or four of us *chavis* on the ship and tried to talk to us. She could not speak Romany, Roumanian, or Albanian, but she made by signs an invitation for us to take *habben* and we went inside and had a sumptuous feed. Even now I remember that it was salt beef, pickles, and a rice pudding. That is the only clue which now, so many years afterwards, makes me think it must have been an English ship. At that time I could not speak English, although my father spoke English and Welsh, being the son of Tinker Jasper Petulengro immortalized by George Borrow in his books. But he never used the language when with us for the simple reason that my mother, who was a pure-bred Berber Roumanian tsigane, could not understand it. Always they *rokkered* Romany together. We stayed so long on the ship that a commotion was caused in our camp and a search sent out for us. When eventually we were found there was not a very pleasant reception awaiting. I think that must be why my recollections begin at this period, for I can remember the thrashing I got to this day.

I have said that the lady was to me more beautiful than it is possible to imagine any one in the world could be. She was tall and fair as a lily, with hair the colour of butter, eyes blue as flowers, and teeth that shone like mother of pearl. We could not believe that she was an ordinary mortal and we felt she must be a queen from wherever she came. When we spoke of her together, she was the Big-Ship-Queen. The elder boy in our little party besought our lady to take us with her when the *beren* went away again. She could not understand him, so he made signs and pointed out to sea and then a finger to ourselves. The lady laughed a long time and called her *rom*, as I supposed he would be. He shook his head and also laughed, and with our quick, natural intuition we knew that it was *nanti-jal* : no go ! He made a sign putting his hand about five feet from the floor, which we understood to mean that when we were so tall we could go with him. He gave us each a present of money, some figs, and a bottle of sweets, the first sweets I had ever tasted not made by my own people. In spite of the chastisement we received for causing our folk alarm we risked it again the next day, but this time we were unlucky. The lovely Big-Ship-Queen and her fine *rom* had gone ashore and we were soon cuffed off by a rough-looking *beren-engro* with a drunken face who swore at us in French and shouted : ' *Allez-vous-en, sales voleurs.*' We departed crestfallen, but put our faith in the morrow. Alas, we were to be again disappointed ! The big ship had gone over the sea.

That is the first real memory of my life. As I have said, I do not know how old I was, but from what took place shortly afterwards—the departure of my twin brother from our *tan* to relatives in England—I must have been about four years old.

II

EVEN to the poorest *gorgio* child, working at four years of age would be a terrible hardship, but to the Romany boy and girl work comes as the natural order of the day from the moment they can stand on their feet.

While the *sors* are out fortune-telling or peddling their wares, the children are the home-tenders. Those of from séven to ten years *dikkas dur gryes*, tend the horses ; the girls of anything up to ten years are preparing the meals and cleaning-up generally ; the younger children as soon as they can toddle, are taught to *chorah de kash*, steal the wood, for the fire from the side of the river where there is always a plentiful supply of sea drift-wood, which the children take to the *tans*, chop up and use for the *yag* on which all the food is prepared and the water boiled.

In some camps the *yag* is communal. Together children of every *tan* make a great heap of wood, especially when a *bouri-pennen* is being held by the elders, and near the glowing embers of the *yag* the fiddles are brought out and singing, dancing, and merry-making rouse the night. Those are the nights the *chavis* live for ! In little groups of their own, the *chis* and *chals* sit together and play the simple games of *chingar-piera*, a game similar to your English game of five stones, or with little cubes of wood made by themselves play the game called *opré t'a télé* : ups and downs. The elder boys of from, say, ten to fifteen years, play another game using feathers stuck in the end of a piece of *puvengra* with which they play a game much like battledore and shuttlecock, using two pieces of stick as bat. The idea is to knock the potato to a certain height and try to make it fall in a marked circle, scoring points the nearer it falls to the centre. Great skill is needed to excel at this game and no Romany *chal* is considered of any standing until he can toss the potato to perfection. The bigger girls, the *juvvals*, seldom join in any games, but sit in their own circle and are content to tell fortunes and talk to each other of their desires in life, meaning lovers. Like the cinderella of your *gorgio chavis*, they are mostly in favour of marrying a *tarno roy*, a prince, and they relate to each other with great joy and greater imagination how the *boro-rye* and his *chal* gave them the *kooshti akha*, the lingering look. And great is the jealousy caused if a *juvval* can prove that she received a look from a bigger personage than the others. They also prepare and compare their creams and beauty secrets. A Romany *chi* would not risk the doubtful things *gorgio* ladies smear on their faces because told to do so. She likes to know what she puts on her flesh. She is very conservative in these things and not being able to read all the alluring advertisements, she continues with the creams her ancestors used 5,000 years ago. So they sit together gossiping and comparing and even massaging each other's faces with the *Rikkeni Chis Churlo*, literally translated : the Lovely Girls' Cream. The *juvval* is setting the snare.

Usually things go off merrily and peacefully at a *bouri-pennen*, and the finale is the *bosa-veno* playing the fast Romany step-music that puts fire in your feet and sets the blood pounding in your heart as the whole tribe joins in a wild good-night dance before turning reluctantly to their tents. It is when the different tribes meet and when they argue about the rights of territory at the *bouri-pennen* that trouble starts. Then is the time when blood is spilled, heads are cracked, tents torn to ribbons, and the Romany equivalent to the Corsican vendetta begins. Of these I have seen many, and even a few among the peaceful English gipsies who to-day are mostly *diddikais*, and whose nomad life is tame indeed compared with the adventure and hardship which is the lot of the Continental Romany.

It is not necessary to have a row to start a fight. A fight can begin most agreeably, as with the Irish. You can have a good-natured fight at any time and any age by going up to a youth and saying for all to hear : ' You couldn't do now what you did to me two years ago ! ' A challenge irresistible to any Romany ! And then while the others sit round, you have a nice little set-to. But in a real mêlée it always means a fight to the finish, and the quicker they are knocked out the better we like it. It is the women, here, who make the most havoc. Indeed, they turn it into a massacre. Even the men are more afraid of the women than of the men, and do not really like it when the women rush in. One thing you can be sure of when the women take a hand—the fight will soon be over. It never lasts long after their wild entry. What scares the men is, of course, that the women have nails. Men use only their fists. And many is the man I have seen with his face like a ploughed field after the women have leapt in and done for him. Moreover, a man does not fight at his best against a woman, he usually contents himself with warding off her blows and concentrates more on defending himself than on attacking her. It is not a fair fight and the women know it and, being women, they do not bother how fair it is so long as they win it. When I have heard *gorgios* talk of the gladiators of Rome, I have often thought that to a Romany mêlée they would have looked a picnic. To see the women leaping in and tearing handfuls of hair off each other's heads and pulling each other's ear-rings out so that for the rest of their lives the old women proudly carry with them their slit ears as battle trophies, you would begin to understand how perfectly business can be combined with pleasure !

III

IT was in the spring following the incident of the Big-Ship-Queen that I remember my first real highway *trek*. The tents were loaded up on the carts. The tinkering tools were all prepared, new soldering-irons, bottles of flux for making the solder run, sheets of copper bought for making kettles, and coils of wire for making all the necessary articles eventually to be sold in the *tarno-gavastes* through which we must pass. Flour, suet, which would be rolled in flour and sealed down, had been bought from the *mastengro*, and the dozen and one little things which the Zingari *rovel* uses for preparing her family's food, were all placed on a separate cart. The organization a good Romany *rovel* puts into her commissariat would beat the efforts of many a quartermaster of a regiment of soldiers. Nothing it seems possible to imagine is ever forgotten. Who but a real Romany when travelling would think of including such things as whole peppercorns and whole mustard seed to be ground by the *chavis* as pepper and mustard are needed by their elders ?

When families of the tribe come to a forked road, lots are usually cast to see who shall go to the right and who take the left. No other method of decision would be possible, so great a part do Fate and superstition play in the lives of the *tatcho* Zingari. If one has already gone ahead, he has taken his choice, and it is then that the *patteran* is brought into use. The *patteran* is used in every country where there are gipsies. I use the word *patteran* here because it is the word used in this country. They say it means a leaf, but gipsies of Hungary and Germany call it the *zinken* or sign. The French gipsies call it *dessin*, and I think myself the word *patteran* is a gipsy corruption of the word pattern or design. Let me explain how the *patteran* is used. Each member of a tribe has his own design, that is to say the *rom* or head of the particular family, as you *gorgios* have your crests, arms, armorial bearings. Our *patterans* are often every bit as elaborate and certainly are treated with as great a respect, though we put ours on the trees and roadways rather than on note-paper and silver. If a *rom* or husband of the family decided to take a certain road he marks his *patteran* on the ground with a piece of wood or iron or chalk. If he has any other members of the family with him he puts their marks and their number and sex in long and short strokes down the tail of his *patteran* so that the family following will then take the other road, thus avoiding working on each other's territory, and all other families following would have to pass along the *boro-drom* till they came to free roads where they could place their own signs. It is the rule of the road not to go down the fork-road where the *patteran* is marked and it is rare that Romanys poach on each other's preserves, so troubles are not usual from this cause.

I cannot tell the names of the *tarno-gavastes* or *boro-gavastes* through which I travelled in Roumania, Bosnia, Herzegovina, and other countries through which I *trekked* in my childhood days. The big days were the fiestas and fairs. My father would be bartering for ponies and goats and from what I can remember he found it a difficult task. The various Romani dialects of gipsies from different countries take a lot of understanding and it was my mother who came in useful then as interpreter. The reason my father found it difficult was that he was brought up in England and Wales. His name indicated his trade, and the trade of his ancestors : *Petul-engro*, horseshoe maker, or smith. As a young man he started out as a *grye-kuper*, horse-dealer, trading Welsh and Exmoor ponies in Hungary and Roumania, and it was while engaged in his business that he met and married my mother. He never really mastered the difficult *chib* of the Roumanian Zingari, but love speaks all languages and love won. He stayed in Roumania for some time, but would leave us suddenly for months at a time, and finally decided to take us back with him for good. There were times when my mother and the family were left so long alone that it seemed almost as though we had been deserted, but since, of course, I have learnt that they were the times my father had to travel to Inyanterra or Wolsenya for more *gryes* and ponies, and to take back

8

the Hungarian horses he had either bought or taken in exchange.

During these absences we were all placed under the care of a brother and a sister-in-law of my mother's. My uncle's name was Mascka Zlerak, Zlerak being the family name of my maternal grandmother and grandfather. Mascka was a giant, six foot four, and looked mightier still beside his wife, Lavanya, who was scarcely five foot high. He was enormous-shouldered, with hair not black but slightly iron grey and tough as horsehair. He had peculiarly thick eyebrows, the hairs hanging down over his great hazel eyes, the whites of which were vivid as egg-white. He had a heavy military moustache, and a broad neck which hung slightly forward, giving it a belligerent look, ready to attack, the battering centre of his great strength.

Lavanya, his wife, had a skin like ivory and hair as black as a raven's feather. She was extremely superstitious even for a Romany and everything to her was a sign of luck or disaster. A crow alone would bring sorrow and she would hide her face. A croaking raven, a sure sign of death. Indeed, in all our lives the croaking raven as messenger of death has had a deep and uncanny significance for our family. The *cherikko*, the wagtail, which is the lucky bird of the Romani, would bring old friends to your *tan*. To find a broken flower on the road and pick it up would mean news of a sickness to a relative. The moth flying around the house and which is not the one that gets in clothes, must not be killed for it is the soul of a dead *gorgio* seeking something. A toad walking across the road, a sure sign of an enemy. A croaking frog, news of a birth. A *juvval* finding a bird's egg on the road would have a child before the year was out. A black ear of rye in a field, a gift of gold. A black man first thing in the morning was good luck ; a grey horse likewise. A man with a wooden leg was lucky ; a wooden-legged woman a curse. A cross-eyed man would bring us great luck ; a cross-eyed

9

woman would take our luck away. To this day Lavanya's fears and joys at simple everyday things hedge me in, impatient as I get with myself at times. I would not care to count the times I have given up work in disgust for the day on meeting a cross-eyed woman, for no stronger reason than that when I was a *chavi* Lavanya would have shaken her head in sign of evil, and foretold disaster to all our plans.

IV

MASCKA ruled us with a will of iron, and we *chavis* were always anxious for the return of our father, who, although not big and impressive as Mascka, could take his own part and would never tolerate any interference from him.

The first serious fight I ever saw was between these two.

Lavanya was an exceedingly attractive-looking woman. She had been out peddling, and a young farmer, charmed by her smile, had asked her to take a glass of wine with him on the bench outside his door. She sat a while in the afternoon sunshine sipping her wine and smiling at the good deal which no doubt she had just made, all unaware that Mascka was watching her from a distance with eyes like thunder. The wine finished, she said good-bye and probably added some amiable words of Romany good luck, and went on down the road with her peddling.

Now it must be understood that *gorgio* people have been wilfully and stupidly misled about the morals of Romany women. Their code of behaviour is so strict from early childhood that to look seriously at any man but their *rom* does not enter their thoughts. To look seriously at a *gorgio* would make them a pariah. Their smiles and glances are part of their charm, and as unconscious. They smile when they approach you for the obvious reason that if you have something to peddle or a fortune to tell, you will not get very far with a frown.

Lavanya, then, was doubly wrong. Not only had she accepted a glass of wine from a man but from a *gorgio* man. Innocent as it all was, she deserved by Romany law the beating-up that was in store for her. Mascka, his heart black with anger and his jaw set savagely, waited for her to come home, and as soon as she entered the tent he rose and went straight up to her. Mascka said no word and made no sound. He got hold of her hair with one twist of his huge hand and pulled her to him, and with his clenched fist he gave her a blow like a hammer full in the face. Then he took a closer grip on her hair, jerked her off her feet, swung her round, and flung her in a corner as he would fling a dead hare. He was just going to give her some more when my father came up.

My father went straight to where Lavanya lay, obviously to help her, and Mascka made a blow at him. My father immediately threw his coat away and they set about each other, while we children squatted in a huddle like little sheep, strained and frightened. Fear mingled with doom in our little hearts for we thought Mascka would make short work of our father who, though a tall man, was thin and wiry and not thick and heavy like the powerful Mascka. But what a surprise we got. In the first few minutes it was clear to us all that my father was by far the better fighter of the two. He was cool and unhurried, where Mascka was furious and uncalculating. He struck out in all directions, his head down, his aim wild. My father dodged and side-stepped, timing his blows and hitting hard and frequently. It was the first time we had ever seen brain pitted against brawn and neither we nor Mascka ever forgot it. Suddenly Mascka got a lucky one home, made a lunge and split my father's ear across so that the lobe hung in ribbons. My father wore gold ear-rings, but the ear-ring was torn clean out by the blow. Never had I seen such blood as poured down over my father's face and neck. Blood seemed everywhere and we thought it was indeed the end. But the sight of his own blood seemed only to make my father fight more savagely still. The more blood, the more blows. We youngsters could distinguish nothing of the fighters. Only the thud-thud-thud of the blows as they went home. I remember vividly that everything about us seemed aware of the fight. The tension communicated itself to our very beasts. Our dogs were yelping and straining at the leash to get free and have a scrap themselves. Even the birds, to my small mind, seemed all at once to be whistling madly. The mules and donkeys turned round to watch and stamp with impatience and bewilderment. My father's great dog, half-mastiff half-wolfhound, that could have torn Mascka to bits, barked and howled and clanged his heavy chain. But not a sound from their own lips, not a murmur, not a groan. Only the thud-thud of the blows and the scraping of their feet as they fought for a hold.

They must have been fighting a good half-hour when my father crashed his fist on Mascka's jaw and Mascka went down like a log. He lay with his eyes closed and blood welling over his face and we all thought him dead. I remember well thinking as I squatted there watching : Where shall we bury Mascka ? That was all I worried about. A few days before we had buried a goat and dug a hole in a hedge and there had been great excitement among us *chavis* to whom digging a hole and putting something big in it had strange novelty and charm. Also I had heard from the bigger *chals* what fun a funeral fiesta was with the fiddles and dancing till dawn and more to eat than you could put away. I had just decided on the best place to dig the hole, when Mascka opened his eyes and did us out of the treat, and my mother ran to him and helped him round and made up poultices of chopped raw meat and a herb which had in it a little red flower.

When Mascka was on his feet and had got his balance back

he went sulkily to my father's tent and held out his hand. With this gesture he acknowledged my father the victor and put aside all ill will. Small as I was I was very wide awake and alert and I knew that my father had more than just won a stiff fight. He had seemingly done the impossible and had proved something that made us all not only admire his victory but respect him. Whenever I saw my father fight after that I had no fear for him and no doubts. He told me long afterwards that he spent some years with the sparring pavilions on the fair-grounds of Wales and Lancashire. And I have never forgotten his words to me : ' Never be afraid of a big un, son. There's more to hit ! '

No gipsy woman would dream of having a man who could not fight. She will go out and peddle and work herself to the bone and bring him back every farthing without question or murmur. But he must fight. Her one boast to another woman is always : my man can fight your man ! She takes the blows herself often enough, but at least she tells herself she knows the weight of her man's fist, and that consoles her for a lot of pain. Could one have read at the bottom of Lavanya's heart one would have seen that all her desire was to go and help Mascka against my father. Afterwards she was far more sorry to see Mascka smashed than ever he was himself. But my mother was rightly proud. It was her day. She held her fine head even higher. With every one concerned and all who heard of it, her stock went up from that time one hundred per cent.

Mascka and my father were now good friends again, and though I saw them argue and quarrel many a time afterwards I never saw them fight. Mascka seemed to realize that my father had a technique, probably acquired in that foreign country of his he boasted so much of, that was proof against all his brute force, and he wisely accepted his beating as final.

There had always been a certain tension between these two, and although the fight had eased it, it could not entirely banish

13

it. Mascka never tolerated competition or the slightest hint that any one could do something which he could not do and he was envious of the way my father used to boast of his far-away country. My father would sit over the *yag* at night and tell of the great people of the land who came to speak with him, and of how he had seen the Queen, and of how London was the greatest city in all the world. He could not keep a certain disdain from his voice at the ' provincials ' among whom he found himself. (He was wrong about this, as I was to learn later.) He would extol the virtues of the English and praise their sense of honour and gentleness of character. He spoke well, the fire of a Welsh enthusiasm added to a natural gipsy eloquence. He told them how enlightened were the people of England and of how, by comparison with other tribes, the English Romany were the more educated and more respected. He would boast to them of his father who was in the *boro-ryes lil*, the big gentleman's book, and so had become the most famous gipsy who ever lived. You could see Mascka scowl as he sat in the firelight looking through his heavy brows, and you could see my father pretending not to see Mascka's scowls and rubbing his triumph in like salt.

Moreover, my father had learnt little secrets at the English fairs which even Mascka, who seemingly knew all things, did not know. Little bits of fake magic, some neat conjuring tricks, card and domino swindles, and some small inventions which he had found and brought over with him. When he started on his mock magic he had Mascka beat without raising his fist. Mascka would sit like a small boy watching intently for the catch, showing by his contemptuous grin around his nose that he knew it was a fake and an easy fake at that, but never able to catch my father out.

Our greatest delight and astonishment was for the trick of the disappearing penny which my father would repeat again and again, pleased with our cries of dismay. This particular one had a great irritation for Mascka, and after watching closely

and finding no clue to how it could be done, he would turn
on his heel saying : ' What a stupid trick ! There is nothing
sensible in it ! To make a penny *disappear*. Make one
come, that would be a trick ! '

Now Mascka had a curious power over fish. He was a
wizard at tickling trout and he could charm even pike out of
the water, a thing my father never could do. Sometimes,
when my father had had more than usual success, and the
laughter and cries of admiration were more than Mascka
could bear, he would be heard to murmur scornfully : ' Much
more sense in getting a fish out of water than making a penny
disappear ! Much more sense, much more difficult ! '

But one night my father varied his trick. Not only did
the penny disappear, but a bright silver florin appeared in
its stead. And after that, of course, there was never any
argument about it !

V

I WAS saying that we came under Mascka's rule when my father
was away. He had not been gone five minutes but Mascka
seemed to take on a new personality. Before our astonished
young eyes he would appear to add five more inches to his
already magnificent height. Back would go his shoulders
and he would strut masterfully around us and we would get
our first lecture : ' I'm the *sherengro*. I'm the Big Man.
The chief. The Great I am.' And as he spoke he seemed to
tower above the earth like a moving mountain.

But what an apprenticeship ! What good fortune to have
begun life in the shadow of such a man ! I wonder if a day
in my life has passed that I have not had to thank Mascka for
something I had learned from him. For Mascka was, without
exaggeration, the most versatile man I ever saw. He was an

expert coppersmith. There was nothing he could not carve from wood. I have seen him carve a chair from one great solid block of the wood of the *akhor kopaci*, the walnut tree. He had no elaborate tools, not even tools which a poorer working-class man takes to his work. He had only a home-made chisel and a pocket-knife. Instead of the augers and bits and braces of the carpenter, Mascka relied on hot irons, and the result was a masterpiece for a museum. Round the legs and back he carved grapes and stems and leaves with their veins finely marked in a manner that would have given Grin-ling Gibbons something to think about. On the seat of the chair he carved his *gryes'* heads and a couple of dogs—lurchers, leaping—and all around the outside bevelled edge he carved dog roses. Mascka would never part with this chair, he loved it dearly. It took all his spare time and when he wanted to take his temper out he would be seen cutting and carving and polishing at his extraordinary chair till the mood was over. It took him two years to make and I would give a hundred pounds to know where it is now and to possess it. Mascka invented his hinged-moulds of plaster of Paris in which he cast the Saints and Virgins and Apostles he modelled and which we sold from door to door after giving them a licking of paint. He was the smith of the crowd. He could make a horseshoe quicker than I have ever seen an English black-smith make one, and many a time I watched admiringly as he placed his *sastra* on the *covantza* and *coored* for all he was worth.

I have seen him kill and dress a pig and snare every known vermin and bird you could name in field or tree, for he was a wonderful poacher, a great accomplishment with the Romani. He could make mats, carpets, nets, banjoes, fiddles. It used to be wonderful to us to hear Mascka get tunes from his home-made violins, and when he used to go to the taverns to *kil-i-bosh* he used to explain to us that he did it for two reasons. There were the times, he said, when he ' felt like

16

music,' but he was not going to play and waste the tunes : the peasant had to pay for them ! He would choose the time of the fairs, for those were good times for the peasants. The gold would be jingling, they had sold the old *gryes*, the calves, and those woolly pigs that look more like sheep than pigs. Their *pocis* would be filled and now for filling their stomachs —the tavern, the women, the wine, and the gipsy fiddler. Mascka would play the lead, the others would play second, sustaining the notes. Wine flowed and the *gorgios* would chant the *gillie* that Mascka would be playing. Suddenly he would break out into a different strain, weird unreal notes would come, first low, then rising higher, then low again, and the *gorgios* would or could not sing. They seemed to go dumb and nearly asleep. Mascka would then quickly go round with his sea-shell collecting the coins, and none was able to deny him. If a peasant seemed to give grudgingly, the wenches, the *gorgio racklers*, would take the money from the peasants' bulging purses and Mascka would make a good night of it. But Mascka used to say when they said to him : ' Why don't you go often and play your fiddle at the tavern ? '—' Oh, no, one can't always play. It's the *mullahs* of the long gone *bosa-venos* who invite me out, and only then do I go.' Mascka did not know a note of music, but no note of music ever escaped him, and there was no tune, real or invented, that he could not play at will.

Mascka used also to make rings from coins for the peasants at the fairs by a method as old as ring-making itself. He used to drill a hole in the centre of the coin and with a rawhide hammer, which he had made himself, he would hammer the rings into shape. If he hadn't a file he would rough it down with a certain kind of stone, then he would make us do the polishing, and no goldsmith in the world can polish a ring like a Romany boy. Mascka would save up every grain of the metal dust ; the gold going into one little bag, the silver into another. These bags were Mascka's savings bank and he had a considerable store of precious metal.

Mascka had a natural way of pushing points home and he was a wonderful teacher. During our working hours, in the evenings when the day's peddling was done, Mascka would gather the *chals* together and hand out the different work. The younger ones would be given the job of cutting old tins into strips for binding around clothes pegs. The next group would be given the job of whittling the pegs into shape. Mascka would then do the tricky part of the work, the cutting of the notch in the peg and he would make them with a speed and accuracy wonderful to watch. When the youngsters got behind in their work, Mascka would start on something new, for there were always a hundred things to make and a hundred jobs to be learnt. He never let you tire, knowing that a tired worker is a poor worker, but his fingers were never at rest and he saw to it that yours were not either. Mascka would scrutinize each piece of our childish work with long and minute care. If it were not up to his standard of what he thought such work should be he returned it to you. He never explained ; he returned it. If you asked him what was wrong he would say : ' My brains are for my body, your brains are for yours.' And you soon set to and found your mistake out by yourself. Romanys waste few words.

Wonderful as his work was, it was never perfect. In every thing Mascka made there was a fault. That was one of the earliest things he impressed on us as he taught us our work, the Romany ruling that none shall make a perfect work. In all our work, therefore, there is a fault, an intentional fault, perhaps one side less straight than the other, four holes where there should be only three. We never compete with the Creator. We Romanys say that He alone may permit Himself perfection in His work.

Mascka, besides his skill in making all things, was an expert at glass-blowing. He would take small rods of glass, put them

18

in flames from a special blow-lamp with two burners facing each other, and make all kinds of glass fantasies. He would fashion small birds in white or opaque glass, then he would put the wings of the bird in a different colour, pink or green, a yellow beak, and two little dots of black to form the eyes. These birds he would then fix while in the molten state at the bottom of a long pin, and they would be sold as tiepins to the peasants. He had also a contraption like an ordinary grinding barrow which he would pedal exactly as for knives and scissors. He would melt the end of a glass rod in the flame and pedalling quickly would make spun glass as fine as silken threads gather on the face of the wheel and the silk-like glass would become the tails of the birds or be braided into neckties.

Mascka also had a little glass *Beng*, devil, which placed in an ordinary bottle could be made to do all sorts of fantastic gyrations inside it. He taught me the secret of how it was worked, and I have made and sold many thousands of them in all the fairs of the world.

But Mascka's masterpiece was an especially large *Beng*, which he would ' graft ' with at the fairs and fêtes, and with which he never failed to cause a sensation among the superstitious peasants, and townsfolk too for that matter. He claimed that his *Beng* had supernatural powers, could read all thoughts and answer all questions. He had a very large glass cylinder about eighteen inches tall and six inches wide. This was fixed into a walnut base and filled with water. The big *Beng* would be at the bottom of the cylinder, watching out and seeming to meditate. A big leaden top supplied the necessary pressure for making the *Beng* gyrate as Mascka told him to, giving the correct note of black magic and hocus-pocus. Mascka, having put his *Beng* through weird or amusing motions, would then call on the peasants standing around to ask his *Beng* any question they desired. The peasants would hand over a couple of lei and to the astonishment of all who tried their luck the *Beng* never failed to give a satisfactory answer to their queries.

This was Mascka's secret. Upon what looked like plain bits of paper he had written (or, rather, had had written for him, for he could not even make his own mark) with a solution of lead, four infallible answers to any question it is possible to ask. *Yes. No. Very Soon. Not at present.* If you think those out you will find that they will answer to your perfect satisfaction any question put to them with a subtlety which at least the Devil could not surpass. Mascka would place one of these slips of paper in the receptacle at the top of the lead cap. As he raised the cap and took off the pressure the *Beng* would obligingly rise to the top of the bottle. Mascka, with much elaborate politeness, would then ask him to write his answer to the questioner's secret thoughts, and behold ! written on the blank paper by the obedient and captive *Beng*, the answer would be handed to the awe-struck crowd. Of course the supposedly clear paper with the sugar of lead writing had been developed by ammonia during its stay in the receptacle, but as no one knew this but Mascka it seemed to the crowd of onlookers that Mascka was in league with the Devil in person and was getting his answers straight from hell itself.

To add to this impression of all hell at his beck and call, Mascka had cleverly had his four infallible answers written in many languages, for among the peoples of Roumania there were different nationalities by the score at the fairs we visited : Croats, Slovenes, Serbians, Montenegrins, Greeks, and many reading only French. So before getting the blank paper out Mascka would make great play of asking his client in what language he would like his answer and it looked even more occult and sulphurous to the *joskins* to see the papers come out in their different tongues. But one day Mascka caught a tartar. A foreign *rye* said in answer to Mascka's question : 'English.' Now Mascka hadn't any papers written in English, but nothing could ever catch him off his guard. So he said :

'I am sorry, noble sir, but the Devil he doesn't understand English.' The Englishman and his friends had a good laugh at this and he was eventually persuaded to try one in French. But when he had read it he said loudly : ' Well, I don't know what language they do speak in hell, but his French is damn' bad too ! ' Mascka still had his reply and came back quickly with : ' Well, you must understand, gentlemen, that the Devil never had a schoolmaster when he was a boy. He's had to teach himself all he knows ! ' The Englishmen roared with laughter, but it didn't worry Mascka, who went on collecting the lei.

That was another lesson I learnt from watching Mascka. Never be at a loss for a reply, and that a quick retort will save many a difficult situation. I had my training early, too. Once as a lad I was out peddling mottoes and cards at the cottage doors in some remote Somerset villages, Bible texts and pretty sayings about love and good weather coming soon and not to get up late, lazybones, or the day will be done. We *chavis* peddling these ' smudges ' as they are called, naturally could not read and we relied on the country-women who answered the door to take her choice and tell us what they said. But one day even the country-woman was baffled. She looked at the motto a long time and then looked at me and said : ' Well, this is a funny one ! I'm sure I can't make head nor tail of it ! ' ' Spell it out, missus,' I told her, wondering what was coming next. She spelt out laboriously with a shake of her head : *Ici on parle Français.* ' Ah ! ' I said quickly before she could get her breath back, ' that's the lucky Romany card, and it means God Bless our Happy Home ! '

Anyway, I cleared my stock all out, so you can see a Romany will always find his way out of a tight situation.

VI

BUT with all Mascka's teaching there was still another who put us through our paces. Everything my mother made in lace-work or wool-work the *chals* and *chis* had to learn. She used to make a lot of woollen bootees for baby wear with a crochet-hook, which was also hand-made, either by Mascka or one of the children, from an old razor handle. My mother would crochet the bootees while we *chavis* would help by braiding the tie-up and making the tassels. My mother always said you could not learn too much, and next we were taught by her to make daisy-mats. These were made on a wooden frame studded with nails or pieces of wire which projected from the frame about one inch. Backwards and forwards we would wind the wool, then the squares would be knotted and finally cut, making the entire mat a mass of daisy flowers. We soon could turn out these mats very quickly, even the smallest children making six to seven in an evening. In the morning they would be sold by the *juvvals*, the young girls of fifteen to eighteen, at the doors.

Then we were put to net-making. Potato nets, fishing nets, poaching nets, and my mother would examine our work with a severe eye. However well a Romany can do a thing it is a boast that the next time it shall be done just twice as well. None would ever think of passing off a piece of inferior work. We say : There is always room for improvement or embellish-ment, so try it next time. In this the *gorgio* worker seems lazy and careless to us, and knows little that is of real practical use to man or woman. A Romany without a penny in his pocket can travel the world, a hundred trades at his finger-tips, a thousand tricks in his head. We Romany *chavis* learn twenty-four hours of the day and night from the age of three, and thenceforth are able for the rest of our lives to pick our way about the world, knowing that wherever we may find ourselves we have our livelihood in our nimble fingers and our sharp wits. The *gorgio chavi* by comparison wastes his most impressionable years, learning nothing of use to him till the age of fifteen or, if rich, twenty-three, and is then a slave for the rest of his life, nailed to the one spot, able only to do one job and trembling for that from the moment he gets it.

Our training was Spartan. No emotion was lavished on us. There were more blows than kisses, for we are a race that does not kiss but can always take or give a beating. No matter how excellent the work, no rewards were given. None were expected. There was never any praise for good work, only severe scoldings for a *wafodi* piece. Romany *chis* and *chals* are not pampered and the harder the knock he or she can take the better thought of by all. It is no use howling if in making a peg the knife slips and gashes your thumb. Better not draw attention to it, however deep the wound, or you'd get a cuff on the ear as well. What were you doing to get the cut? Thinking of something other than your work. That'll teach you to concentrate in the future. No frantic mamma or school-marm rushing about with bottles of disinfectant and bandages in alarm, reading up in the daily paper what to do when your child cuts itself. No sympathy was given : none was asked. Although my mother was the finest parent a child could wish for she lavished no unnecessary emotion on us. The idea was to keep us from becoming *bilaco*, soft or effeminate. It is a hard world you have to face, she would say, so start facing it young.

Evenings, after the daily toil, would be passed away with my mother telling legends, queer happenings, and little stories of mythical birds and animals, and always with the hero, a boy with a bald head, who could catch birds as they flew, charm wild animals and dragons, and for whom no difficulty was too great to overcome. She would teach us of the habits of animals and insects by telling us the Romany superstitions

c   23

concerning them. As, for instance, the reason why we must never kill a spider, as there was once a Romany princess called *Aranyi* (our word for spider) who boasted that she had from the gods the gift of making silk finer than the silkworm. She was told by a gipsy *choovahanee* that only one insect in the world could do that. The princess jeered at the old woman who then told her that since she could spin more finely than the silkworm and since only the spider could do that, she would be turned into a spider. Hence the reason no Romany will kill a spider and bring on himself Aranyi's curse of evil luck.

I remember also my mother telling us of the old Romany legend handed down since the Crucifixion of why we gipsies are allowed to steal once every seven years. My mother said that while the procession was resting on its way to Calvary, an old gipsy woman came into the crowd and asked what was happening. She was told, and when she saw the look of anguish on the Saviour's face she took pity on Him and thought she would like to prevent the crucifixion. 'If only I could steal those nails,' she thought. She stole one and threw it away. But at the second attempt she was caught by the soldiers and thrashed. The old Romany begged for mercy, saying : ' I haven't stolen anything for seven years ! ' One of the Disciples standing near said to her : ' You are blessed, now. The Saviour allows you to steal once every seven years from now onward ! ' My mother used to tell us as *chavis* that that was the reason why only three nails were used and why the feet of Jesus were crossed.

She would tell us of the old gipsy woman who told the great King : ' You are like the half-moon but your rival the other King is like to the full moon,' and just as the King was having her cast into prison she explained that he was like the half-moon growing ever bigger and more powerful, whereas his rival was the full moon who must grow ever smaller till it fades to nothingness, and, the King was so pleased, he gave her

24

a bag of gold. Kings were always rewarding us gipsies in those days, if my mother's stories were anything to go by. It was the unlucky brother who went to play with the rest before the King. The King was so charmed that he said : ' Fill up their instruments with gold ! ' The unlucky brother played the piccolo. The next time they played to the King he was in a foul temper and said : ' Ram all their instruments down their throats ! ' And the unlucky brother was the only one whose instrument would go down his throat ! This last story made a great impression on me as a *chavi* and I never would learn any musical instrument but the melodeon. However badly I played it, I felt at least no one would ever be able to ram it down my throat !

So versatile was my mother that she seemed to me even then a female counterpart of Mascka. But she had far greater knowledge than he, knowledge and intuition and a wisdom that had no bounds and a patience bordering on the miraculous. Handed down to her from centuries of Berber ancestry was her unrivalled knowledge of herbs and healing. She knew every herb and wild plant, and, as though it were a sacred charge and duty, she insisted on our learning the names and uses of them. She was the doctor of the community and every one came to her in their difficulties. She was the midwife, the mender of broken joints, the wise woman whose touch was magic and who knew the cure of all ailments.

My mother had great faith in the *Duvel*, God, and never did anything without a little request for His help in the curing of her patients. For my mother was *Duveleskoe*, and was not afraid to tell all the world about it. The hard-heads who derided religion would chaff her and make fun of some of her beliefs, but no chaff or laughter could turn her from her faith in the *kooshti-Duval*, and she carried her faith to the grave. My mother's faith was simple and true. She taught us never to take what was not ours. A rabbit, a pheasant, a partridge, she said, the good God gave to us as well as to the *gorgio*.

25

The *boro-ryes*, the gentlemen, she thought were the biggest thieves because they stole the land from the poor. That was her opinion. She believed that when *Duvel* created the earth and peopled it He meant that every one should share in the fruits of the earth, but that with the coming of the mighty-men, the greedy *sherengros*, things changed. They wanted the double share but did not want to do the single share of work. So she said, to take what *Duvel* sends is right. But to take what another man grows is wrong. In this way we were taught to get the rabbits and hares and other game, but always to respect the property of those who have earned and worked it.

To my mother's way of thinking Mascka was, of course, a black sheep, the blot on her family's good name. Mascka did not keep very narrowly to the path of honesty. He was, as I have said, a most versatile man. He could always earn money. How he chose to earn it now and again was his own affair. He did strange things, often more for excitement than for gain. Mascka boasted that he never let any one get the better of him and he would wait years to get his own back, but mostly Mascka got somebody else's back. Many a time I have heard my mother plead with him and entreat him to mend his ways. He would promise good-humouredly, but he would never *coor dur duk*, strike the hand, on it, which is the Romany oath broken only at death. So we all knew that Mascka would be as bad as ever in his own arrogant way.

The winters for the Roumanian Romani are very trying, and combined with the rough method of living and the activ-ities of petty police officials, things are made very difficult. There was always some trouble over certain pitches, but graft and baksheesh are rife in Roumania and it was always the twenty-lei notes that would act like a gipsy balm on a sore face. My father was pretty headstrong and, having been bred in England and Wales where graft with the gipsies was a thing unknown, was always in difficulties with the police authorities.

It was always either Mascka or my mother who would have to do the clearing away of trouble. It would always be my father who by his stubbornness and refusal to understand that petty Roumanian police are not easy-going English village constables, would push them head first into it again.

Once my father was taken before a local judge on some trumped-up charge about allowing some horses or some ponies to be on prohibited ground, and was fined fifty lei or their equivalent in ' time '. At the very last moment Mascka arrived triumphantly on the scene with the necessary lei. My father, trained as I say in England, was furious at the injustice of the charge and was perfectly willing to do ' time ' rather than pay them what they asked. He remonstrated with Mascka for wasting our hard-earned money on them, when Mascka shrugged his shoulders and said with a grin : ' Don't make a fuss ! I've just had fifty lei worth of his geese this morning ! '

VII

WE had been *trekking* for about a month (stopping only a day or two at the various small fêtes, mostly to enable Mascka to work his *Beng*, and the other members of the *trek*, Lavanya, Thoda, Horda, and Mirella, to peddle their wares and tell fortunes) when our people decided to lay up for a week on the outskirts of a big town where Mascka knew of a free camping-ground.

Our party mustered about thirty-five all told, including the *chavis*. A distant relation of Lavanya's had joined us. He was a splendid specimen of a man and his name was Tonescu. He had with him his son, a youth of about eighteen years, and his two daughters, Pakotav and Zafora. They were twin sisters, a glowing olive colour, and very tall and supple. These

27

girls were *sapengros*, snake charmers, handling anacondas and boa-constrictors, and they could always be relied on to create a furore at the fairs we visited. They also did an acrobatic turn with their brother and their boast was that the trio in strength was a match for six ordinary people. Events were always happening to prove their boast well founded ! Mascka, Lavanya, and their *chavis* went on ahead to map out the pitch. Our *vardo* with our family was a mile or two behind, followed by Tonescu, his family, and another Romany whom we had nicknamed Humpty. Humpty used to work as a weight-lifter, fire-eater, and wrestler. He had attached himself to our party and was general handy-man in return for food and accommodation.

When Mascka arrived at the camping-ground he found that another tribe of Transylvanian Romanys had already pitched in one corner. Mascka gave them the friendly greeting and the secret sign, but they turned very hostile, explaining to Mascka that they expected another contingent of friends to arrive shortly. Mascka tried to point out that there was room for all and explained that he had a priority on the pitch, having been there every year for many years past. Having explained this he turned his back and without further ado began to drive in his stakes and erect his billy-hook. Just then we arrived on the scene. As Mascka was bent over his stakes a member of the rival tribe went up to Mascka's billy-hook, pulled it from the ground, and kicked over his water-can. Immediately Mascka straightened up, took on a fighting attitude, and pushed him away. That started the fight. The two men hammered savagely at each other for a few minutes till other members of the rival tribe came to their man's aid and Mascka was surrounded by four or five of them. My father, seeing Mascka's plight, left our horses and went to his assistance, pushing the other men away and leaving Mascka and his rival to fight it out alone. With this they started on my father. My father used the expression : 'One dog, one bone !' and

' *Our* vardo *with our family was a mile or two behind. . . .*'

picked on the largest remaining of the four. But it was no use. The others tried to trip him up and one gave him a blow on the back of the head from behind. When Lavanya saw this she picked up a heavy steel-lined whip that my father had dropped and took a hand in the matter. Now Lavanya was only a small piece of a woman but with the butt-end of that whip she played havoc. She was quick as lightning in her movements and she struck a younger member of the rival tribe a terrific blow on the head and he went down like a log.

That brought the women of the other tribe into the fight and then my mother joined in. Her weapon was a soldering-iron, a lump of copper attached to an iron handle. The other women brought into play tent stakes, bits of iron rod, and anything they could lay hands on. Our party was heavily outnumbered and things began to look serious. Mascka had just got his man well beaten, when a woman of the opposite tribe hit him across the forehead with an iron stake and once again I thought poor Mascka's number was up. Just then Humpty and Tonescu and his family came up. Humpty seemed to take in the situation at once. He seized two females of the opposite side, one in each hand, and banged their heads together like coco-nuts. I think Humpty's face scared them more than the knocks, for he was not too pleasant to look at. The two women screamed and fled to their *tans*. Mascka's opponent then joined his mate to help knock out my father but Humpty gave him a blow that nearly broke him in two and down he went. My father by this time had his opponent beaten to a frazzle, and then the two Tonescu girls joined in, fresh and fit. They fought the other women like tigers. They punched, they scratched, they bit, they tore handfuls of hair from them, and within five minutes our side was master of the field. Immediately a truce was called, wounds were dressed, my mother being doctor, and the next morning the rivals departed, leaving us in sole possession.

VIII

THIS was the first real fight with another tribe that I had ever seen and it is one I have never forgotten. Starting out that morning Lavanya had seen a rat hopping on three legs and had said : 'A bad omen. We shall see blood spilled before sunset.' Only Tonescu was upset by the fight. He sulked all day and said he would not sleep that night as he and his son had missed a treat. Not a blow had they been able to strike. A big disappointment for a Romany !

Shocking as such fights must sound to fireside-sitting people, they are seldom to the death. The reason for this is that a Romany does not fight like a *gorgio*. He never hits a man when he is down. As soon as his man drops he leaves him and turns to the next one. Moreover, a Romany never kicks. I do not know why this is, but you will never find a Romany man kick. He will fight, scratch, pummel, wrestle, bite, but he will not kick. An ordinary single stand-up fight between two gipsies is fought with more decorum and more straightforward honesty than in any stadium in the world. Never would a Romany dream of hitting below the belt. He would not understand such tactics. He knows the inevitable law : one must win and one must lose. A good loser is often better thought of than the winner. And there is never any ill feeling afterwards. A youth will train and practise secretly for months to challenge his successful rival again, but without malice and with nothing underhand in his intentions. At sixteen I joined the militia purposely to get some good scientific training in boxing and self-defence, to get my own back on three youths who had bested me in some fights, though also to escape a gamekeeper whom I had just bested in a fight. I had always admired my father for his knowledge and science in fighting and for the way he got the better of men twice his size by his more intelligent methods. I jumped at the chance. I had seven weeks of bullying sergeants and not altogether gentle gymnasium instructors, and all the rest of the army nonsense, but I accomplished what I set out to do. I came back knowing how to fight, and I took them all on and surprised the lot of them. Later, in the army, I used to fight a world-champion club-swinger, a Sergeant Batterby. I was no good at swinging clubs but I certainly could lay him out !

Fighting is essential to the Romany. It is essential to his prestige and reputation. Just as millionaires want champagne and yachts and country houses, so a Romany must have his prestige. He can do without the champagne and the yachts but he cannot do without the reputation of being a fearless man. Besides, how otherwise could he get his women ? He must be looked up to and able to protect his own. He must be known as a man whose fists are to be reckoned with and whose shadow is an assured sign of protection.

But supposing, at a general fight, something serious has happened and some one dies. There is no such thing as running and fetching the police. The Romany has a fear of the law. A fear of its stupidities, its lack of understanding, and its waste of everybody's time. As soon as the police are brought in you get inquiries and detentions, and hours of blockhead interrogation, all leading nowhere. Who knows who did it ? Who knows who began it or ended it ? Who knows anything but that it was a fight to the finish and one side won and the other lost ? So the rivals give each other the sign of peace, call a truce, and take their man away for burial.

We Romanys do not weep at our funerals. We leave that to the sentimental and illogical *gorgio*, who delights in tears when faced with the serious issues of life, which, according to our way of thinking, they seem to have no philosophy to meet. We do not weep for our departed, because we believe that they have gone to a happier world. A world in which there are no policemen, no judges, no gamekeepers, and where angels have no finger-nails. We need nothing to remember him by. All that was ever his has been burnt so that his spirit shall not be earth-bound. We keep not a lock of hair and even his gold is boiled down before it is shared up among his relatives. He leaves no will, no tangles for lawyers to batten on, no enormous fees, no legal squabbles. We all know the dead man's wishes because they are the wishes of the tribe. All shall share in his wealth in equal parts, the same as our own shall be shared when we are gone.

When we have gathered in our dead, we prepare for the feast which must take place immediately after burial. We dig the grave. A coffin is made and the dead man placed in it, and according to Romany custom seven holes are then drilled in the lid. Each hole has a peculiar mystic significance. The first hole lies above the forehead, the hole through which the soul can leave. Two are for the eyes to see. Two for the ears to hear the music of the *bosaveno* playing the requiem. Two are lower still, below the heart, so that as the body disseminates it can pass through. They also bury a pair of heavy *chockas* with the corpse to enable him to travel over the burning wastes to Paradise. The coffin is then placed in the ground.

When this is done the fiddlers, the *bosavenos*, strike up and slowly, slowly the sad music conveys to the dead what the hearts of the living feel and their eyes do not shed. It becomes more wild, more wailing, drawn out like the long moment of a pain that can no longer be borne in silence. To the wild mournful scraping of the fiddles the muted clappers join, more subtle than castanets. Slowly the dance begins, the Death of the Spirit Dance, with slow reverent movements the spirit is wooed from its body, patiently at first, and then more wildly, angrily, furiously, louder and still more loud, the spirit of the dead man is invoked to leave its body. He

32

sees the dance. He hears the music. Through the last of the holes his spirit wrenches itself free from his body. Quickly the music changes, the dancers stop, the coffin is covered in with earth.

He has gone to his favourite tent or to his caravan, and the music follows him. The mourners surround his tent, oil and lumps of fat are thrown in, and after them his clothes and everything that has been his. Not a button may be kept: all that he has used, all that he has worn, must be consumed by the flames. His *vardo* also must be *yagged* for his spirit to be freed. As the flames leap higher and higher, so the music of the fiddles grows more wild and more eerie, as the spirit, freed from all earthly cares, takes the long *trek*, the *boro-trek*, to the sound of the *mullah gillie*, the Song of Hope.

There is more wild dancing and yet wilder music as we sing the song that accompanies the departed on his long journey. *Vov sos bichala dur cherinos t'a soli-pala andre dur boro-ceel lel soldo nanti coor, Trusal odi dur kooshti-Duval rigs lekki mullah nanicoored, ki-kavaki guglo-bashes san, t'a ki-kavaki dur tarno-roy da boshavenos kils.* [He who guides the stars and sun on their ways so that two shall never meet among all the millions of these worlds, the good God, shall take his spirit through unharmed to where a sweeter music is and where the prince of fiddlers plays.]

Music is played after the burial not only to guide the spirit on its way but to injure any enemy who may be around. To the Romany way of thinking the *bosh* must not be played vainly, for we think that the melody when played does not fade away but remains in the air and for ever hovers around the *mullah* of the departed. My mother used to tell us a story of how in her tribe seven Berber *chis* and seven Berber *chals* had to chant a certain *gillie* to make water flow and they would sing for seven hours without a break, and water would rise round their feet. She said they also used a special chant to exorcize evil spirits from people afflicted with certain com-

33

plaints, mostly mental. My mother would also tell how the
Berber Romanys could resuscitate their dead by mystic rites
and mystic music. She vowed that she had seen a corpse
return to life more than once and made to dance ; she spoke of
heliotrope lights streaming out from the reviver into the
corpse, and that the dead would sit up and answer questions
revealing the future, though it had been dead several moons,
and that then it was made to dance, and that afterwards they
would cut out the tongue and fill the mouth with some herbs,
possibly a kind of garlic, and later they would bury the corpse
again.

We had never known my mother to tell a lie and she was
so sincere in her descriptions of these rites that I for one
never doubted her.

IX

MEN with peaked caps and bright buttons and gold braid
looking over our carts and turning everything upside-down,
and suddenly things would go none too smoothly and we
would be compelled to camp on the same spot for a long time,
and then one day all would be excitement and we were off
again.

I did not know then that these were frontiers and that we
were passing through many countries, Serbia, Bosnia, Mon-
tenegro, Herzegovina, Albania, making for a port called
Antwerp which was the door to my father's land. Such a
trek is slow work and it is hard work. A Romany's day in
any case begins with the first faint indication of light on the
sky and ends when it is too dark to see the piece of work
held in the hand. On a *trek* a day has no beginning and no
end.

There were the small excitements of local fairs, and there

was one incident which stood out in my small mind, magnified by the promise it seemed to hold of a land of continuous feasting and gentlemen of great wealth. It was at the frontier of Herzegovina, when suddenly Mascka and my mother and all those who had done the talking in the various tongues before were struck dumb and it was my father's day. A man came up and spoke to us in English and at once my father came into his own. He spoke to my father of Cambridge and of its surroundings which my father knew well. He spoke of George Borrow and of Tinker Jasper Petulengro, my father's father. They were delighted with each other, and my father then announced that the *boro-rye*, the big gentleman, had asked us all to a feast in our honour that night and that we were to give of our best. What a feast that was ! Whole sucking-pig the big gentleman had had roasted for us, and the heavy peasant wine of the country flowed in our tankards. All the fiddles were brought out, the dancers twirled and clapped their hands, our singers sang their throats dry, and my father strutted like a peacock. This, his silent swaggering told us, was England. This was a great English gentleman and this was how he treated us. Had the others, the barbarian people of these crude lands, treated us to anything but impertinent condescension or downright ill-tempered abuse ? But this was an Englishman, said his arrogantly-held neck. The gentleman had brought his friends to show them a real gipsy festa, and they threw us gold pieces and laughed and drank to us and we were dazed with wine and happiness and showing off, and the fun only ended when we were too exhausted for it to continue. When I crept into bed with the other *chavis* very late that night I prayed that the *trek* would be over quickly and that soon, very soon, we would be in the land where sucking-pigs were roasted in our honour by great gentlemen and we were spoken to with soft voices and smiling eyes.

But the *boro-trek* had a long way yet to wind. We made

35

our way peddling from door to door the little plaster statuettes of the Virgin and Saints and Apostles which Mascka had made and cast and we had coloured. Or walnut-picking and shelling them for the markets, and the usual trades of lace-making, herb-selling and hand-reading.

It was about this time that I made myself my first fur cap. I do not know what its equivalent in joy would be to a *gorgio* child, but the first dream of a Romany boy is to catch a rabbit or a hare, skin and dress it himself. With these skins we make our caps, and bigger and expert lads make waistcoats and jackets in which they strut, the envy and admiration of us all, for the waistcoat and jacket are the sign of your prowess as hunter and poacher, greatest distinction of all to a Romany. When we had caught our rabbit or hare and skinned it, we would rub the skin with alum and lay it to dry in the sun where it became as hard as brick. We then rubbed it with olive oil and beat it with a raw-hide hammer, laying it on the fleshy part of the leg and hitting it as a shoemaker knocks nails into a sole. Then we would rub it gently between our hands till it became soft and supple. Thus was our first skin caught and cured and our ambition was now to get enough to make ourselves a waistcoat and jacket and give our elders proof that already we could catch, feed and clothe ourselves. The girls, meanwhile, would be collecting every small feather they could find and placing them in bags. They were collecting an important part of their marriage dowry. Every feather plucked from a bird would be carefully dried and powdered with bitter apple to prevent insects and preserve the feather, and at last enough would be hoarded to make a bed : the great feather bed of the Romany weighing at its lightest sixty pounds. I still have the bed my mother made of the feathers she picked as a girl, for no matter what the discomforts or how hard the way, no gipsy will ever leave his bed behind, whether it has to travel by donkey, mule, or hand-cart.

Two years and two months after leaving Roumania we arrived in Brussels, our last stop on our *trek* to the sea. Here for the first time we began to understand that parting was inevitable. Mascka was working the big fair and, as always, we *chis* and *chals* were doing what we could to wrest pennies from the tight-fisted Belgians by our tricks and *tatting*. The fair ended, we *trekked* to Antwerp.

We were sad as we made our way nearer and nearer to where the ships were that would separate us, for nothing that Lavanya had been able to say could move Mascka from his dislike of England. He would not come with us, that was final. Lavanya coaxed and threatened and cajoled, again and again she spoke of the blood-tie, more deep in the Romany than in any Italian or Jew ; but always Mascka shook his head and turned away. He had many reasons for refusing. To begin with what he had heard of England from my father he did not like. Above all, he said, he would not give up his freedom. And he had never heard anything like the laws and regulations and police interference as when listening to my father telling how by English law you had to have a local police permit for a pitch at the markets and fairs, and how you may stop in a field only by permission of the farmer, and all under the eye of the various petty authorities. Mascka could not understand all this. It seemed to him a tyranny no true Romany could submit to. He was shocked and decided. Besides, he said, the place was too small. I suspect, too, that the idea of England was repugnant to him because he did not know the language and for all his great versatility and talent, language-learning was not Mascka's forte. He felt, rightly, that there he would never be master, he would always be playing second fiddle to my father ; and although Mascka could take a beating and shake hands on it, he could play second fiddle to no one. Another reason was that Mascka had a strange dislike of the sea. He could see absolutely no reason for the sea at all. He would go anywhere on land but he would not cross the sea. He used to say that it was not right for people to cross the sea ; why, he never explained, but he knew that it was not right. Lavanya would willingly have come with us, but Mascka's stubborn belief that his freedom would end if he crossed the sea, told her that it was useless to insist. He told her banteringly that they would soon see us back again, as after the freedom of other countries my father would not be able to stand England for long. Lavanya was the most heart-broken of us all, and she was not comforted even when Mascka, who was a great one for stealing geese, said contemptuously : ' There aren't even any geese to get over there ! Why, they even have to import their geese ! What a country ! '

At Antwerp came the parting, and the final farewells were the signal for a general celebration. When there is a big parting each Romany puts a certain amount of money in the kitty and there is a big smoke and drink. Gipsies from France, Holland, Brussels all joined in. The first night of the rejoicing is for men only. They sit drinking and smoking and telling the tale until all the money is gone, all the words used up, and their legs will just stagger back with them to their *vardos*. The second night they let the women in on the fun. This is the big farewell with music, tambourines, singing, and dancing in which all must join. Now is when you see the Romany's kiss for the first time. Not the *chumidav*, the betrothal kiss, the sacred kiss full on the mouth. But the kiss on both cheeks and on the neck, holding each other by the ears and singing the tsigane parting song : ' The *vardos* may never be collected together again as now, but when they are all *yagged* and our spirits freed, we shall meet again in another form. . . .'

Lavanya was cut to the heart to see my mother, Anyeta, looking at her with all her sorrow in her eyes. The two of them clung together, held each other by the ears, kissed each other on the neck and cheeks, and wished each other the future happiness of luck and love. They rubbed each other's ears and said : 'May your ears burn for ever and may we never cease to talk of you.' They crossed thumbs for a speedy return. It was the first time I had ever seen two women cry ; there was no moaning and no sound, but I remember the stream of tears running down my mother's face. Mascka was very affected, but he would not show it. He blew his nose repeatedly and would turn gruffly aside, clearing his throat. Nothing on earth could have made Mascka show the tears in his eyes. He even made a joke about all these tears of the women helping the ship over. He didn't want to say good-bye, yet was obviously impatient for it all to be ended and to get away as far as he could from all these tearful farewells.

Meanwhile, our bulky beds, and barrels filled with our goods, were placed on board, and our little caravan led down the hold. This sudden smallness of our caravan impressed us *chavis* even more than the farewells. We peered down after our big home, so vast in size to us when we put our little shoulders against a wheel that had stuck in the mud or had to be helped uphill, and far away down in the hold it looked to us no larger than a perambulator. And as we looked suddenly it was covered up by other and bulkier goods and we were sure it had fallen through the big hole down through the bottom of the ship into the sea, and that we had seen the last of it. Final farewells were still to be said on the ship, with Mascka bringing his fiddle into play, and we each exchanging little tokens and gifts we had made ourselves specially for the occasion and which we all promised never to be parted from. I know that Mascka's last words were a joke, for I remember him laughing back at my father as he went down the gang-plank. We huddled together waving till Mascka and Lavanya were too small to be seen ; all the *gorgios* around staring at us as though we were beings from another and a very peculiar world. As, of course, we were.

X

MY first memory of England is a group of labourers on the quay-side at Harwich offering us sandwiches and drinks of tea and cocoa from their billy-cans. They laughed and chaffed us, and I suppose now that they were saying something like : ' Gor blime, Bert, just look at these 'ere kids,' grinning at our antics as though we were large puppies, for we were just as friendly and unself-conscious. We were, of course, exceedingly curious and had our noses in everything. I remember that we had a very long wait and that our goods had to pass much inspection, and my father had to talk with many officials. But where a *gorgio* child is bored and impatient if it has a two-hour wait and is usually slapped and told to sit still and *behave* itself, a Romany *chavi* is delighted if it has to wait ten hours, so much is there to see and nose into.

I remember that the sun was shining, for I know my mother said to my father : ' The sun is giving us a welcome, an omen of the joys to come.' I remember, above all, that the sun seemed to be also in the faces of the people about us. For there were no black looks. That was extraordinary to us, so used to peremptory voices and being elbowed roughly aside so that others might pass first. Here in my father's land people seemed amused by us, but not unkindly. They smiled and offered us their food and drink without our asking for anything ; and I can remember in my keen little brain thinking that here was an easy crowd and what a living there was to be picked up among people who smiled just on looking at you.

At last everything was settled and the 'all clear' given and away we went, once more free from all care. We passed through many towns and villages, making for our first real stop, a place called Barnet. My father was anxious to get there on time for a big fair which he said was important to him, but of which I remember nothing. But I well remember our first meetings on the road with other members of my father's family, and how we were introduced to the dealers and the British Roumani. I remember that the British Roumani treated us as though we were little gods. We were the new arrivals. Above all, we were the *puro-rati*, the pure blooded. I have heard since that we were the last of the pure-blooded Roumanian Zingari ever to enter England and stay here. There have been some through the country since, but they have not been allowed to stay for any length of time, making for America via Liverpool. My mother would tell me this, and I myself have never met any of the *puro-rati* on the English road.

Anyeta, my mother, was nearly heart-broken. She missed Lavanya and Mascka and their family. She struggled along using the few words of English she knew then. She was sad also because she could no longer *dukker*, read hands, at which she was expert and uncanny. After the rough times she had had the last two years she had thought that now life would be softer, and all she knew was that she was a stranger in a land unlike anything she had known before. She never opened her lips to complain, but for the first few months it was obvious to us that she was pining. She tried to converse with the Romany *racklers*, but they were using *kant*, and slang, and knew little of the true Romany *chib*, which we used.

Truth to tell, we secretly thought the British Romany an anæmic fellow compared with those we had left behind. He was good at specializing in one thing or trade, but life seemed soft here and he had not had to use his wits and fingers to such purpose as we had. I early saw that there was not a Mascka among them. But what saddened and disconcerted my mother was that their *kant* and slip-shod talk threatened to oust our true Romany *chib*. She was saddened because, as she explained to me, it was a hundred against one. It was no use our holding out, we could never teach them the pure *chib*,

so we must fall in and learn their impure *kant.* They spoke a
form of mongrel cockney Romani, as they still do. To pitch
your caravan is to *archav* the *vardo.* To them it was to *hatch*
the *vardo.* They would speak of having no place to *hatch.*
The *plastramengro,* the policeman, had become the *plasteringra.*
A *puvengra,* potato, a *puveningra. Juggal,* dog, they called
jukeler ; *kash,* wood, was *kosh* ; a tree, *kopaci,* was now *pucey.*
This is the sort of mongrel *chib* the British Romany talks ;
slip-shod and with the least of effort needed, and to this he
adds the dialect from whatever part of the country he comes.
I can tell a Lancashire, Norfolk, Devon Romany the moment
he opens his mouth. From any part of Wales or England I
can spot him, adding to his already corrupt speech the lilt or
sing-song of his district.

Apart from his comparative softness, laziness, inferior speech
and easy living, we found the British Romany friendly and
far less aggressive than foreign Romanys, especially those of
Middle Europe. The customs were much the same, except
that they knew little or nothing of herbal lore. They had
forgotten it, so little new and true blood had mixed with
theirs, that they had lost most of the ancient wisdom. My
father was very proud of my mother's knowledge of herbs
and healing and would show her off, his pure-bred Berber
woman, to the envy and admiration of all the Romanys we
met. All came to my mother for healing and her fame soon
spread among our brothers of the road. Centuries of secret
knowledge were behind her almost magic healing qualities.
She knew the way to make every ointment, balm, salve, and
though she could not tell the names in English of the herbs
she knew them by sight. She made much money gathering
and drying herbs : nothing escaped her eye. She used to tell
us that nothing could do us harm but belladonna. She said
that if a herb was not good for you it would taste so bitter
and unpleasant that in any case you would not persist in
drinking it.

It interests me to recall how I alone was singled out by my mother as her pupil. All that she knew of herbs she passed on to me, but she never bothered to teach my father, or my brother Ruperto, or my sister Lorenza. I was the lucky one. It may have been that I was an exceptionally live and intelligent lad. I was two when they gave me my nickname, Tarno Siani, and certainly all that there was to learn or see I learned and saw.

But it may also have been just luck. It may have been just that I was her constant companion and I was the one to whom she talked and explained things. She was a fine sight to see, my mother, her basket of wares on her arm, her walk like a queen, if a queen could walk half as well. Not fine in the large sense, for she was a small, dapper woman ; but fine in her movements and alertness, and the intelligent expression on her beautiful, serious face. Her hair was as black as a raven's feather to the day she died, and she had every one of her teeth. She bore her first child at seventeen and her last at fifty.

It was surprising how soon she picked up English words and idiom. We would start off down the village street, I taking one side, she taking the other. Perhaps she was naturally gifted for language, or perhaps it was just that she had to learn this strange tongue, so she set her mind to it, but I have seen her reading hands in broken English in one street and trotting out the same thing in perfect English on the return journey in a month's time.

My mother had a wonderful way with hands. She never told them as other gipsies tell them, or even as I tell them myself, with too many words and flourishes. She would say one thing and leave it at that. But she would say everything. She would look at the hand for several seconds intently and then look as intently into the person's eyes. Then she would say : ' *You have had the sun in your blood, and there has been a shadow, but it will be lifted at your first grey hair.*' No more

43

than that. She had short, lovely little sentences like that with which to sum up what she saw and the women loved her for it. It was curious that while with other fortune-tellers, and with myself I notice it constantly, women never cease asking you to explain or elaborate or tell them more, with my mother they never asked a question or wanted her to describe more fully what she had meant. It was as though they were hypnotized by her intent look and the prophetic quality of her utterances. One word of hers seemed more eloquent than all the blarney and the smiles we could give them.

This quality in my mother of being reverenced and accepted by quite stupid, unlettered people as something they could not understand but knew to be far above the ordinary run of Romany, or of *gorgio* for that matter, was a thing I was conscious of early and very proud of. They regarded her more as a wise woman, a prophetess. Village women would wait eagerly for her to come back again, and would have many things to ask her about health, or their children, or their homes. I often think now, with the caravans dying out and the gipsies forbidden the lanes and commons, how much is lost to the modern villager. In my mother's day and right up to just before the war, the women at the cottage doors got a hundred times value for their money. What do they get to-day? They take an omnibus to the nearest town and slouch about in cheap shops where a lot of bored girls wrap things up for them in bags, all part of routine and commercial machinery. The omnibus costs them already from twopence to sixpence or a shilling. Well, for twopence we used to give them a dozen clothes pegs when I was a lad. Not cheap factory made goods that the shops sell, coming from Japanese cheap labour, and God-knows-where-or-how produced. But fine strong pegs, made in the fresh clean fields, as work was meant to be done. We gave them lace, beautiful hand-made coarse lace from patterns centuries old. We made them whips from rushes which grow in the ponds. And we made

44

flowers from the pith of the rushes and carved them from *coggies*, white roses from the white turnip, cream ones from the swede variety. We carved them all by hand, intricate and appealing work, and with a drop of cochineal would have them any colour you could desire. We would set them to advantage against ivy leaves and they would last for weeks and be far more pleasing to the eye than the garish cardboardy artificial flowers they decorate their little homes with to-day. We could do every form of mending and tinkering and bartering. Our big brush wagons carried everything to rejoice the heart of the housewife—pans, kettles, rush-mats, crockery, all the best of their kind, all the cheapest on any market.

The woman who came to the door when we would knock would get a bit of colour in her life, a smile, a momentary welcome, excitement. She used to get goods just as cheap as she rushes off to buy to-day and much better in quality. Above all, she would get a woman like my mother who had wits and common sense developed far, far beyond anything the *gorgio* woman can ever attain, and to it all the knowledge old as her race, and a wisdom that cannot be taught. For her twopence, or sixpence, or shilling, she would have the goods she had chosen, plus a quick glance at the hand and a word of warning or a compliment, a recipe for lumbago, a word of advice on the baby's sore eyes, a herb to treat nerve trouble, a hint on how to cure an erring husband, and a smile or a gibe that would keep her heart warmed till we passed that way again.

XI

BAD as I am at remembering names of villages and towns where I spent my early childhood, one name I shall never forget. Lavenham, in Suffolk. It was here that for the first time in my life I wept bitterly as though my heart were broken and cursed the day I had been born a Romany. (I have grown wiser since !)

I was about nine years old and had been in England nearly two years. I had been quick at picking up the language and could now answer my father in English almost as good as his own. But, like all Romanys, I knew nothing of reading or writing, and had no knowledge of the alphabet or even what it could mean.

I used to fraternize quickly with the *gorgio chavis* of my own age and picked up their games, and now and then I would teach them something a little more difficult and intelligent such as our games. But I was always brought dead up against their silly question : Can you say your alphabet ? They seemed to set great store by this alphabet thing, for they would call to each other : 'Hi, Bill or Jim or Ted, see that boy ? He don't know his A B C yet !' And this was always the signal for a huge laugh, every one pointing at me and sniggering and enjoying their joke.

One day, when they were laughing at me, a little girl stood near. She was looking at me very seriously, her finger in her mouth, and then she came near to me and said : 'Can't you really say the alphabet, little boy ?' I said no, that I couldn't, and didn't even know what it was. So she said : 'I'll teach you, if you like, and then they won't laugh at you any more.' She was a little girl such as you see on the oleographs of that time. Fair curly hair with a fringe, a white frilly pinafore, bonnie cheeks, and blue eyes. Her people kept a little store near the village green and we sat outside on the grass, she threading daisies into a chain and teaching me my letters. Things seemed very rosy for me then and the time slipped by so very quickly that before I realized the day was gone I saw my people returning from their daily round of peddling. I had forgotten the *yag*. I had not fed the *gryes*. I had not milked the goats or prepared the food.

46

I had done nothing. But in spite of the *cooring* I got, I was happy that I knew somewhere up to O and was having another lesson to-morrow. I remember lying awake nearly all the night running over A B C D . . . A B C D . . . and falling asleep, the first time in my short life, just as it was time to get up.

But when the morning came the sun was gone and the rain streaming down. I knew that all hope of my people going out was gone and that it meant no meeting with my little teacher. *Gorgios* don't like the *parni*. The day seemed years to me. I asked my mother ten times an hour if there was anything she wanted from the shop. No, nothing. And why was I suddenly so active and why especially to that shop ? I must have blushed and my mother's wits were sharp. There was much laughter and my brother teased me and asked in Romany when was the *rommerin* and such little things as : ' Fancy our Xavier [my first name] and his *gorgio rovel* ! ' And I had to ignore it and bear it like every child in every family all the way round the world.

The next day broke warm and fine and it was a Saturday. I saw my teacher coming along keeping well to the other side of the road. I beckoned her, she beckoned back. Then I went bravely across and we sat on the edge of a dry ditch under the shade of a *boro kopaci*, and I went on with my lesson. I conquered it. I could say the alphabet before the morning was out ! But this time I did not forget to keep the *yag* well alight and the big pot on the boil. No chastisement this time but a pat on the back of the head, a rare thing for me. Truly, my lucky star was over me. I went to bed, my life was bliss, my sleep was good, my dreams were peaceful.

The bells were tolling the early morning worshippers to the little church when I got on the green next morning. The good Christians armed with their prayer-books and best bonnets were off to their prayers. I saw amongst them the aunt of my little teacher and her father. I had never seen

47

inside a church and often had wondered what they did there.
I walked to the porch of the church and peeped inside, and
then went slowly back to our *vardo*. I thought how soft-
hearted and kind such people must be who went so early in
the morning to pray for themselves and others. I inwardly
said a prayer for myself. The morning passed and afternoon
came. My mother was busy inside the *vardo*. My father
was on the *puv* busy with his *gryes*. My brother was engrossed
in making a new catapult. I had nothing to do, for I must
mention that my mother would never allow us to do unnecessary work on a Sunday. She was *Duveleskoe*, and we had to
keep Sunday quietly and be as idle as it is possible for a Romany
to be.

I wandered into the village, keeping near to the green,
hoping to see my little teacher. All at once I saw her coming
round the corner. She had on a bright blue dress with a
white sash, and I was soon near her. We were making plans
for the morrow and I had just repeated the twenty-six magical
letters, when the aunt, the one I had seen going to church,
came out of her door. At the sight of us her face went red
with fury and her mouth went in a mean thin line that made
your heart beat faster. She hurried across and seized the
little girl roughly by the arm, keeping away from me as
though I were a rattlesnake. She shook my little teacher
like a rabbit and said in a loud angry voice as she dragged her
away: ' Millie, how *dare* you ! I'm *ashamed* of you ! How
DARE you stand there talking to that dirty gipsy brat !
NEVER let me catch you doing such a wicked thing again ! '

I'd had some bad thrashings in my time but never in my
life was I so completely broken. My little heart seemed to
stop and my stomach felt sick. Everything went dark and
cold to me. I watched the hatchet-faced old *busni* till she
turned into the pathway, and I went across the field and lay
on the grass and sobbed as I had never sobbed before. Again
and again I went over the words she had shouted out loud.

I wondered why I was born a Romany *chal*, despised by people, pointed at and warned against, while other *chavis* were petted and guarded. It seemed very cruel and wrong to my young mind. I had no wish to go on living, for, for a moment and to my quick child's mind, I had understood how unequal the fight. I thought, too, how these were a people who prayed in the morning and hated in the afternoon. I must have stayed a long time sobbing in the meadow, but at last I knew I dared stay no longer. I dried my eyes and washed them in the brook to take away all traces of tears. Romany children are not encouraged to cry and I had no desire to meet with a second rebuff when I got home.

I sneaked in, sheepishly, trying to look my ordinary self. But my mother was not deceived. She took one look at me and asked me in a matter-of-fact voice what was the matter. I rubbed my finger in my eye and said gruffly : ' Nothing. I've got some dust in my eyes, that's all.'

Something in my woebegone appearance must have touched my mother, for she watched me a long time. I am sure she knew the kind of incident that had provoked my tears and how bitter they had been, for after a while she put a gentle hand on my shoulder and said in her quiet voice : *Si, ma kooshti chavi ; mandi kek. Mandis t'aa len cik andre merno akhas !* [*Yes, my good son. I know. I, too, have had that kind of dust in my eye many a time !*]

XII

ALTHOUGH, childishly, I was always expecting him to come running round the next corner to meet me, it was not till three years after I came to England that I saw my brother Waldo again.

I was now ten years old and we had been parted when we

were four, after the incident of the Big-Ship-Queen ; he, my twin brother, the elder by six hours. Did he know I was in England with our mother ? Romanys are unable either to write letters or receive them, but surely he must have heard from friends and relatives we had met at fairs and on the road that we were here. Was he as eager to find me as I was to find him ? What had they made of him here ? I felt he would be beyond me now, and that by comparison I must look humble and foolish. In my eagerness there was a diffidence. I was not used to playing second fiddle nor to feeling inferior to *chavis* of my own age.

My father had brought Waldo to England on one of his trips from Roumania, for he had a sister who though a Romany *racklo* had married a *gorgio*. They had a daughter, Annie Laurie, but no son, and had begged of my father to let them bring up one of us. They had so often pointed out the advantage it would be to us, to be brought up in England and not in the haphazard Continental way of continuous hardship and wandering, that at last my father had been convinced. So strongly indeed, that he had even succeeded in convincing my mother, especially, he pointed out, as the separation would not be for ever and we would all meet again when we reached England. It was some time before they could make up their minds which one of us to send, but finally Waldo was chosen. My father did not like to risk sending me, for I was the dare-devil of the two and would not make much of an impression on his relatives. Waldo was chosen because even at that age he was more docile and could be relied on to behave himself at the right moments.

We were *trekking* between Norwich and Lincolnshire when we passed near the town where he lived, and my father decided we would break our *trek* and find him. Waldo had been brought up as the son of my father's relative, so we were supposedly cousins. My father explained that this relative had been trying to drop the Romany associations and become as *gorgio* as possible. He seemed to be breaking it to us gently that our meetings would have to be as clandestine as possible and as infrequent. This may have been why he had spared us the meeting for these past three years. Anyway, we reached the town and camped on its outskirts. My father was right. My respectable relations were abashed at our clothes and our manners. And Waldo was a shock which it took me a long time to recover from or believe.

Perhaps the difference can best be explained by giving an idea of our clothes. I was a miniature of the men of our tribe, for it is the pride of the men that their *chals* be dressed like themselves, even down to the tiny whip I carried in imitation of my father at the horse fairs, and the imitation swagger. I wore little bell-bottomed trousers of a velvety corduroy and black ; a coat of a thick pilot cloth, slaty-blue ; a waistcoat of ivy-green. I had many pockets, all outlined with dark braid in a fancy design, four pockets to the waistcoat, four on the coat, three buttons on each. The buttons on my clothes were from coins, centimes, lire, lei, big and small, punched and flattened by Mascka. Mascka again had carved the ring which I wore round my kinsman scarf ; it was cut from a piece of bone from the leg of a sheep and carved with a figure resembling a Maltese Cross. On my feet I still wore the hide sandals Mascka had cut for me. To complete it all was my hat, a soft, black, high-crowned, felt hat with a wide band of silk ribbon on it, embroidered in roses and other flowers.

Waldo came gingerly towards us wearing his eight-and-elevenpenny reach-me-downs, his penny-half-penny Silvers Drift hat, a stiff Eton collar, and a bow under his chin. They had polished his face up so that the skin seemed to have come up red and been nearly rubbed away. His hair was parted in the middle and stuck down with plenty of soap and water. His big baby eyes were open wide to see what sort of a cousin he had, rolled up from the other side of the world.

My mother, I think, was the most surprised when she saw Waldo. I remember her staring at him with a small frown between her brows, for a long time as though she did not believe him real. I do not know exactly what she thought, for she rarely said her thoughts aloud, but I made a shrewd guess. He had been taught to call her ' Aunt,' and until he was a middle-aged man I never told him differently. She herself never wished him to be told at all, after that first sight of him.

Wally, as he had become, was quite a nice boy. He and his *gorgio* friend, Hubby, were regular attendants at the local chapel. The teacher used to bribe them to be good boys, they told me proudly. The reward was a half-pint of monkey nuts. They were always bad boys again when the monkey nut season was done. My mother taught us, her other children, her way of religion. We were open air and sun worshippers and could not understand that God would think better of us if we herded together in a dark-looking building to pay our respects and tell our troubles. My mother taught us that if we prayed we had to ask the *kooshti-Duval* direct for anything we wanted and not to be ashamed or afraid to ask. Every night we were taught to ask for Good Luck, Good Health, and a Wish for Wisdom. In my prayers, at this period, I did a great deal of thanking the good God that I had not been the lucky one chosen that day six years ago in Galatz. I had always had rather a grievance on this score when I thought of it, but now my gratitude knew no bounds. Also, my mother's eye would soften as she looked on me, as though she quite agreed with me as to what a man should be.

Civilization had made Wally exceedingly self-conscious. He blushed easily, especially when he saw my clothes, which took him some time to get used to. But I was secretly as ashamed of him, and not merely for his outward appearance and *gorgio* clothes, but for his complete inability to do anything useful and the blankness of his brains. I, who had envied him his joys at living among hospitable people as one of themselves, was soon to find out that like the pet bird in a cage with all the advantages of having his food found for him, Wally was helpless if you opened the cage door. I was the wild bird having to forage for myself, and happy I was not to have been trapped and left defenceless.

Although my father's relative, Ahny, was full of her Romany traditions and still peddled her wares in the district in which she had settled down, Wally had been turned into a semi-*gorgio* with *gorgio* ideas. A semi-anything is always a mistake, as it means that one is torn in two and not a complete whole with instincts and likes all running in the same direction. Dulled and useless as my brother Waldo was he never lost all through his life his inborn taste for wandering and yet was never happy and never wandered except in talk and threats. His big, kind-hearted *gorgio* father had completely altered his character. He was shy and *bilaco*, and I thought him quite ridiculous with the many things he was afraid of and the stupid thing he thought it daring to do.

To my shame I found Wally worked in a gang. Boys used to work in gangs in those days, when first I came to England. His apprenticeship was picking up twitch at sixpence a day and cutting thistles in the fields, picking up stones, singling out turnips, and tearing out weeds. The boys would work down the field, a supervisor walking behind them, hitting with a stick on their backsides if they did not keep bent double and at work. That was my *gorgio* brother! I would go out with my *tatting*-bag, easy and free, with no masters to wave their sticks behind me, and swop for rabbit skins, white rags, lead, all of which I sold to a marine-store dealer, and whatever more was wanted at the moment. I would make five times what Wally made, and even had I made half as much I would not have traded my freedom for his broken spirit. I was out even at ten years of age to be my own master, and very soon was to become it. Yet my way of living was disgusting to my cousins, my post office relatives, with their reach-me-downs and respectability. They are the ones who still hesitate when they meet me, and beg me, when we do, not to say anything about this gipsy-business and not to shock their home-dress-making friends by referring to the road or using Romany words while in their house.

I can remember vividly that what shocked me most about Wally and his work was that with his cutting of thistles and picking up of stones, he had also to dig up dock and burn it. To see him doing this, showed me the distance which separated us and would never be crossed. He was maliciously and ignorantly spoiling and burning what my mother had told me was the most valuable curative medicine among herbs and the foundation of many of her most successful cures. Here he was ignorantly burning and wasting what the very *gorgios* he was working for paid pounds to procure at the herbalist or chemist. He was spoiling something he could have sold for one shilling an ounce instead of destroying for sixpence a day. But he hadn't the sense or the knowledge of where to sell it. And this is still being done everywhere to-day by the unenlightened *gorgio*.

The plan grew in my mind to try and reclaim my brother and give him his freedom again. I was to be his teacher, and with the faith of youth decided to take on the part of Mascka and remould him nearer to the Romany idea of what a boy should be. He was an apt pupil in spite of his self-conscious-ness and quite grateful and eager to learn, but he had forgotten the rough Spartan training and his few years of easy life had so completely altered him and softened his spine that it was years before he was even as proficient as a Romany beginner. I believe that in his half-hearted way he admired and envied me, but the damage had been done and he was not old enough to reason and so would not admit it. He graduated, his next step, to working in an iron foundry, from six till six, for twelve shillings a week. Quite the most difficult and unpleasant work one could imagine. I became a youth and at fourteen graduated into a goat and donkey owner. I had property and freedom. He had still slavery and servility.

Much later, I did persuade him to try the road, and freedom. I cannot to this day give myself a reason for insisting as I did on rescuing him, as I called it. It may have been just my natural inborn stubbornness that goes at a task, however difficult, till I have got the better of it. It may have been that Wally was not merely a brother, but my twin brother, and I felt a deep personal shame to see a replica of myself having the manners and outlook and dependence of a twopenny tradesman. Stubbornness or vanity, persist I did. I went as far as buying him a caravan. I taught him photography and bought him a camera, tripod, plates, and all the necessary gadgets by which to make it a paying proposition and earn a good living on the road. Failure was inevitable and served me right for interfering.

In any case, even had Wally had the strength of purpose to renounce his lower-middle-class respectability and *gorgio* ways for ours, there was his wife to reckon with. He had married a really handsome girl, daughter of a *gorgio* farmer and horse-breeder. She had fine flaxen hair and was tall and very good to look on. She consented to try the life for a while, but it did not suit the petulant temper of the woman who has married beneath her. So Wally settled down again in a humdrum town, hiding his unmentionable ancestry beneath the disguise of small tradesman. It was not so much of a disguise either, as he had little claim but blood to be one of us, and he deserved his punishment. For some reason I cannot explain, when a *gorgio* marries a Romany, they always try to hush the Romany part up. It is these who whisper anxiously when they see you : ' Don't say you're a Romany. These people don't know it, and we'd rather it wasn't mentioned.' This is a trait peculiar to the British Romany. He goes soft and snob after a few years, a creature full of small shames and unreal fears.

Waldo was blessed with two handsome sons, both bearing the good old Romany traits which mother and father were so anxious to deny. The elder, particularly, was keen and alert, a shrewd buyer, a good seller, a lad who could see and drive a bargain. He came to me of his own accord and I taught him many things. He was quick and always turned his knowledge to advantage. He was a go-getter. The other possessed the cool, calm, never-get-excited nature of his surroundings but had a keen nose for a bargain and a flair that could be only Romany for exaggerating the marvels of whatever he wished to sell and getting double its value for it. But the *gorgio* influence had made them both self-conscious and taken from them all desire or initiative. I know that in their hearts they longed for freedom and the open *boro-drom*, and that they were not content with their caterpillar-on-the-cabbage-leaf existence. But convention has claimed them and they are shackled. Here is a lesson to the missionary who tries to save the heathen and who brings the aspidistra outlook of Balham to bear upon the savage. Both of us are true-born Berber Romanys, born in the *pus* as tradition demands. All his life my brother has been ashamed and envious of the life I lead and of myself. All my life I have been unable to understand why a stiff collar and a bow under it should have made of one child a servile nit-wit as limited as the average workman; and why a kinsman scarf slotted through a carved bone ring should have made of the other an arrogant independent being, jack of many trades, master of all.

XIII

My mother's memories may have been too long for her to become early reconciled to my father's land, but I was at home in it within a year.

I well recall my first day of work in the new *puv Inyatarra*. I had heard my father tell my mother so often that we were now in a land where an easier time was in store for us, and I was soon to prove it. I had my little basket on my arm and I called very timidly at a house with steps to it that had just been whitened and on which there was as yet no speck of dust. I hesitated for fear I should soil it and offend the owner of the house who might chase me away with a stick or angry words. But from behind the curtains of her little window she must have been watching me and seen my look of fear and perplexity, for before I could make up my mind she had opened the door, a beaming smile on her face. She said in a sweet motherly voice : ' Come along, what have you got to show me ? ' and I knew at once that I was among the big-hearted folk my father used to boast of to make Mascka angry.

I displayed my wares. I told her the prices, timidly, in new-found English of which I was still unsure. She seemed to wish for the privilege of buying something from me. Here was none of your hard-bargaining viragos of France and Belgium who beat you down for a sou or a centime and use high shrill voices as an added terror to a small child. Here was a buyer with a sense of value who knew what excellent wares she was getting and was willing to buy at the correct price. I had found my first customer. I cannot remember what I told her or what it was she chose, but I remember this : when she had paid me and I had with difficulty counted the coins of my new and strange-looking wealth, she said : ' Could you eat a piece of cake, boy ? ' Could I eat a piece of cake ? What manner of people were these who, after paying you the full price, with no attempt at bargaining, asked *chavis*, famed for their appetites, if they would like pieces of cake ? I was invited in the little kitchen, and to the cake was added a glass of milk. I ate and drank and my only thought was that I should soon stretch out my arms and find my blanket over me, and that this was just another pleasing dream

that comes to a boy who sleeps peacefully after a day that starts
with the rise of the sun and ends only when the evening
shadows fall. But no, it was real. Here, then, we were in
the paradise my father had told us so much about as a reward
for the hardships of the *trek*. I wondered why he ever left
this to go over the sea among the folks we had left, and the
dusty roads that had seemed without end. I thought of
Mascka and Lavanya and the Tonescu girls. What a treat
they had missed with Mascka's stubbornness ! How could
one let them know that this was what they had dreamed of
and did not know existed ? What a place for Mascka's
statuettes and Lavanya's beautiful lace ! I was sorry to think
that we might never see them again to tell them that after all
the good things and the hospitality my father had boasted of
were true.

After that first experience, I had no fear. As the weeks went
by I made many sales in the villages and many friends, and
heard many remarks passed about me. I heard such remarks
as ' roguish,' ' sweet little dear,' ' poor little child,' and
mothers saying to their *gorgio chavis* : ' How would you like
to have to get your own living like this little boy ? ' They
liked my little round face with its quick eyes and quicker
smile, the silver buttons all over my pockets, the little scarf
knotted round my neck, and the flat raw-hide sandals Mascka
made and which I still wore.

It must seem strange, perhaps even unbelievable, to the
gorgio reading this, that a child of eight was out on the roads
peddling wares, many of which he had made himself, from
morning when the first windows were opened to evening
when the lights were put on the tables and the doors bolted
against all knocking. But judged by *gorgio* standards I was a
boy of fourteen, and not a sloppy boy of fourteen such as you
see about to-day, but a boy of fifty years ago who worked and
earned his living from the day he left school at eleven years of
age. To a Romany *chal*, especially a true-bred foreign

Romany *chavi* trained by Mascka and my mother, a *gorgio* child of seven is a baby in arms and a wasted opportunity. We learn value early. Already at the age of five, as we make the rounds with our elders, we are shown what is a bargain ; what has been a good deal and what has been the reverse ; we are taught that it is right to give certain things away for food, and that we can trade this or that for eggs and bread. Every move a grown-up Romany makes he explains to us children. Our elders do not treat us as sweet little things but as those to whom their knowledge must descend and who must work from the moment of standing steadily on their small legs, and must be taught that the world is a harsh place in which if you do not get the better of it, it will get the better of you.

I do not say that you will find children working to-day as they worked then. Even the Romany dare not put his child through the mill as we knew it. If, to-day, he takes his *chavis* out with him on his peddling rounds and one of them looks five minutes under fourteen, half the inspectors of the local police force, to say nothing of the nearest branch of the R.S.P.C.C., will be on his track giving him £10 or a month. Yet it is a good life for a *chavi*. I was not out alone. My mother was always with me, for it was always me she chose as her companion ; she doing one side of the street ; I the other. They would greet me with a smile because she had just passed, or would say to her : ' Your little boy has been here before you.' We paved the way for each other's wares. There was always an elder of the tribe with the *chis* or *chals*. Always some one to keep an eye on you, to see that you are not cheated ; to see that you are learning your lesson ; to watch your progress and explain your set-backs. The English Romany is born soft and bred soft and they do not even fight like we used to. But the *gorgio* boys are also deteriorating. In the schools and the home the spare the rod and spoil the child is showing its ill effects. A child seems to be kept longer at school not to enlarge the capacity of its brain or to put its intelligence up, but to keep it out of work and put the rates up. So you see great gawky boys of eighteen still sucking bits of toffee down the street with their satchels under their arms. The average twenty-three-years-old to-day was the average fourteen with us. These are easy times and although it may look very nice to those who are always running other people's lives for them, to me, as observer, the boys of to-day are both less hardy and less alert than they were when I was a boy. Admittedly it was a much harder life, but it turned out harder men. A boy could look after himself at once, yet he is helpless to-day and getting every year more so. When I was a *chavi* the *gorgio* boys left school at eleven, passing the fourth standard, or if they were dunces they had to stop till thirteen. Then they set off to earn their first money by doing half-time work in the factories. From the modern sentimental point of view it may have been wrong, but from a human, practical point of view boys were turned into men and not kept soft-spoken like girls and with no greater effort to make in life than one which any girl can compete and beat them at. Many a milling I got at home and very sore I have felt after it, but it was always to teach me something, and I learnt it, and I never repeated the mistake again. Never raise your hand against a child because you are in a bad temper or irritated with yourself, for that is a mean and cowardly act for which there is no forgiveness. But a whacking never did any boy any harm in my experience. My training was hard but it was essential. A *chavi* must be trained as a dog must be trained. You can still have an untrained dog and it will correct itself by instinct. But the child has not that instinct and learns only what it is taught. An untrained child is a half-being all its life, and the latest educational authorities' findings are only just discovering or admitting what we Romanys have known and practised for centuries : that a child learns from the moment it is aware of the world about it.

So that I was not an object for pity, up as I was at the first

'I was not out alone. My mother was with me, for it was
always me she chose as her companion.'

grey light of the winter morning or carrying my basket from door to door through the hot summer afternoon. I did not sell and bargain wares all the time, or through all seasons. When there was nothing for me to sell that we had made ourselves, I used to go to the local fish shop. There we would buy up bloaters at half a crown a hundred and peddle those. Actually we would get 120 for half a crown, and if you asked for a half-hundred you were given sixty. These we would sell for one penny each or three-halfpence for two, throwing in extras if there were children in the house. In the autumn, also, we would peddle nuts and we were famed for always giving our customers a square deal.

XIV

CATCHING people is just as interesting as catching rabbits or pheasants, and after all that is very much what it is like to a child, sniffing down a rabbit-hole to see if Mr. *Shooshie* is at home and catchable, or knocking at a door and wondering which of us will be enough. To a Romany boy things are not nearly so bad as they seem to the *gorgio*. We get used to snubs as well as to praise, and it does not take us long to know where to expect temper or kindness. Besides, we early develop yet another sense to help us. We learn to weigh up on sight, a gift that saves many a disappointment and un-necessary haggle. Perhaps because we have never been taught to read and write we need the assurance of our own eyes to guide us, as we cannot afford to go by hearsay or chance.

Everything that happens to us we profit by. And going to rounds with our elders is a lesson in elementary psychology which lasts us all our lives, never fails us, and about which *gorgios* would write learned books full of discovery. We *chavis* quickly learn how to tell who lives in a house without knocking at the door. Any true Romany will tell you more about the woman who lives next door to you by glancing at her windows or garden than you will learn in a lifetime of 'good morning' over the wall. Say her windows are the first things we study. We like the curtains to be generous in material and the blinds rolled up just a little crooked. That means that the person within is rather an untidy, impetuous, can't-be-bothered-with-detail-kind of person, a good giver, and kind-hearted. When the curtains are draped in exact loops and the blinds pulled up tightly in a straight line, we know that it is a house where everything has a place and heaven help whoever displaces it or the unhappy husband who drops ash on the carpet. We know that the owner is calculating, a tyrant for detail, and altogether a tough nut to crack. Where the curtains are skimped, the last quarter of a yard missing somewhere and the blinds always half-way down the window, we know the owners to be mean and mistrustful, from whom we can confidently expect no sale. Then there are the door-knockers, door-knobs, and door-scrapers. Nine times out of ten it is the woman with the badly-polished door-knocker and ill-kept door-knob and door-scraper full of weeks-old dirt, who opens her front door with a rush and barks : ' We don't want any tramps and that sort in *this* house ! '

Gardens are an unending source of information to us and cannot lie. You know the old maid's garden as soon as you have placed your hand on her gate-latch. To begin with she sticks plants in anywhere. People give her cuttings from theirs or presents of bulbs and she is so grateful that they go in wherever there is a vacant space. So you can tell her garden at once by its lack of conscious design. She will put pansies among the geraniums and larkspur among the wall-flowers and be surprised when they grow up together. Also in an old maid's garden nothing is ever thinned out, for her kindness of heart seems to think it a sacrilege to cut or trim, especially if a friend gave the root. In these gardens you rarely get level rows but always one big mass of flowers without order, tall ones in front of little ones. It is always a generous riot of colour, and usually the prettiest of all gardens and the most loved. There is always a good sale here, an invitation to come in, and a talk that goes on for hours.

Then there is the calculating garden. This is usually run by the retired clerk or schoolmistress. It gives you no emotion of pleasure whatsoever but makes you sit up and take notice. It is prim, austere, the roses trained to a nicety, and everything at the square angle and mathematically accurate. Unlike the old maid's garden, here everything on the subject has been consulted and read. There is never a tall flower hiding a bunch of little ones ; all that has been grown has been grown correctly, but more as though to teach it a lesson than to get an emotion from looking at it. This is a lady who needs much persuasion and has to be in a very amenable temper indeed to consent to listen or buy. And when she doesn't buy and won't listen, it is always on principle.

Then there are the placid people who like rock-gardens. No work to do, no digging. The best effect possible with the smallest amount of work to be done ; and once done, it doesn't need to be repeated, watched, or cajoled. It will just go on growing and spreading and looking better every year with a quarter the bother the neighbours use, digging and complaining. These are nice easy-going people and where there is a rock-garden there is nearly always a good-tempered owner and a sale.

There are the contradictory gardens, in which the plants are always dying off. The husband plants them and the wife moves them on. And generally moves them on in the middle of the season. This is a house where both are keen gardeners, and where, though so many flowers seem always to be drooping and dying, both take delight in them. This is the sort of garden which when we enter we exclaim : ' Ah, the ladies have been at work again ! ' The lady is born generally under the sign of Sagittarius. Jupiter is her planet, and he is always moving things on, and she does the same with hubby's plants. She may move you on and she may be the most generous of the lot.

We always, of course, keep an eye open for the *chavis* gardens ; those little corner patches with a bit of everything in, and the odd onion growing among the pink daisies and the potato-plant side by side with something nondescript growing with a lot of green leaves and probably planted from a pip or stone. Where there are children there is rarely a harsh rebuff and we can nearly always be sure of a welcome.

Then there is the man's garden, full of show-off and superiority. Here there will be everything in season ; every-thing just set out with dahlias and asters ; the chrysanthemums set well to the back for the autumn ; evergreen shrubs framing the gaudier flowers ; the front of the beds kept for changeable plants, jonquils, violas, daffodils, everything in rotation, and lots of labels. We know him at once. The business man who cannot relax. The more prosperous clerk, sales or depart-ment-manager type, caught young and unable to see anything free or rebellious, even in his plants. Everything treated like a letter lost or answered, everything filed and tabulated, nothing is done for the fun of it, and there are no or few mistakes. The wives in these houses are uppish and you may get a snub ; on the other hand if her husband has not retired and she is alone all day she may be glad of a talk and will always buy something of the embroidery type, or rug-making with instructions on how it can be done.

Beware of the house where apples lie thick on the floor under the trees. These are the people who will let forty bushels of apples rot and think they are conferring the kingdom of the world plus the Koh-i-noor on you if they give you a wormy half-dozen. These are the people who waste and do not want till you suggest to them what you would like ; then the wasting fruit becomes more precious than gold. These are the people too mean to give what they waste away, but if a couple of school-children sneak in for a treat, they set their dogs and magistrates on them. If you see apples rotting on the ground in their hundreds, you may be sure that the people in the house are curt and ungenerous. And you will never be wrong.

XV

PETS are easy gaugers of character. The old lady with the parrot will always have a son abroad and keep you for an hour with stories of how wonderful a son he is. Love-birds are for romantic old couples and single sentimentalists. (As a *chavi* I once sneaked a handsome cockatoo walking majestic-ally about the front lawn and took it round to the kitchen door and said I'd found their bird and brought it back again. They made a great fuss of me and gave me five shillings. Although only a *chavi* I remember that the cockatoo belonged to Rear-Admiral Hammond, for the importance of the name and tip impressed me greatly !) Where people are kind-hearted and easy-going they will let their child keep rabbits or guinea-pigs, and that is always a sure good sign for us. If you find a man keeping pet mice and guinea-pigs you know he is the experimental type. He's a bit queer and delighted to see you. He will listen to you for hours and beg you to come again, and he will always buy whatever you are persuading him to take. People with unusual pets are nearly always queer and original and easy to get along with. Romanys understand them instinctively and they always like us. People who do not like animals we rarely get along with. They are the people who do not like a little trouble whether it is cleaning out a bird-cage or to give a dog or cat the little attention that it needs to keep its fur clean. Of course there are exceptions, and they may be the poor unfortunates who have lost a loved pet and refuse to put another on the pedestal again.

The age of the dog is the age of the owners. If it is young and frisky, it is a young frisky couple ; if heavy and overfed and none too active we know they are getting old. We do not like fat heavy dogs, for that means that it is being killed with kindness and overfeeding. These are the heartless people who think nothing too good for a dog although their fellow men may starve and children are forbidden a penny-worth of sweets. We know when we see an overfed piece of dog-flesh that there is no cake for us—he has had it all ! There is the sportsman's dog, the bull-terrier, chalk-white, and looking as though it had spent the morning peeling onions. No man without considerable pluck would care to take one about. But its owner is of no use to us. We know the type, spending its money on the race-course and in the pubs, always a gambler, always broke. When we see a bull-terrier we know that he must have cost a lot, but that the man who bought him keeps his wife short, exceptions apart.

The type we like best of all is the little man with the big dog. This is a generous soul. He is a good-hearted man and he knows he has taken on a big-sized job feeding and caring for such a dog, but he loves it and would make the sacrifice of an extra pint or half-ounce any day for his friend. From their experience Romanys say that people who keep big dogs are generous and unselfish people and one is always treated kindly in dealings with them.

Of course a comfortable home always has a sleek well-fed cat. If it is thin and bedraggled you know that it has had to do its own catering and that there is little left over for you. One of the first things we learn is that if a cat sits comfortably unmoved on the step when you knock, it is a house where the people are kind-hearted and nice-tempered. That cat has never been kicked and has no fear of strangers. But if a cat leaps up the nearest tree at the sight of you, do not bother to go on. When I see an angry and suspicious cat preferring the company of a tree to the company of human beings, I know it is useless to go farther and I generally turn back at the gate. I know the type and am sorrier for the cat than for myself. People say it is a sign of bad luck if a cat runs away from you up a tree. All it means is that the cat has had enough of human beings and at the mere sight of another two-legged brute it leaps to solitude and safety.

XVI

IF you want the people who do not know anything and do not want to know anything, look for the No Hawkers, No Circulars, No Street Noises plate. This is a silly sign for Romanys because they cannot read and having found out that the writing on the mat means WELCOME they march hopefully in. All signs mean much the same to them. But here they soon find their mistake. It is possible to overcome every prejudice on the road and even to talk a blustering fetch-the-police-my-man householder into listening to you. But it is never possible to put one over on the snob. We soon find this type out and then we need no warning signs to keep us away. We have another certain sign for snobbery in a house, but I will not tell it or it might be altered and spoiled. Here are the people who do all their buying on the telephone and are well stung for their stupidity, for shopkeepers are just as good psychologists as gipsies. It is on these gates that you will see our chalk mark warning our brothers who follow what to expect. This particular mark is something like a pair of spectacles with a line through it, meaning : Keep off. *Wafodi*. Bad people !

We learn early to judge women by the type and quantity of jewellery they wear. When we see four or five massive rings on one hand we know she has not been used to money in her youth and now is making a good show of it. Romanys know a great deal about precious stones and diamonds, at least it was so with the old Romanys, and even a Duchess wearing paste would not escape our eagle eye. We are also quick to judge bad taste by the badly matched colours of clothes and rooms. This always offends a Romany, as he takes his colouring from Nature and has a keen appreciation of beauty in colour. Rarely do we see women whose colours harmonize as do the colours on the flowers. *Gorgio* women seem to have little natural sense of line or beauty and their idea of colour is a disagreeable and perpetual shock to eyes trained to the blending of earth's colours, skies, animals, and seasons.

Smell, which is a highly developed sense with us and almost animal in its intensity, is early adapted to inform us of the type of people who inhabit the houses at which we call. We arrive at a house, the door of which is ajar, a smell of stale tobacco smoke hangs around and tells of an old widower living alone, the very curtains impregnated with smoke. He is pleased to see us for he likes to tell us once again that it ' don't seem quite the same-like now,' and also to ask a remedy for the ' dratted screws ' as he calls his rheumatism. There is the elderly widow, she of the musty house, kind-hearted, her home overrun with mice. Her children are always living away from home, married, and her son especially is always in ' a good position in London.' This paragon of a son is never in a humdrum job, but always is manager of some giant store, cock-o'-the-walk in a factory, or rapidly becoming head of a government department. To the question : ' Do they look after you, ma'am ? ' the reply is invariably : ' Well, you see, he has married a *real* lady and they have their position to keep up.' Ageing spinsters, their gardens filled with old-world flowers, sweet-williams, cornflowers, cabbage roses, a sprig of rosemary, have the house smelling of fresh soap and cut flowers. These are the ones who, when their hands are read, must always be reminded of a lost love or told to expect a future one. Their faces colour with embarrassment and pleasure at the chance to speak of their love of a long-past day. You can tell the gipsy everything ! They will even bring out his photograph and ask your opinion on him. Usually they blame their parents for having parted them and tell you sadly that perhaps had he been more persistent she would have taken less notice of her parents' threats. How loyal they are, these lonely and innumerable women ! Many a time I have been shown bundles of faded letters tied in faded ribbon. Often they will say that the lover died and they were to have been married in the spring. I have often wondered how much of a consolation it would be if I told them that from what I hear from the women who got their men, they are probably happier with their dreams than they would have been with realities. While on the subject of elderly spinsters, many is the old maid of sixty I have met who still hopes to meet the man of her dreams. These always manage to pick up the courage to ask : ' Do you see marriage in my hand ? ' And I reply : ' There is still romance in your hand, lady, and an unexpected joy is on its way to you.' I hear a sigh of relief and they want always to pay me more than I ask. Or these old ladies will say : ' The only man I ever loved married a cousin of mine. Do you think, gipsy, I shall still have him ? Is there any sign of the death of this woman ? She treats him terribly ! ' They are always very sorry for their old lovers. I have never heard of so many ill-used men as those who did not marry these old women. I have often wondered would she treat him any better if she got him ? She would probably make him pay in full. Women are strange creatures, anyway.

XVII

PEOPLE are taught so little how to observe or to put to value what they see, that often our simplest feats of summing-up are put down almost to Black Magic. I know a very great deal about magic, white and black, and I can assure you this using our eyes and ears and noses has very little indeed to do with it. An old lady will open her door and we will at once speak to her of India and a son or daughter far away. She will be in ecstasies and unable to credit our powers of clairvoyance. But we do not need clairvoyance here. We have seen through the open sitting-room door that good old row of carved elephants ambling along the mantelpiece, and over the settee the silver-embroidered cloth that comes from Calcutta via Coventry. Or the busy housewife will give us a smile as she opens the door, her sleeves rolled up. We will read her hand and tell her the number, ages, and sex of her children, and even her husband's profession, and be at the next door while she is still recovering her breath. Here also we need call on no psychic powers. We just take a look sideways at her washing line. There are the little dresses in three different sizes : three girls. A little shirt or washable suit : one boy. A pair of blue overalls on the line : the husband is a mechanic, big man or little man we see by the length of his arm sleeves and pants. We know the state of the home's finances by another quick glance at the dustbin. Salmon tins and cucumber peelings tell their story ; corned-beef tins more plainly than words that fresh meat is a luxury reserved for one or two days of the week. Every Romany is a miniature Sherlock Holmes.

Then again we Romanys have our signs marked up or chalked on walls, and we glance at their gate-posts to find what others have left for our information. We have our signs for every occasion. A savage dog, a death, a birth, husbands or sons at sea, newly married, separated, scandal, mean, generous, good, bad. We read the sign left for us on their doors or gate-posts which the Romany places for his *prala* who follows after him, just as he places his *patteran* on the ground to tell the road he has taken.

As to their hearts, we can read them as you *gorgios* read a book. Yet even in this we are helped, not only by the signs we leave on their walls, but by the villagers themselves. For all the *dukkerin* my mother taught me, and the psychic powers she developed in me and the training experience has perfected, I sometimes think you could go through any small town or village knowing nothing but how to pick up a hand and stare in it. Practically all your work is done for you at the first door at which you knock. The village people are gossipers who love to tell a stranger of some one else's downfall or ill luck. Not so much that they gloat over it, as that they have nothing else to speak of and very few people to speak to. Here is their life, and nothing within its narrow radius escapes them. The villagers will find out everything there is to know ; no need for the Romany to bother. Almost their first question is : Have you been to the house at the end of the row ? You reply in the negative. ' Ah, poor woman,' she will begin, ' she has just had such a trouble.' Here they lower their voices. ' Her daughter has just had a baby . . . you know . . .' Then they will tell you who they think is the father. Or a young married man has gone from the narrow track of respectability. If they don't know why, they'll make a shrewd guess. Or this young married woman wears silk clothing which she cannot possibly afford on her husband's salary ; the ' big man ' in the village comes into this somewhere. The people at the Hall are nearly always ' a queer lot,' particularly if they have not been there long and come from somewhere ' furrin.' The young lady is not all she should be and is seen at strange times with the *boro-rye* of a neighbouring village. 'My husband saw them together in the wood the other night.' Or they went away together last week-end. 'My son who is the porter at the railway station says he went on the nine o'clock train and she went on the eleven-fifteen on Saturday, and she came back on the three o'clock Monday and he on the six-forty-five.' They work it out to every one's satisfaction. Even the parson does not escape. We know where he makes the most calls, how long he stays, who gets two hundredweight of coal at Christmas instead of one, and where his old suits go.

After the first two or three houses, therefore, there is no more work to be done. We know the affairs of the village as though we had lived in it a lifetime. And in the face of all the local magistrates, fines and restrictions, I will say that people need us at their door. Many a man has cried to me and told me his fears and worries. Many a woman has told me the secret things in her heart and felt that a burden has been taken from her. Wealthy folk pay fashionable doctors hundreds and thousands of pounds to cure their nerves. We Romanys have never heard of the newfangled cures of getting people to tell you everything about themselves and asking a hundred guineas a time for the pleasure of listening. We take a shilling or two and do as much good, because nothing will ever make me believe that a rich man gets anything but doubly ill and irritated having to pay away so much of his gold to keep his stomach working and his thoughts clean. We Romanys are a form of ambulant father confessor, curing sick souls. I have often been asked: Do Romanys divulge the secrets they hear on their way ? Never. I knew the secret love affairs of dozens of people before I was twelve years old. I know of hundreds of thousands now, and some love affairs are pretty grim dramas, believe me. We guard your secrets far more closely than you guard them yourselves. For love may be blind, but I can assure you that the villagers are not.

Big strong men are the delight of a Romany's heart. Distinguished visitors and all film stars say after their first day, the classic : ' I think your police are *wonderful* ! ' No one asks our opinion, but we found that out many years ago. Never as a *chavi* or a man have I failed to sell something to a policeman. The bigger they are the more soft-hearted and easier to persuade. We are taught to know them by the little blue and white plate on the door, saying County Police. The *moocher* shuns them, but the Romany always works them and seldom is there a failure. Incidentally, this easy-going spirit is found in most tall men, and very tall men are childlike in their generosity. The small man is always more difficult to convince ; he is not so lazy as the tall man, nor so stupid ; he seems to think you are trying to get the better of him and it needs hard work and much time to allay his suspicions.

Many were the offers of adoption from lonely spinsters and kind-hearted old ladies my mother received for me. I used always to be grateful to these old ladies as a *chavi* because they made my task so much lighter and more pleasant. There were the benevolent little old women filled with surprise at finding you so small and already at work, who would offer a coin and say they did not want to buy anything. But this no true-bred Romany would allow. I was never flattered and always gave them more than the value of the coin if I took it. When I had mastered the language so that I could express myself beyond the formal names of goods and prices, I would explain to them gravely that I was a seller, not a beggar. We Romanys consider ourselves traders. There is only this difference between ourselves and shopkeepers. We carry our wares to the doors, display them, and have made most of them ourselves. There are big traders now who are following our example and countries now send ships to other countries with goods on show for which they want orders. The true Romany has a great spirit of independence. We extol the virtues of our goods and try to make a sale. The big stores of to-day employ teachers to teach their staff salesmanship, and by

heaven they need to. They are not natural salesmen and sales-
women. And that is just what we are. We are born knowing that there is nothing better than to bring off a deal. If a
woman has no money by her, but keeps chickens, then we
chop our goods for eggs, and if we can get a bigger value in
eggs than we could by taking cash, we like it. Many and
many a time I have come home from the days *peddling* with no
money in my pocket but with my basket filled with eggs,
butter, cheese, pork, ham, and even pickled onions. What
matter ? We can eat these and we cannot eat coppers. We
are taught this barter as part of our childhood's training and
once we have learnt our lesson in values it is rare for any one to
get the better of us. If they did, we should never be able to
forget it. Our elders would see to that ! We like a *chop*, and
by that is not meant one of pork or mutton, but a deal or
exchange. *Gorgio* boys do it with penknives and marbles,
whistles and trinkets. We *chop* for more serious things—food,
chickens, goats, donkeys—and the grown-ups for horses and
ponies. We will haggle for hours to get that extra sixpence on
a deal. Not that we need the sixpence, but we need the honour
of beating our opponent. Many a time I have seen my father
haggle an afternoon away to get a shilling off the price of the
horse and then spend ten times as much in celebrating his
victory !

XVIII

A ROMANY mother in her lullabies makes her child promise
three things : to *rokker* Romany, to *kil-i-bosh*, and *nanti
della gorgio vek a kash*.

And when he has learned these three things, and can speak
his own language, play the fiddle, and understand that he
must never hit a *gorgio* with a stick (hit him with your fists !)
he goes on to the next step in his education.

74

'*I have seen my father haggle to get a shilling off the price of the horse and then spend ten times as much in celebrating.*'

He learns to catch his food and he learns to cook it. Among the Romanys boys are taught the arts and preparation of food as well as the girls. Cooking is not considered a specifically feminine task, and even the *gorgio* agrees with us there, for the best and first-class cooks are men the world over. But it is not because cooking is an art or a luxury that we boys must take our turn at the cook-pot. Our education is not based on arts and elegances. Our elders say : ' You will always have to eat, so you may as well learn to cook it, and the sooner the better.' No Romany parents can say that they will come back each night, however strongly they intend to. They may be lost or some misfortune may befall them and they may return at midnight instead of at seven. And it is thanks to their early training that in the meantime their *chavis* will have caught their food and cooked it and tucked themselves up in bed without night-lights left burning or reassuring good-night kisses.

One of the passions of the Romany is his cup of hot coffee. It is one of the first things we are taught to make and prepare. Our coffee is dandelion coffee, though, if we did not tell you so, you would never know that it was not the best that Brazil or Kenya have to offer. In looks and taste it is the same. In the spring-time, when the dandelion has flowered and is at its best, the roots are dug up, washed, and dried in the sun. They are then cut into pieces, these pieces placed in a tin and roasted over the hot embers of a fire, pounded on a heavy stone, rubbed carefully through a sieve, and put in a tin and stored for the winter. This is the Romanys coffee, and it is not only equal to the most expensive shop brands, but is a drink which is a fine tonic and one of the best nerve builders and liver rejuvenators in the world.

One of the first dishes a *chavi* is taught to prepare for himself is the potato-sweet. This is so very simple and so very good that his parents know that while there is a potato lying about he will never go hungry. We first make a corer with a piece

75

of bent tin ; stick it in, turn it round, and make a hole clean through the middle of the potato, which has been half-boiled. The piece of potato that comes out we cut off at the end and stick back again ; we then fill the hole up with jam nearly to the top, put in the other cored top, and there is our potato filled with jam and closed top and bottom. We then bake it. The jam impregnates the potato, and you have a sweet to delight any child and far more wholesome than suety thick puddings.

Moreover, we do not pinch the potatoes, as you have just been thinking. We would have a deal for them. One of the girls would go down to an old farm-house and trade the old lady a couple of yards of lace and get perhaps a stone of potatoes in return. Romany shopping is always done on the barter system. You get more that way.

Another sweet the child soon learns to make itself is the *buni-manricli*, or honey-cake. You take oatmeal, or wheat, or barley-meal, parboil it and dry it. Then mix it with honey, ground walnuts and a little nut, the barcelona nut, which has been ground, chopped, or hammered out and cut up. Mix with honey and meal and butter and walnuts, and bake. In addition to being extremely nourishing, these last indefinitely. Sweet biscuits, also, are made that way. Plenty of fat, oil, or hedgehog fat for preference, some ground oatmeal, some treacle or syrup, a pinch of salt, and mix together and bake.

We go in a great deal for soups, and everything you can think of goes into the *sastra* pot—the big iron pot on the tripod. Pork, mutton, anything that has been left over—sparrows, rooks, wood-pigeons, moor-hen ; turnips—always lots of turnips for the Romany—onions, wild thyme, fennel, marjoram, garlic, and any fat that comes to the top we skim off and use for cooking snails.

Among the first things the Romany *chavi* is taught, is to hunt for his dinner. Among the easiest hunting is sparrows.

Sparrow-pie is a toothsome morsel, but we children need not starve wondering how to make pie-crust. When we had caught them, the girls would pluck and clean them, thread them through a piece of wire, which would then be strung between two forked sticks over the fire. As the row of roasting sparrows would drop its little sizzles of fat on the fire below, the smell was almost unbearably tempting to the *chavis* sitting round in a ring. One sparrow is just right for a *chavi* mouthful. How do you catch a sparrow ? We used to catch them around the haystacks of a night time, with a sieve, and a candle and a wooden spoon to hit them on the head with.

A winter dish no Romany can resist is the *parni-cannie*, moor-hen. The moor-hen is particularly easy to catch. In the winter when the ponds are covered in ice the moor-hen seems to think it is an ostrich. It is so taken by surprise at having no water to take to, that it runs across the ice and sticks its head in a hole in the bank, convinced that it cannot be seen. So you need never be at a loss for a dish of moor-hen, roasted with fennel, marjoram, wild thyme, and a touch of garlic or shallot. Furthermore, the eggs of the moor-hen make a very special kind of omelet. To the beaten eggs the Romany woman grates some pieces of cheese, adds tiny pieces of bacon, chopped garlic or shallot, and a little piece of thyme. This cannot be bettered by any *gorgio* omelet and hot from the pan has an odour that would give even a dyspeptic old millionaire an appetite beyond his mineral water and dry biscuit.

XIX

WITH our training of how to catch our food we are also taught where to find that food. Early the Romany *chavi* learns where to find pheasant eggs, partridge eggs, and the succulent *hotchi-witchi*. The *hotchi-witchi*, or hedgehog, is highly prized by the gipsy. Not only is he wonderful to eat but his fat is used in some of our oldest herbal cures. I do not know exactly why his fat is so important a basis for our ointments, but I do know that you cannot poison him. Gamekeepers have told me over and over again that they can put enough strychnine to kill half a dozen men in their pheasants eggs to catch the hedge-hog, but he can eat the lot and no harm come of it.

As a dish the *hotchi-witchi* is unrivalled. It is more succulent than a rabbit and more tasty than a pig. Also it does not eat the filth a pig eats ; it is clean in its habits, and pure in its food. It eats only the best of everything—pheasant eggs, cow's milk which it sucks direct from the ever-handy cow, and apples which it takes home by rolling over on them and pinning them to its back. The hedgehog makes a perfect little nest in the hedge and covers himself with grass, and like the criminal he covers up all his tracks with care and forethought. But, unfortunately, when he leaves his nest he always backs himself out, hind legs first, and in backing out he makes a big broad trail and pulls the grass along with his spines. He has to back out like this because his nose is so exceedingly sensitive that the smallest rap with a finger will kill him instantly. Now the *gorgio* would not notice these tracks, but that is exactly what the Romany child is taught to look for, and once you have found your nest you have only to wait till the gentleman comes home drunk with milk and fat living. The trick is, of course, once you have caught the little devil, to get him undone. You have to handle him very gingerly and the pet trick of a Romany is to put him inside somebody's bed. That teaches you to feel inside your bed next time and keep your wits about you ! It is really very simple to get a hedgehog to uncurl. You only have to know his weakness. For the hedgehog is like a lady, he loves to be tickled. All you need do is rub your finger or a stick up and down his back and he uncurls. The gentlest tap on the nose and he is unconscious. He is not as difficult to skin as you might imagine. You run a red-hot poker over him and burn his spines, hang him on a hook, and take his skin off. Some Romanys prefer to leave him un-skinned, roll him in wet clay, rub him in the embers of the fire, and when baked, break the clay, which comes apart with the bristles and skin. This is the best way of keeping the luscious juices intact and the flavour of the meat unimpaired. However, he can be very pleasantly cooked in the simpler way with herbs, particularly agrimony and sorrel which permeate the flesh and are as essential to Romany cooking as is garlic to the Greek or Italian. I well remember once as we sat round the *boro-yag* eating our *hotchi-witchi*, some gentlemen belonging to a shooting-party on a neighbouring estate passed near us and were curious to see what smelt so good. They con-gratulated us, and added enviously, that their luncheon, which was only pheasant, would not be half so good.

Ah, but had it been pheasant we would not have allowed them so near ! We should have been hidden away, secretly bid to the feast. Not merely that we would have come by our pheasant unlawfully and the more hidden we were the better, but that pheasant to a Romany is a right royal dish and not to be shared by any but the family, and certainly never offered to a passer-by. We have many tricks for getting our pheasant, but one which pleases us most is the raisin trick : raisins, a fish-hook, a stake in the ground, a piece of horsehair. The raisin is attached to the fish-hook, which is attached to the horsehair, which in turn is attached to the stake thrust invisibly in the earth and covered over. As the shadows fall the pheasants come out of the wood for a last feed before bed. It's the old cock we want to get. He has a fine life and being polygamous always has his harem of females within call. The first evening we scatter handfuls of innocent raisins over the ground, with-out intent to deceive or defraud. Out comes Mr. Pheasant with his lordly old strut looking to the left and right to see that the way is clear. Satisfied that there is no danger he gives the signal : cork-up, cork-up, cork-up. Out come the ladies. By now he has seen the raisins and gets quite excited, and a good time is had by all. In the middle of the day, when they come out again, we have strewn more handfuls of raisins. But the third time is always unlucky to Mr. Pheasant. The raisins are there, but so are the fish-hooks attached by their horsehair thread to the stake. He is ours. The sun goes down and we go up. The Romany loves roast pheasant, and, unlike the *gorgio* epicure, he likes his pheasant free from lead. He does not think that because a bird is peppered with shot it makes better eating, or that the half-dozen lead pellets conferred on it by its gentlemen owners make it more desirable or worth its unnecessarily high price.

XX

WE also don't like shot in our *shooshie*, either. Here again we use two of the senses the *gorgio* no longer needs and rarely uses : observation and smell. Our sense of smell is particularly keen and when we are anywhere near a rabbit-hole we can always tell whether Mr. *Shooshie* is at home or not. If he is not at home the rabbit-hole is empty and gives off a damp cold smell ; but if he is, there comes out a warm pungent smell not unlike that of a litter of puppies huddled together. If Mr. *Shooshie* is at home we get to the windward side and set what we call a smoker. The smoker is made by cutting coarse brown paper into strips about eighteen inches long and three inches wide, which is then steeped in a solution of vinegar and saltpetre, and dusted with Cayenne pepper, dried, and rolled up. This smoker we now light and the wind blows it down into Mr. *Shooshie*'s home, starts him sneezing, and away through the bolt-hole he runs and into our net he goes. He tastes better caught like this than mutilated with shot or tortured in the steel trap. Besides, we should so hate to disturb the game-keeper from his sleep !

The catching of hare also is based primarily on observation. For first of all you have to catch your hare, as Mrs. Beeton says in her recipe for cooking it. Fortunately for the *gorgio* there are always a million of his fellow men willing or paid to do things for him, but should these millions ever fail him and he has to catch his hare before he can follow the rest of the recipe, this is how we do it and it may help him. A hare runs in tracks across fields. He also looks backwards as he runs forwards. These are the two things that matter about Sally the *caneegra* to us. (For some reason unknown to me a hare is always a she to a gipsy, and always Sally.) She makes her 'roads' herself, for the hare has a remarkable sense of location and can regain her home from the opposite side of the field in a flash, and always from the shortest angle or straightest route. So we have to play Red Indian and seek out Sally's tracks. To see whether Sally still uses a road we set what we call a *tester kash*, or a gager. A gager is a piece of stick cut from a bramble bush for preference, and these we set leaning over her road in the grass at opposite angles and at distances of two yards apart. As I have said, a hare, like a gipsy, can see backwards. She knows her road by heart so she streaks along it, eyes at the back of her head, bumping into the brambles which catch her fur as she passes, and tell us what we want to know. The next day we can see by the brambles tipped with fur which road Sally uses and set our snare accordingly, for we never waste a snare on an empty road or knock at an empty house. The next night we still keep the little sticks there, but at a distance of three yards farther along we place our snare. A snare is four, five or six strands of brass wire. We make a loop in the end, and at the other end put a pail, and as the pail revolves it twists the wire perfectly level, kinkless, more evenly than any machine

could wind; then we take away the pail and put the end
through the loop. This is then set in the road three yards
ahead of the thorns. Sally, the *caneegra*, has been pricked the
night before; she does not know what attacked her, but as she
runs down her road to-night she looks behind her for the
enemy, keeps to one side, and is in the noose before she can
look round again. Early in the morning we make our way
to the fields and from afar can see her scattered about the grass,
the stiff white belly shining in the early light.

Hare is best with crab-apple jelly and stuffed with agrimony,
sorrel, and other herbs which impart a flavour to the flesh that
would be an object lesson to the highest-paid *gorgio* chef you
can name me. The hare skin we use for articles of clothing,
for linings of overcoats, for caps, and particularly for belts, of
which the Romany is inordinately fond. These belts are
studded with nails, metal buttons, and coins, and are very
strong and handsome. They are also extremely useful in a
tight corner, and many a *cannie-moosh* has had a slosh with a
belt made from one of his own hares.

And here is something else about the hare which the *gorgio*
does not know and which we found out centuries ago. The
entrails of a hare, cleaned out, treated with formaldehyde, and
twisted, make the finest possible catgut strings for the fiddle or
banjo. This catgut is far superior to that of the *gorgio's* sheep
catgut, and according to the old Roumanian, Hungarian and
Magyar gipsies, who are the best fiddlers in all the world and
can do things with their fiddles that make your fashionable
five-hundred-guinea-a-time violinists look like children
scratching, hare catgut treated in the secret Romany manner
gives a quality to the music unprocurable by other means and
makes the notes sweeter and more resonant.

And while on the subject of music, you should see the
Romany lad lure snails with his special call which brings them
out of their shells and makes them sway and dance like a snake
before its charmer. Romanys are very fond of snails; we

treat them with garlic and boil them in salt water, stuff with
fat, and bake them. But we pick only those that grow near
the hawthorn hedges ; never any that are near ivy. There is
an old Romany belief that one can charm away warts and
carbuncles by rubbing them with the spittle of the snail.

<h3 style="text-align:center">XXI</h3>

FISH also the Romany has to catch before he can eat. Eels are
a useful dish as they are probably the most vital and health-
giving of all fish and can be cooked in so many different ways.
In every pond in England there are eels which the *gorgio* knows
nothing about. We make a basket with osiers, for every
chavi is taught basket-making for many reasons. For eels we
make a circular trap, very like a lobster basket, only that it is
made in a more skilful way, the sticks arranged in such a
manner that it is easy to swim in and practically impossible to
swim out. In the basket we put the entrails of a sheep.
When the eel wriggles through it seems easy enough, but soon
he gets so fat that it is impossible for him to wriggle out again,
and he has not the sense to get out of the hole at the top. Eel
jelly, eel soup, fried eel, all these are delicacies pleasant to eat.
We also treat eels with herbs, and particularly with the root of
the buttercup which, when cooked with eel, is similar in taste
to a truffle. Buttercup root is also used raw by us for many
dishes. Scraped, it is rather like ginger, and hot and pungent,
and yet used in salads it is rather like a mild garlic.

But if eels require no brains to catch, other fish need plenty.
And that is why we Romanys like fishing ; we like using our
wits and getting the better of our opponent. Most *gorgio*
husbands know nothing about fishing. He usually catches two
things : the nine-thirty out and the six-thirty back. But no

fish.   And to make it worse he goes fishing on a Sunday when the fish shops are shut.   Once I went fishing with a *gorgio*, and after watching him sitting patiently for six hours without a bite and consoled only by his pipe, I realized that we Romanys would soon starve if we left it to the fish to make up its mind. I decided that to a *gorgio* gentleman fishing, which he calls sport, mostly means idling the day away, knowing that at the end of it, even if he didn't catch fish, he would find partridge and lamb cutlets and what-not awaiting him on his return. So it didn't matter much, anyway.   It seemed a matter of vanity and laziness.   Especially when he told me the *gorgio* angler's prayer :

> God grant that I may catch a fish
>   So large that even I,
> When speaking of it afterwards,
>   May have no need to lie !

I suppose that the difference between catching fish in a business-like way and not catching them in a gentlemanly way is that in the first instance you have to eat and in the second you have only to boast.   The *gorgio* likes to stuff his fish with wadding and formaldehyde and put him in a glass case to shine in front of his friends.   We stuff ours with herbs and bread-crumbs and live on the memories.   We don't boast of the size of our catch or wave our arms about and measure off imaginary lengths, but our friends know of our prowess by sitting around the *yag* and sharing it.

The correct *gorgio* angler has a whole armoury of flies and battery of hooks, but if we made a game of it like that we'd just naturally starve to death, like the monks on Friday.   We don't invite the fish on our hook, we make him invite himself by giving him things he cannot resist.

Take trout.   We catch trout by tickling or by making for it an irresistible dish.   The best fish bait for trout (and incidentally

84

for eels) is equal parts of oil of rodium, oil of juniper, oil of cedarwood. Sprinkle a little of this mixture over a handful of moss and place the worms in the moss for at least twelve hours so that they get thoroughly saturated. If you must use your own bait, mix a drop of the oils with it, and turn it from a bait into a lure. Trout, of course, needs no additional charms in the cooking. The best way is always the natural way; straight from the hook into the frying-pan and into the mouth.

Bait for perch or roach is best made of equal parts of oil of spike, oil of fennel, oil of thyme. Mix well before using and add a drop to any living or other bait.

A fish the gipsy is very fond of is pike, the fresh-water shark. For some reason I cannot fathom, unless that he wastes so much that he may as well waste a little more, the *gorgio* does not eat pike. This is a mistake for it makes good eating and is a great nuisance to other fish wherever it is found. We get a pike in several different ways, but the most successful is when he lies idly in the shallow streams moving his fins gently but otherwise not moving. We drop a three-angled hook weighted with a small leaden ball the size of a marble, unbaited, on a thick line, about a foot away from it, then give a quick pull with a particular and deft movement of the wrist, and he is hooked in the gills and landed. We do not wait for him to bite. We bite him. Sometimes we even grease the bullet and shoot with a Winchester repeater. (There are no game laws where we are!) Greased, the bullet flies straight, otherwise immediately on contact with the water it ricochets. We wash him with fresh water to take away the muddy taste; clean him; stuff him with marjoram, thyme, agrimony, breadcrumbs and fat. A pike is a first-class eating fish.

Carp is a much despised fish in England. Yet it is treated with the respect due to it in all other countries in the world, particularly in Japan where it is the symbol of good luck. Carp is a bit bony to eat but its flesh is an epicure's dream and it would repay a millionfold any interest taken in it. It is at its best cooked with onions. Stuff with sliced onions, herbs, a sprinkling of flour, and bake in a moderate oven. I have often wondered why cookery books ignore this succulent fish. The carp figures in many legends in the Far East, in Italy, where there is some story relating to the magic powers of its head, and also with us. Our *juvvals* fish for carp, and fine anglers they make too. Romany girls are very superstitious about the carp and at certain dates or certain hours they set themselves to catch one and count the scales. They say you can count the carp's age by its scales. What the Romany girls count is, of course, the year in which they shall be married. This legend can be taken too seriously. I remember one girl belonging to my father's tribe who caught an enormous carp and then threatened suicide because she would be well over sixty before she got a sweetheart according to its scales! They had great difficulty in keeping her from jumping in the river and drowning herself, she took it so to heart, fishing up the old monster!

XXII

OUR vegetables, of course, we have all around us, nettles being our favourite. Young nettles are finer to the palate than spinach and wonderful for stamina and all blood troubles. An Austrian prince a hundred years or so ago made half a million sterling by selling to the army nettles and saying it was spinach. He was not only giving them something far better than spinach but was curing their skin troubles and softening their arteries. You will never have hardening of the arteries if you have nettles in your diet. Dandelion root and leaf, such a nuisance to the *gorgio*, is a godsend to us and excessively useful. In flower we make our own wine of it, fine as the best hock or sparkling if you prefer it like champagne; its root we use in a hundred and one medicines ; the nicest leaves we eat in our salads. Indeed, the *parney-kip-lulagi*, the piddle-bed-flower, is heaven's own gift to hungry or suffering humanity, and if you still think it is a weed I assure you that it is a magic weed and can do with a little more respect from the *gorgio*.

Bills have not to be passed through the Commons to help the Romany to get his own allotment. I have grown marrows and gourds for years which have never cost me a penny, nor inconvenienced the farmer. We plan our kitchen garden like this. In the spring-time, when the wheat is sown, we used to go down the drills of the corn and measure out certain paces and set out seeds. A Romany measures in the simplest way, naturally. He paces out a certain number of feet, which he remembers by picking his age and the month of his birth. Say his age is thirty-five and he was born in December. You pace out 35 feet by 12 feet and there is your kitchen patch. You put in your seeds. As the corn grows higher the pumpkins grow larger in the rich shade, no one to see them and the birds cannot see them. We would then roll round again in the autumn—and I once had such a patch that we filled a cart with them from only one field. It sounds strange to say that all this is done without detriment to the farmer. It harms no one. No one ever enters a cornfield till perhaps May, when they cut the thistles, then we set the pips, and no one visits that cornfield till the reapers arrive on the scene. We have been before they come and harvested on our own. Should any one by chance find our patch they put it down to the birds. Birds are always getting blamed for carrying the seeds the Romany sows ! Romanys do not do that to-day, I'm told. But we did, for in my day there was still fun to be got out of using our brains and scheming. And fine jams and preserves to be made from our pumpkins and gourds. Boiled pumpkin pips, incidentally, are good for colic ; pound them up, boil them, and strain the water off.

Lest you should think that this is simple fare I will surprise you by saying that in certain parts of England, more numerous than you would believe, the much-coveted truffle can still be found. It is the easiest thing in the world to train a dog to get truffles. Among the places I might mention—ah, no, my Romany friends would not thank me for that betrayal. Anyway, have a try now and then under your own elm trees !

XXIII

ROMANYS are not only particular about the cooking of their food, they are particular about its eating. Here I would like to say that we think the *gorgio* a messy, even an unpleasant, eater. It is not merely that he eats far too much and without giving thought to what he is eating. It is that he piles up so many foods on the same plate. Whether it is roast beef and Yorkshire pudding and roast potatoes and several kinds of vegetables, and onion sauce and lamb and the same amount of potatoes and vegetables, the whole drowned in a vinegar and sugar called mint sauce, or his puddings and hors-d'œuvres, everything he eats is messed up in a jumble on his plate. We are taught from infancy to have at most two things on our plates. We are taught that more than this would spoil the palate, the sense of taste, and the sense of smell. If we are to have two vegetables, we eat them separately, as do the French. We also eat from our own plate or bowl and from no one else's. Mascka used to make our little wooden bowls as children. Only chestnut and sycamore was good enough for him. Crockery was useless on the rough roads over which we had to jolt and our eating utensils were of wood and enamel. Each of us was taught to do his own washing-up and there was quite a little rivalry as to which of us could make the wood cleanest and whitest with our little wire brushes which we would turn always in the one direction so as to make the grain of the wood still more beautiful. We were never allowed to eat too much nor to tempt ourselves to eat. What we asked for we got and that we had to eat. The English child may have the world's best table manners and live in holy fear lest he spill his food on the nice clean tablecloth, but he knows nothing of the hygiene of eating and lives and dies in an ignorance of his food that would shock a true-bred Romany of six years old. Greed is a natural *gorgio* vice. It is a trait unknown among Romany children. Not that we do not like sweets and food, but that we have been trained differently. They do not loom as mysteries in our lives, nor are they used as rewards or punishments, so that we do not gorge or dream on them.

As we sit in our circle around the fire, our keen appetites excited by our keener noses, we have one unbreakable rule : the eldest first. Whether it is a man or a woman it does not matter, the eldest gets served first, and so on in age down to the children. While I am on the subject of old people, I would like to say how much we Romanys love old age. We have no fear of it, nor contempt for it. Especially do the *chavis* adore the old. To us they are wise, greatly wise ; we measure their knowledge and their experience by our own small knowledge and experience and we understand how much they must know. The Romany does not just worship youth and beauty in the vulgar *gorgio* way. They do not turn from wrinkles. The more wrinkled, the more reverenced, for the harder life has been. What is a terror and a tragedy to the *gorgio* woman is to us a sign of honour and not disgrace. We love our old people. (I will say they are much more picturesque than yours, except your country folk who have a natural earthy look still about them.) We are sorry for the *gorgio* old who seem to us always lonely and of use to no one ; unwanted and unclaimed. Family pride and tradition are strong in us. Moreover, our old people really are more wise and knowledgeable than ourselves, not like some of the *gorgio* old, who know no more than they did as young people and are merely senile. Whereas the *gorgio chavi* would turn away in disgust or not know where to hide his shame if he saw his old granny smoking a pipe, the Romany *chavi* is delighted to see the old ladies drawing placidly at their pipes. When the Romany woman takes to the pipe—(my mother smoked strong cigarettes years before the *gorgio* woman ever dreamed of such a thing)—it means that she is getting old and settling down, and it is pleasant and soothing to the nerves to have a little sit and a draw at the pipe. Then we know our grandmother is happy, and the great joy of the Romany boy is to save up enough to *dav* the *toovla*, give her a piece of baccy, or *lels tutti a svegla*, buy her a pipe, and see her old eyes gleam and her brown old face take on a hundred new wrinkles as it creases up to grin her thanks and tell us the old, old story that we are the finest and strongest of them all.

XXIV

To be a contractor at the age of eleven would be an unheard of thing to a *gorgio* boy. But I was one.

It happened quite by chance, but I hung on to it. We were staying on the fringe of a town and I was *tatting* and calling at the house of a painter and plumber. I bought some odd scraps of lead from him, some old brass taps and lots of metal oddments. He was a little man with a scraggy beard and moustache. A good-hearted little fellow who was always trying to convert the heathen. They called him Teddy Africa and his name was Secker. He was a prominent member of the local chapel, much concerned in the welfare of the savage in Darkest Africa. So what more natural than that he should take an interest in me, pitched, as though by heaven's design, on his very door-step. He plied me with questions as we did our deal. Did my people treat me kindly ? Did I get enough food ? I told him that Romany parents treat their *chavis* kindly but firmly. I told him I had had the *kash* many a time, but always I had deserved it. I probably would deserve it many times more. I assured him we always had plenty of food. Trust a Romany for that !

As we finished our deal I noticed bits of coloured glass from danger lamps and church windows about his yard. I asked what he did with them and he told me he threw them away. I told him I would like them, because I used also to make model churches and weather houses in which Noah comes out when it rains and his wife when it is fine, and here were just the windows I needed for them. This led him to taking me round his work-yard, in which, to my surprise, were hundreds of street lamps packed tightly together. Teddy told me that he painted them all every year, did the repairs to the broken panes, and refixed them at the end of the summer. He said he wanted a boy to wash them ready for painting. I thought this was where I came in and asked in a very serious voice how much he was prepared to pay. He said a shilling a day, but I held out for so much a lamp. I explained I could work as long as I liked and straight on till I had done them. I did not need to leave off at four on Saturdays and I would work all Sundays and also after tea. We closed the deal at one penny a lamp, and I put down my *tatting* bag and started off at once.

I had to use a spoke brush for the inside strips of metal where the glass was fixed, an ordinary soft brush for the outside, and soda in the water, of which there was a copperful boiling ready. I did an average of three dozen lamps a day and was sorry when they were all finished. I felt considerably important at finishing my ' contract ' so soon, and asked had he other jobs. Teddy suggested I paint the lamp-posts in the street, a job consisting of brushing away the dust and coating them with a buff-coloured paint. How many of these could I do per day ? What was my price ? I drew myself up to my full

height, which was not considerable, and suggested twopence a
post. But he said : ' No. I'll give you more than that. I'll
give you threepence.' I thought him a form of lunatic.
Fancy a man giving you more than you asked. He must be
bilaco. But I know now that if a man had undertaken the
work he would have been paid from one shilling to one-and-
sixpence at the very least.

Now for the first time in my life I hired labour. I soon
found that it took longer to dust them than to paint them, and
I begrudged the time I had to spend on these preliminary
preparations. An idea occurred to me : why not get a *gorgio*
boy to do the rough work ? *Gorgio* boys were not too
plentiful as they were mostly at school, but I soon found one
who was willing to play truant next day and I paid him a
penny for each post he cleaned for me. Then things began to
hum. As an employer of labour I had a difficult time. The
schoolmaster took a hand and I had to engage a fresh boy
nearly every day. But on Saturdays I had all the hands I
needed and I had a couple of streets all ready ahead. When
Teddy inspected the work he could find no fault with it, and
only once or twice did I have to go back and dab a little on a
place I had missed. I did not like being rebuked so took great
care he had no chance of finding fault again. I was now earning more than a tradesman. Teddy told me that Andrew, his
workman, only got fourpence an hour, so I must not tell him
how much I made in a day. I felt master and millionaire in
one ! I finished my contract and had roughly three pounds
in cash. I had earned about twenty-two-and-sixpence a week
clear, painting from fifteen to eighteen lamp-posts a day.
Sometimes it was only an ordinary gas pipe fixed to a wall,
but it all counted at threepence a time. No little dog ever
wished a town more full of lamp-posts than I did !

My next contract was dog kennels. Not little wooden
kennels, the home of one dog, but a building where some local
wealthy man kept a pack of foxhounds. These were boarded

out to neighbouring farmers and sportsmen while the kennels were being painted. I was to do the kennels in red oxide paint, and it was mostly a matter of iron railings and doors, rain-water gutters and iron tanks. These kennels were four miles from anywhere in complete isolation and I could not afford to pay for a room or waste the time walking miles to the caravan and back, so I decided to sleep in the kennels, put in a stock of food, and for Teddy to bring me more from time to time when he came to inspect the work. I do not want to boast, but I do not know of a *gorgio* boy of eleven years who could spend night after night in a lonely spot four miles from anywhere and not give the job up next morning if still alive. Teddy was fair to me. He told me that the last time the kennels were painted it had cost him three men at half a crown a day for three weeks. Fifteen shillings a week was a grown man's good wage in those days. It went a good deal further than three pounds will go to-day. Many a 7 lb. pot of jam I had for one-and-ninepence from a famous grocery chain-store, with threepence returned on the jar. Cheese was mostly fourpence a pound and the best Canadian fourpence-halfpenny. Lard was fourpence a pound and currants one penny. Tea was fourpence-halfpenny a quarter, with an enamel wash-basin or teapot or saucepan thrown in as an inducement to buy. At one time I had so many of these free gifts from groceries that I stocked my caravan kitchen for years. It was mainly the cause of the Romany going out of the china and hardware trade, this giving away of mantel ornaments with quarter-pounds of butter, teacups and plates with certain brands of tea. So if fifteen shillings a week was paid for a grown man's full wage, and three of them taking six pounds all told in three weeks, it looked to a Romany lad to ask for four pounds on completion of the job. But Teddy was firm. He promised me five. I went to work at the first light of dawn and worked till darkness made it impossible for me even to feel my way about. I did not go to the Hole in the

Wall, as they called the little public-house where you bought beer handed to you through a hole in the wall and where Teddy's three grown men had spent most of their time. I was not a workman but a contractor, and the sooner the work was over the more profit I would make on it. I finished the work in a fortnight and Teddy was as pleased as he was surprised.

Clinking my five golden sovereigns in my pocket and following the *patteran* which I picked up a few miles down the road, I *trekked* the nineteen miles to where our caravan had moved and great was my mother's joy when she saw me swinging down the road looking as if I might buy everything in sight. I showed her my fortune and told how I had come by it and her eyes flashed as she listened to me. She took my little capital and put it safely away to my account in the bolster with the communal wealth. In those days we slept on our gold and the family pillow was solid, believe me. I once saw at a Romany wedding a quarter of a peck of gold given to the bride as a wedding dowry and they could hardly lift it.

XXV

I was beginning to realize my worth. To *tatting* I added other activities and decided early to become a dealer and an owner of live stock. A young Romany's one ambition used to be to possess a *grye*, and he has to get it, starting perhaps with a couple of *cannies*, and a *brockrie*. He *chops* and *chops* until he gets to the *dickey* stage, which is owning a donkey, and then there is no stopping him.

To hear a Romany *chal* describe the merits of his *dickey* is an education in itself. Every good point is brought out, but hear him buying a *dickey* instead and you'd never believe the animal could live with so many alleged ailments. I've seen a Romany buy a donkey one day which, according to his account, had spavins, cracked hoof, was windy, had a touch of mange, was a cribber, jibber, and a roarer all in one, and the next day at a different fair-ground he had transformed that *dickey* into one that was docile, sound in every way, wind and limb, a good feeder, could run like a racehorse, and pull a ton. With all these qualifications, who could resist handing over another donkey or pony with all the before-mentioned complaints and a dollar to boot, which means five bob as an extra ?

My first real property was an old girl called Nanny. No, not the old soul that you *gorgio* folk put all the bother of your *chavis* on, but a goat who, although she came from a well-bred family, had not got the best of tempers. Her biggest aversion was a stick, and to wave one in front of her nose was courting trouble. Nanny would buck and put herself in a fighting attitude at the mere sight of a stick and with head well in would give a perfect imitation of a champion boxer about to do some body work. Nanny eventually presented me with twins, and I used to take my small flock out to feed it in the lanes. I had been out with the three of them early one Sunday morning and was returning through the village when I had the misfortune, on the green, to pass a Salvation Army band. As soon as I saw that drummer I knew there would be trouble. Nanny saw him too, doing all the real stuff with two sticks at once and treble noise, and she was off like a race-horse in a bee-line for him and his drum, and that drum was never banged harder either before or after than when banged by Nanny. No sooner had I got her horns out than she seemed to know there was still another side left to the drum, and she backed me into the village pond in trying to get a good run at it ! Nanny not only broke up the drum but broke up the party, and it cost me fifteen shillings, and I nearly retired from the goat trade.

Still, goats were cheap in those days. Nanny had cost me only a half-crown and then presented me with twins; and many a goat I have bought for one shilling. I always got a good price for my goats when I sold them as I used to decorate their horns with brass, and with the twisted spiralling rings and the gleaming balls on each horn; they looked so handsome as to be worth the small extra I charged.

A Toggenburg Nanny I bought from a jeweller in Sudbury for two shillings used to give three pints of milk a day. I recall her particularly because, young as I was, I have never forgotten the man who sold her to me. H— was his name and his father used to go to the fairs and markets for miles around dressed like a Chinaman, in a little cart with four-in-hand donkeys drawing it with a great jangle of harness through the lanes and commons. H— used to sell a plate-powder which he had christened Carboniferous Ooze, a name which never failed when he hissed it out to have the effect on the yokels he had anticipated. He used to tell them that it was a miraculous Chinese powder, whose recipe was lost in the mists of time but had been rediscovered (presumably on a clear morning !) by him in time to save the plate of the world and particularly that of the housewives present. Actually his Carboniferous Ooze was a plate-powder made from a recipe given him by some passing gipsies to whom he had done a good turn. It certainly is miraculous stuff and very simple to make, and I will give you the old Romany recipe when I have finished with H—. H— had a long thin face, dark, the kind known as cadaverous, particularly suited to his Chinese impersonation. He waxed his long thin moustaches to hang down the corners of his mouth and droop over his chin, and he wore an inverted lamp-shade on his head with an edging of tassels which bobbed about as he spoke and reassured every one that he was telling the truth and really came the hundreds of thousands of miles he claimed to have come. Often for the fun of it, meeting him at a fair, I would *spiel* for him, helping him to work up a crowd, and translating the Chinese he mouthed at me so earnestly. We would begin with a Chinese song in high falsetto tones,

calculated to deceive the scholar let alone the *joskin,* and soon
we would have them rolling up.

Wonga wonga won ahee
Nan yan nan o you o me . . .

we would intone with correct Oriental monotony and break off
to discuss the crowd in our strange native tongue. ' *Wen*
ching pong ping poo ? ' he would say to me excitedly, and I
would soothe him with : ' *Yang ling chang ching loo,*' and then
translate it to the *gorgios.* We created a furore with our magic
Chinese powder, which, I would tell them, was the invention of
a Chinese priest 7,000 years ago. His name, I remember, was
Won Hi. It was only threepence a box and still, after
centuries, it was being used to clean the plate in the temples of
China. All the silver and gold in the temples of Confucius
had been cleaned with this for thousands of years and this was
the reason why it had never been worn away and was still
to-day one of the chief wonders of the world. And now the
housewives of So-and-so were being allowed to share in its
secret ! H— must have made a small fortune out of his
Carboniferous Ooze and he certainly deserved it, for though
he sold them mock-Chinese he sold them the best plate-powder
it is possible to use. It is also very simple to make, and as the
gipsies gave it to him, another gipsy can give it to you. All
you need is a penny ball of whiting and some goldsmith's
rouge. Put the whiting in a pail with about two gallons
of cold water, stir till dissolved and the water milky. Now
strain it from one pail into another, the rough sediment
remaining in the first pail and milky water in the second.
Leave it to settle a while, then stir it up again, then leave to
settle again, then strain off a second time. It will be finer still
now. Finally strain water off, when the wet paste will be at
the bottom of the pail, spread it on sheets of paper and it will
dry into a fine powder, after its purification by water. Mix it

up with ordinary goldsmith's rouge and you have the finest
plate-powder in the world, made from an old Romany recipe
and given away without any tassels on the hat !

XXVI

I HAD got to the donkey stage of ownership when we *chals*
made friends with a *gorgio* boy from a near-by school who was
taking chemistry.   He was always hanging about our caravan,
and one day brought us a chemistry outfit, and to our astonishment tinted a bit of my *dickey's* ear.   We were delighted, saw
its possibilities, and swopped some Romany conjuring tricks
and some windmills for the outfit and a lesson on how to use it.
Then off we went to see if Hoddy's donkey was in its stable.
Hoddy was the samphire man of Dersingham, Norfolk, and
as usual was on the booze.   We put blue stripes round his
dickey's legs and pink and green spots over the rest of him, and
when Hoddy came down the following day, imagining he was
sober, he thought he had properly got rats.   Just another touch
of the old d.t. for Hoddy, for they used to booze properly in
those days and they used to get it.   Meanwhile we had gone
round to the *gorgio* boys and charged them pennies for seeing
the only coloured zebra in the world !   This dodge was so
successful that it occurred to me that there was money to be
made in showing coloured donkeys and I told Dolfy Grey that
I was going into the show business for a month or so.   Dolfy
Grey was a Romany boy, but of English stock and therefore
bilaco, so that although he was eighteen and I only fourteen I
ruled him easily and he always looked to me for advice and
leadership.   So we had a *chop* for Hoddy's donkey.   First of
all we put the fear of God up Hoddy by telling him that the
police would be after him for cruelty.   That brought the price

down considerably ! I gave Hoddy a goat and two kids and Dolfy Grey put the other fifteen shillings, so we had a half-share in the thirty-shilling coloured *dickey*. We borrowed a tent from a little fellow, Toby Grey (every one knew Toby, who used to work a side-show called 'How Mary Secured her Mutton '), and set off to exhibit our donkey. We charged twopence a time to see ' The Only Donkey of its Kind in Europe.' We called it 'Balaam's Ass, the wonder-striped donkey from Cairo. An Actual Descendant of the Donkeys of Biblical Days ! ' When I *spieled* for it I used to explain how all donkeys had a cross on their backs from the old legend of carrying our Lord into Jerusalem. Ours hadn't a cross (because he had been first whitewashed then dyed !) because he was an earlier donkey than any met with in Europe. He was the donkey who came long before the Jerusalem story. In fact he was on hand when the daughter of Pharaoh found the infant Moses in the bulrushes and had helped to carry him back to the palace. So he needed no mark on his back ! Our success was phenomenal, and Dolfy and I were staggered at our luck and my foresight. Only one thing worried us and that was getting him home at nights from his tent. Every one followed him down the street and had a free look. We must have lost quite a lot of local twopences before we had the brain-wave to cover him up. We made him a beautiful overcoat of blanket and we bound up his legs with sacking. This in-creased his value forty per cent, for the sensation he made going home at night in his new clothes was almost as great as when they saw him naked. He never used to cost us anything for his food as every one brought him gifts of carrots and oats and all the local *chavis* used to raid their parents' kitchen gardens and stables for food for our *dickey* ! We took good care to tell the children that it was very lucky to give him a carrot and the donkey enjoyed the fun. All we were afraid of was what would happen when the colour wore off. Eventually we got to a place called Wisbech "Statters," where a fellow was anxious to do a deal, and although the tent did not quite belong to us, we sold *dickey*, tent, handbills, and *flash* painting of *dickey* for ten pounds, and Dolfy and I *trekked* home with two months' takings of fifteen pounds each in our pockets.

When we got back to our people Hoddy met us with a reproachful look in his eye. He had gone straight back on the booze on finding that it was not d.t. this time but a trick played on him. Yet he bore us no grudge. Hoddy never bore a grudge, for he always had his best friend to fall back on —drink. He had a coat full of big pearl buttons, big as a florin. He sewed one on every time he went to prison for seven days. He had 361 buttons last time I saw him. Hoddy was five foot high and nearly five foot across, a lion's heart and a camel's thirst. He lived on the wild shore on the Dersingham coast, a few miles from King Edward's place. Hoddy's house was orange-boxes, driftwood, flattened-out biscuit-tins, all covering a big dug-out in the ground, in which he lived with his one son and two daughters and half a dozen fierce dogs chained around his home to guard it for him. Many a time the King's estate agents came to Hoddy, offering to build him a house for nothing if only he would give up his curious dug-out of a home ; but he was stubborn as a mule about it and would not give it up for any one. When, after many years, they succeeded in getting him turned out, it broke old Hoddy's heart and he died of it. Hoddy's daughters were the finest-looking girls it is possible to imagine, even to-day. Then it was nothing short of a vision to see among all the tied-in, lily-white, over-dressed, unhygienic, mincing female creatures, which were the women of those times, two wild, half-dressed animal creatures, made of bronze from constant living in the sea-winds, thin, quick, fleet as Diana, their black hair uncombed falling in their eyes, through which they peered at you more dark and savage than any Romany I ever saw. They were so wild that the sight of a man or a stranger approaching them or even half a mile away on the horizon would send them like hares to their burrow to hide. I suppose these days a benevolent County Council would come and reclaim them, and, at considerable expense to the tax-payers, make them into passable servants and shop-girls. But in those days we were still comparatively free and Hoddy's children went their wild handsome way without interference from local busybodies. They used to help Hoddy collect his cockles and samphire, and he would go round in his pony cart in the towns and villages for twenty miles around. No one could sing cockles like Hoddy. He gave it a peculiar cry all his own, deep and rich. 'Co-co-cockle ali-ive! Coc-co-cockle ali-i-ive! Big cockle, fine cockle, co-co-cockle alive!' Doors would open at Hoddy's voice and all the women come running, and you could hear the echo of it at the farthest end of the town.

XXVII

Now with fifteen pounds in my pocket it was the moment to become a *grye* owner and try my luck in my father's profession. The first horse I bought was a greasy-legged one from an old farmer. He wanted five pounds. After a lot of haggling I bought it for fifty shillings and I think the old man admired my impudence. I was then practising the *grye-kuper* secrets, in which, as is well known, we Romanys excel, and I wanted to see if I could get my horse well. It didn't cost me anything to keep him, for we were in a lonely part and we used to *puv* the *grye*, which means that, ostensibly by accident, the horse has wandered into a field. We never took him in at the gate. We used to train a horse to go through a gap in the fence, and then we would leave him there all night and forget about him. To call a horse back was another of our tricks : we used simply to rattle maize in a tin pail, for after a good graze of grass a pail of maize is to a horse what a glass of tokay is to a *gorgio* after a perfect dinner. 'He comes to a good home when he comes to me !' I used to say earnestly, looking up with my round eyes at the farmer. 'Yes, he'll go to a good home all right if he goes to a gipsy,' the farmer would say. 'He'll go right back in my own field !' And after the deal he would say humorously : 'And now I suppose I shall also be keeping it for you for a month !'

Soon I had cured my horse of greasy legs and sold him for five pounds to pull a man's caravan, and many hundreds of miles he went after that. Time does not count with us, and that is one of the reasons we always have the best of a bargain. Supposing we had spent a month's work on it, we still had no wages to pay ; we had done the work ourselves and put our experience to the test. The two-pound-ten becomes clean profit. I have seen my father sell fifty ponies for one shilling a head profit, and be pleased. I have known him to take two hundred ponies all the way to Roumania and consider himself in luck when he made five shillings profit a head on each. But then, again, I have also seen him buy a horse for fifteen shillings and trim it up so handsomely that it sold for fifty pounds.

I learned a lot from my first horse. No wonder they prophesied a future for me ! Why, I was soon selling horses to my father at a profit ! The grown-ups used to curb my conceit a little by telling me that it was not so much my dealings which were clever as that the sentimental *gorgio* with whom I dealt could not resist me. I believe I was a rosy-cheeked boy with a bright eye and a merry smile, and with my little gipsy suit and its silver buttons and scarf must have softened the hearts of the old farmers who did not really like to get the better of a boy, where they would fight to the last farthing with a grown gipsy. When I would return to the camp with a particularly fine bargain and parade it before my elders sitting round the *yag*, my mother would look up at me and say with a sly smile : ' Well, Pet, if you are going to go on dealing like this you must be careful never to grow up ! '

XXVIII

IT was round about this time that I thought I would try army life. Not that I liked the idea but that I had got myself into a nasty scrape and it was easier to face the militia than the magistrate. I was just turned fifteen at the time. I had been asked to find some squirrel skins, and squirrel skins I determined to find, so with a bunch of *chals* of my own age I set out early one Sunday morning on a real hunting expedition in some near-by woods. We chose Sunday for two reasons. Firstly we could not go out *tatting*, hawking, or dealing on the Sabbath, as the *gorgios* did not work ; secondly, the chances of the gamekeeper being around were less. I had an old-fashioned muzzle-loading gun, which had to be loaded with powder, then a wad of paper, then a charge of shot, then another wad of paper, the whole business rammed down tightly with a ramrod. I had been particularly successful, for squirrels were plentiful and I was an excellent shot. But we had not reckoned on the distance the sound of the report of the gun would travel, and we had not been working an hour when up comes the gamekeeper.

I knew him by sight. And I had heard more than once of how he was feared by the *poachers* and how fierce he was in a scrap. His nickname was Rough Jack and he was said to act up to it with little provocation. Rough Jack made a straight line for me. He had just seen my last shot, so he knew that the gun was not loaded and that he could struggle for my gun without causing an accident. I was tough for a youth, made all of steel and lightness, and best of all I never suffered from nerves. So instead of giving in meekly as he obviously had thought from my size and age, I fought to retain possession of my own property. I tried some of the tricks I knew, such as putting my feet between his legs, treading on his feet to distract his attention, but although Rough Jack was well on in the fifties he was a game one for a struggle. All he feared was that my friends would join in against him. I called across : 'Come on ! Give me a hand !' But they stood in a huddle watching, panic-stricken, obviously hypnotized by this particular game-keeper's reputation, and left me to it as best I could. Suddenly Rough Jack caught hold of the pin that fastened the stock of the gun to the barrel, and the gun came apart. He had the stock, leaving me only the barrel in my hand. He knew the gun was useless without the stock. But he knew more than that. He knew it was irrefutable evidence. I knew that unless I did something violent and quick I was lost. I was in a fighting rage, more for the loss of the stock than for the threat of the court, and as we closed and wrestled I managed to hit him a heavy blow on the mouth with the barrel. The teeth rattled, he blew a few of them out of his mouth, dropped the stock and put both hands to his bleeding mouth. That was my chance. I picked up the stock and in a streak was away and out of the wood.

XXIX

I GUESSED that this time I had gone too far. I would either be hauled up before the magistrate and given a fine that would eat considerably into my capital, or, worse, I would be sent to the *bichardey-pawdel*. So I cleared out my little stock on the Sunday night and Monday morning and said good-bye to all my people. I gave no hint as to what I intended to do or where I was going, only saying vaguely that I had a job to do and would be back as soon as possible. All I knew was that in my mind I seemed to have got the idea that if you joined the army you were safe from arrest.

Not big enough for the regulars, the sergeant told me. Why not try the militia? But I wanted to go abroad and the militia only stayed at home. He explained with a grin that during the seven weeks preliminary training I could grow considerably and then transfer myself to the regulars. Here was another disappointment. I wanted to be in a horse regiment and the militia, I found, had none. Anyway, I took the shilling and walked the three miles to a village to see one of the magistrates who had to swear me in. I got a ticket for the journey, a shilling to ' see me over,' and away I went. On my arrival I had all the usual jokes that the sergeants at the receiving-room trot out in the name of wit. ' What was the trouble? Sweetheart or murder?' I certainly had a very funny feeling in the pit of my stomach just then. What would happen if the old gamekeeper died? Suppose one of my blows proved fatal yet? I hadn't thought of that when I ran away! ' Orl right, old son, don't look so scared,' said the sergeant. ' A bit of a lad like you couldn't 'ave killed no one, so we'll say it's love!' Love? What was love? There was only one woman I had ever loved and that was she whom, by my temper and foolishness in running away, I was causing to worry again. I wasn't homesick, but I was mother-sick. I asked myself again and again what would she do? Would she get to know the reason of it all? Would she think angrily of me? Anyway, I consoled myself, I was only twenty-five miles away. I would soon let her see me, and see me as a real man, too. That would be a surprise for her and would make up for the anxiety I was causing her now. I pictured myself walking to the *vardo* one night in my red coat and my glengarry hat, a little red knob at the top, and two bits of ribbon which cut the ears like a whip when the wind blew hard.

I got past the doctor and when asked gave my age unblush-
ingly as seventeen and a half. I found the whole thing dull and
easy, and the standardized living and the slavish way every one
took orders and allowed themselves to be bullied was new and
disagreeable to me. But I told myself repeatedly that it was
better than being in prison. A fortnight passed and I heard
nothing of the gamekeeper or the police, so obviously they
were not looking for me. I suppose that having been to
the camp and found me gone he had let the matter drop ;
it is one thing to summons villagers but another thing
altogether to search for wandering gipsies. One place where
I worked hard and acquitted myself well was the gymnasium.
Here I knew that I could learn something of use to me. There
were still some *chals* who could give me a beating. But the
lesson of large heavy Mascka and my quick lean father had
never been forgotten. I knew that I must learn the *gorgio*
tricks of fist and footwork and that our own savage impulsive
fighting was not enough. Every night and every spare
moment was spent in boxing practice. One little sergeant
loved to take the floor with me, play ducks and drakes with me,
and watch me stick it. He admired my pluck. He would
smile when he saw me coming and say : ' Wot ! 'Ere agin !
Didn't I give you enough last night ? ' He could not make
out what such persistence was for, till one day I opened my
heart to him. He saw the funny side of it and from that day
set out to teach me all the tricks he knew.

My first week-end leave came round, and I started trudging
away from barracks and wondering in which direction my
people would have gone. I got lifts on the road in all kinds of
conveyances and one lucky lift which must have come straight
from the *kooshti-Duval* Himself. An old pig-dealer coming
from market and hearing my story, told me that some
Romanys were camping on the common near his place. He
did not know their names, but by the shape and colour of the
vardo, and above all the description of my dog, I knew they

were my people. I could scarcely sit still till the cart reached its destination, when I jumped out and ran up to the *vardo*. My dog knew my joy for he barked and capered. My mother came to the door, with a look in her eyes such as deer have. She *rokkered* Romany. I answered. She pulled me close to her and she made me feel six feet high when she said softly : ' What a man ! ' But almost immediately she said : ' But I don't like the colour of your coat.' Meaning that she did not like uniforms. She said : ' It isn't right. Fight for your own, but do not go and shoot and kill people who have done you no harm. If a *gorgio* came to the caravan and interfered with or attacked some one, beat him and defend your goods. But leave other men alone. It is not godly to kill another woman's son, a son you do not even know.' I explained that I would only be away another three weeks. I told her how, in the month that I was gone, I had gained a knowledge that some would not acquire in a lifetime, and how, like my father, I had learned to use 'em. She was pleased. I think I saw her eyes moisten. She caressed me on the neck and pulled my ears and we lit the *yag* and the villagers came and had the time of their lives seeing a gipsy camp entertaining a member of Her Majesty's Forces. At night the fiddle came out, the castanets, the tambourines. I sang and danced with the *juvvals* of the other *vardos*. I was a hero who had been turned from a *chal* to a man in a month.

Best of all, I could fight. Every gipsy girl admires a lad who can take care of himself and of her. I was anxious to find the family owning the two sons who have given me the knock-out. I prayed that they would turn up so that I could give them the old challenge : ' You couldn't do to me what you did last time ! ' But no luck. I was not to be allowed to add to my triumphs by showing off before them all, and had to content myself with looking as heroic as they all thought me.

Sunday passed. I spent it walking in the fields and the woods with a *juvval*. Never had I done such a thing before as

idle a day away with a girl, even listening to what she had to
say. I began to understand what the sergeant had meant when
I went to the receiving-room to be measured and weighed.
'Is it a sweetheart or murder?' I felt shy and lost all my
usual aggressiveness and cocksureness as we exchanged
confidences and told each other of our lives and people.
Gentle emotions stirred in my heart and frightened me by their
strangeness, unlike any emotion I have ever known. I tried to
discover by her way of looking at me and by her voice when
she spoke whether I pleased her and how much she knew of the
warm unaccustomed feelings stirring in me.

I had to be back at midday Monday, which meant an early
rise for I intended to walk it. I rose at four, for I was only
nineteen miles away and even had I to walk all the way, our
training starts at five years of age and distance is not much of
an obstacle to us. But again luck was with me, and lifts on
brewery-drays and farm-wagons got me to barracks three
hours before I was due. Every one was surprised, as it is not
a thing usual for recruits to arrive before their leave is up, and it
was taken as a sign that I was an enthusiast for the army.
This was not true. I disliked restrictions of any kind far too
much to put up with the monotony and stupidities of army life.
But the militia was not too bad, and with your eyes open there
is always something new to learn. They did not make it too
hot, as the soldiers who had joined the regulars were always
complaining. 'They're fishing for you to join the regulars,
then you'll cop it, my lad,' they used to say to us. And they
were right. I joined a cavalry regiment some years later, but
I was never a success as a real soldier. I will not tell you what
I did or did not do in any war that I was in. Mine was a war
from the time I joined till the day they gave me my freedom
as hopeless. That was not exactly the word on my discharge
sheet but it meant much the same. I left the army as I had
entered it, a trooper but unbroken.

XXX

I HAD only three more weeks and when that was finished I rejoined my mother and started dealing again where I had left off. This was the only life for me and I was happy at my regained freedom and at being my own boss once more. I had become great friends with the *juvval* of my father's companion and my life seemed to hold more significance than ever before. We worked together in the villages through the days, and at night we sat apart and talked. Like all Romanys we put our trust in signs and symbols and fate, and we would compare our skill at *dukkerin* and tell of our successes with the hands we read. One evening as we sat together she took my hand and looked into my palm. She said with a laugh : 'You will hold more *racklers' duks* in your *duk* than any man in England.' (And I can truthfully say that she was right. I have held more women's hands in mine than any man living, as many as two hundred a day passing through my hands to be read.) She continued with a serious face : 'You will be a wanderer in many lands. You will be a *lollie*, a soldier, again. And a shadow will come between you and your best friends.' I answered : 'My mother and you are my best friends.' And she said sadly : 'I know. And one of us two will be with the *kooshti-Duval* within twelve moons.'

I stayed with my people till I had my calling-up papers for my second militia training. They got word to me that she had been kicked by a *grye* the day I left and was gravely ill. Without a moment's hesitation I absented myself, walked back home, knew at first glance that her injuries were fatal, and stayed with her till she died, for though she could not speak, her expression told me more than words that she wanted me to be at her bedside as she passed away. When it was all over and she was buried, I went back to my billet, sad at heart and understanding nothing of the ruthless suddenness with which one finds a thing only to lose it. I had a long time to think it out, however, for I was immediately put under arrest and sentenced to 168 hours' detention. They had no sentiment to waste on dead sweethearts or first love. All that, they told me, was nothing to them.

That, I am sure, was the first step to my being so bad a soldier. I believe when I later joined the regulars I did it out of devilment, to get my own back, and to show them that they could not break my heart, which was the sergeant's standard boast. 'We tame lions here,' he used to say to me with a sneer. But I was no lion. I was a Romany. He'd never tried that breed before.

My mother used to tell me that gipsies used to go with the armies into battle, playing to the leaders before and after battle, even in her childhood days, and that they were made heroes of. I wasn't so lucky. I once got seven days C.B. for playing a tin whistle after lights out. I don't dare to think of the sentence I'd have got if it had been a fiddle I'd played instead of a humble whistle. I left the army with an adverse discharge but with my heart as whole as ever. There was a thing called the South African War and one before that. I was in both. All I care to recall is that I came out of it all with four medals, a bad character, twenty-two shillings, and a cheap reach-me-down. And my boast is still that I am one man who has been in the army and come out of it with his spirit unbroken.

XXXI

TROUBLES, people say, never come singly, and with the Romany there is a belief that it must come three times in succession. We believe in the *trin Bengs* : the devil, his wife, and their son. The devil has the first pick at you. His wife, like all females, naturally must have her share. The son has also to be humoured. I think the routine of the *Beng* family was reversed in my case, the son getting his little picking first, the wife second, and the master last. For my troubles were to grow, not diminish.

My father had been out selling some ponies at a country house where there were children, and had come home delighted with life. Besides the profit on the ponies, he told us, he had made a wonderful bargain and his eyes shone with pride. The bargain turned out to be a very handsome-looking fur-lined coat. He emphasized to us all how it had been the property of a *boro-boro-rye*, the equivalent to a lord in Romany and had originally cost well over one hundred pounds. To own a fur-lined coat had always been my father's weakness. The fur itself was in such perfect condition that it was difficult to understand how the people came to part with it.

When my mother realized that my father meant to keep the coat for himself, she did not like it at all. She remonstrated with him and begged of him not to be so foolish. She reminded him of Lavanya's superstition regarding furs and expressed her own horror of them. For my mother loathed and feared furs. Like many Romanys she refused to wear them, for although we will wear rabbit, stoat, or hare which we have snared, cured, and worked ourselves, we will not touch the large animal furs, especially those which have passed from hand to hand and contain chemicals and germs. Lavanya always believed that if you killed a fur-bearing animal, except field vermin for food, its *mullah* would haunt you. This dates from centuries back when gipsies used to travel with dancing bears. The superstition was strong that unless the bear was buried in his skin the devil wore it and cursed its users. The bear seemed half-human, half-devil, and the *Beng* would not sleep without his coat. Actually I believe this

belief was spread among Romanys because at first they must
have kept the bear-skins and they were old and vermin-ridden
and full of germs and the owners of the fur must have died and
people noticed that all who came in contact with it died too.
It was a hygienic measure. Furs, in any case, are not for
Romanys. They understand the wild creatures too well and
have not the civilized greed for always wanting the other
fellow's skin. But the more my mother remonstrated with
him the more my father laughed. A fur-lined coat was the
wish of his heart and the most he would say to reassure her was
a promise to *chop* it for something else the moment he met a
good enough deal. He wore it with a swagger, thinking how
impressed the other dealers would be, and went off to a sale
somewhere.

I have already mentioned Lavanya's superstition of the
croaking raven, and how it applied particularly to ourselves.
My father had not been long gone when one appeared in a
wood not far from our *vardo* and started an eerie croak. My
mother was uneasy, and I could see that she sensed misfortune
by the way she begged me to try and drive the raven away.
I took my catapult and spent a few minutes shooting leaden
bullets at him. He would fly away for a little while and back
he would come croaking, croaking. ' We shall hear news of
some one's death,' said my mother, the worried look never
leaving her face. We wondered who it could be, knowing
that it could not be one of our family. We were all strong
and healthy ; there was no illness for us, mother would see to
that. What with her herbs and her knowledge my mother
would never let one of us get to death until we were timed by
the *kooshti-Duval*, which meant that only old age could finish
our stay on this planet. While my mother was about, so great
was our faith in her healing powers, we were not going off to
where the *tarno-roy* of *bosa-venos* played his sweet music.

But my mother was to have no hand in this. My father did
not return that night nor ever again. No sooner had he got to

the town than some fever had stricken him and they had taken him to a hospital where it was forbidden us to visit him. The raven had not croaked in vain. My mother vowed he and the coat had brought death in their wake, not understanding that the fur had carried deadly germs and that that must have been why the *boro-ryes* had parted with such an expensive thing for a few pounds. We did not then know such things. Death was our word. My father died within a week in what I realize now was an isolation ward for we none of us saw him again. He was sent back to us sealed, and we were left to drill the seven holes, and prepare for the funeral. We did not bury my father with dancing and festivities. It was not a major funeral with several tribes gathered together. It was a solemn burial with none but ourselves to witness the few simple and necessary rites of our race. We drilled our holes and had our *mullah gillie*, the secret rites of music for the departed, ending in the Song of Hope.

XXXII

The loss of my father meant, of course, that our little home must be sacrificed. The *vardo* must be *yagged* for the *mullah* of its owner to find rest, his spirit must be freed before his feet could be placed on the long *trek* to the happy place. In small family burials the *vardo* is not *yagged* immediately as at a large funeral, when, after the body is covered with earth, every one heads for the *vardo* still singing. In such private burials we give the *mullah* a week's grace to stay in his caravan before the burning. This is probably to give the family time to readjust itself to its sudden loss. Although we all used the caravan at some time or other, principally when it was too wet and too cold to live in our tents, it was still the personal property of my father, as owner and master. All his personal belongings were set aside, all that had been used and shared with him, such as cooking utensils, working tools, and no especial personal claim was ours.

The *yagging* was to take place at the break of dawn so that the freed spirit would have all the long day through to *trek*. We placed the straw and belongings inside the *vardo* and as I was the eldest (my twin brother was six hours my elder, but he was not of us) it was upon me that the task of freeing the spirit of my father fell. I had not seen a *yagging* since, as a child of five, I had left Roumania, for mostly we had travelled alone or with small gangs, and deaths were not frequent. My *juvval* friend had died not long since, but they do not *yag* for *chavis*. So I had to learn the ritual from my mother. Everything had to be done correctly, she impressed on me again and again; I must make no mistake and no hitch of any kind must occur if our father was to go on his journey without hurt and in peace. I was nervous enough at the responsibility placed on my shoulders, for in such cases it is indeed having a man's soul on one's conscience, and it was decided that I should have a full dress rehearsal the evening before the *yagging*. There was a little *tan* which my father used to erect and in which he kept his grinding barrow (we always kept one because it was useful when laying-up in the towns in the winter and no fairs were on), and this I chose for my practice. I got some straw and littered it about; I even put some of his minor belongings in it; and at midnight when the *gorgios* were in bed I pronounced the words of the ritual and applied the torch in which were wound hairs from the heads of all our family. The tent flared up and burned out quickly. A good omen; there was no *mullah there.*

The next morning at daybreak, when the first pink flush of light appeared in the sky, we rose to do the real *yagging*. It seemed, in the chill dawn, a responsibility I almost dared not take on. I would willingly have handed the torch to another member of our family, but I knew that my father's soul waited for me and I knew also that I could not disappoint my mother, who had placed on me my first real adult task. All was weird and silent, and a strange and indefinable feeling came over me. I sensed my father near me. I imagined, as we all did, that he was there waiting and watching us, that he was looking to me for release, that he was eager to be freed from the troubles of this world and knew that I was to do this for him. Repeating the secret words, I applied the torch. A sudden flare, like an explosion, like a thunder-clap, and the straw burst into flames. It had been perfectly calm, I had thought, when the torch was applied. Not a breath of wind stirred, but with the first flame a gentle wind seemed to come, the wind that would carry my father's soul on its long flight. I knew that my duty had been well done. I had made no mistakes. My father would not be earth-bound through a fault of mine. The wind came higher and the flames licked round the *vardo*. Through the roar of the flames we could hear the crackling of the wood, the roof crashed in, sending burning sparks of wood and a liquid play of sparks all around us, then the flames roared up again and soon all that could be burnt was ashes. Only the springs, the axles, the metal tyres of the wheels, in a hot tangled mass of smoking metal, were left among the last burning embers.

When all was over my mother came forward and addressed the ashes, the last rite in our burial service. She stood alone in a circle of cooling ash and again I recall wondering where she had learned the simple beautiful words which came always so readily to her lips. ' *Kooshti Duvel*, let the spirit of my man travel unharmed over the strange roads he will tread, but let his eyes ever keep their power to see us here till he shall know the joy of being united with us all once again.' She then stooped and took ashes in each hand and scattered them over her shoulders. The spirit had taken the great high road of the last *trek* and nothing of my father remained with us. The ceremony was ended and all was well with his spirit.

We then buried the metal parts of the wagon, twisting, hammering and defacing them so that no use for them was left and they could not be used again. Even the little iron buttons from his coat were salvaged and buried too. We dug a deep hole at the entrance to a wood, laid in the remains, and poured water over them to start them rusting.

XXXIII

NOT once did my mother cry or act hysterically. She suffered deeply, but she suffered silently. She had lost her man; she was in a land that was always for her a strange land; she knew she could never hope to see her people or her home again. We now had to have a new caravan. Mascka would have built us one had he been here. The *gorgio* van-builder would make us one, but never like Mascka's oak, ash, and walnut one. She thought of all these new troubles and uncertainties, but she did not worry us with them. A lesson to us again, not to worry others with our troubles; they have always enough of their own to contend with. I would not have dared tell her my thoughts. Watching her now I could only think that bad as it was, suppose it had been she! Without our mother where would we have been had the raven called for her instead of for him? While my mother was there we were safe; there was nothing she did not know, nothing she could not set right. And now that she knew English there was no fear for her. We had such confidence in ourselves then, we Romanys. Our philosophy was: You can eat only one dinner a day if you have a million pounds and if you are hungry anything will do. Besides, these people had so much money that there was always a crust of bread, and if you were thirsty and asked for a glass of water there was always a piece of cake forthcoming.

Birds had no coin of the realm, yet they always got their dinner, and whatever it was provided for rabbits would provide for humans. Moreover, we had started so young that getting our own bread was natural to us. The majority of *gorgios*, when they get to fifty, are always wondering sadly what will happen now. The old Romany philosophy was always that if one can get a living at five with no cultivated sense whatsoever, what a marvellous sort of a living one will be able to get oneself at fifty, our own experience and that of our elders behind us. It is while one is alive that one must live. I have never understood the compensation of a marble tombstone. Some one will always bury you when you start to smell.

There is only one thing to do to make you forget your troubles : work, and work hard. Romanys dare not permit themselves the luxury of brooding long on sorrow, remembering the Fool on the Tarot cards with the dog biting at his feet and the crocodile and snake lying in wait, and its words :

> *Souffrir c'est travailler, c'est accomplir sa tâche,*
> *Malheur au paresseux qui dort sur le chemin,*
> *La douleur comme un chien mord les talons du lâche,*
> *Qui, d'un seul jour perdu, surcharge un lendemain*

We rigged everything up in our tents and set ourselves to work again and take up our lives where they had left off. During the rite of *yagging* the *vardo* we had thought we were alone, but *gorgio* eyes had seen us. The big-hearted old country policeman who lived in a cottage about half a mile away had come out to investigate. When he saw it was our caravan he had stood watching out of sight down the lane. Fortunately he had heard that Romanys burn the homes of their dead, he told us afterwards, and did not interfere. Years afterwards, when he was living on his little pension, he told me that it was the most impressive sight he had ever seen or imagined, and he said : ' Your mother looked like a statue ;

while the flames showed up her face she appeared full of courage, but one could see that she was heart-broken.' He spoke to us on the afternoon of the *yagging*, and said that his wife's brother was a wheelwright, a real old-fashioned working tradesman who had practically retired, but who still kept his tools and did a little bit of work to pass the time away. They had been wondering what we would do without our caravan. He told us that his brother-in-law would be pleased to make us one, very reasonable in price, and we could rest assured that the workmanship would be good. My mother gave the order and we were to help him with the work.

It was a rare happiness to us to see the *vardo* grow. We boys roughed the wood and planed it with the big heavy planes. Always vain to show a *gorgio* how Romanys can work, my young brother Rudy and I put all our strength to it, and were complimented by the old man on our skill and capacity for work. He himself was busy on the wheels. It looked a terribly long job to us, watching him mortise the holes in the hub where the spokes would go, then making the felloes, the semicircle bits which form the outside of the wheels. As a great honour I was allowed to plane these down. This was the most difficult of all jobs, he told us. Then came the great day when the heap of planed wood was sorted out, cut to the required sizes, and the framework fixed together. We did our work in the days of the building just as usual. My mother, with her *kipsie* on her arm, would ' call ' the near-by villages with her lace and woolwork ; we others would do *tatting*, hawking, grinding, and in the evenings we would rush round to see what progress the old wheelwright had made during the day. At last came the day when the body was finished. Here again we two came in, rubbing it with sandpaper ready for the first coat, as he called the white lead paint. We again rubbed that paint smooth, and a second coat was put on. It was again rubbed and yet another coat was put on, these with the final colours. The panels were painted in one colour, the ribs another, then the picking out and lining and the little marks of other colours to ' set it off,' and then the whole finished effect varnished. The body was finished and now came the great day for the wheelwright. A huge circular fire of wood in which the iron tires were to be made red-hot was built up. The tires were placed inside and the pile lit. It brought back recent memories, and I remember thinking : For which of us will this be burnt ? The old wheelwright saw my pensive face and asked my thoughts. I forced a smile and said : ' These wheels will travel many thousands of miles.' He said : ' They will last that time out and more, and they're such a pair of wheels that when I'm in the far, far land you'll remember me by them, won't you ? ' I said I would never forget him and I never have. The iron tyres were made red-hot, taken out with long pincers, placed over the wood rim of the wheel and hammered down, then hammered also round the sides, then we boys poured can after can of cold water on the tires to shrink them to the wood, and they were ready for their final touch up and painting.

What a day when they were fixed to the axles, our goods put in the *vardo*, the fire lit, the lamps lit, and we all assembled to christen the new home ! There was my mother, my sister Lorenza, Rudy, myself, a Romany named Gray and his wife Sylvester, his sons Adolphus and Benny, his daughter Zena, the village policeman and his wife, the wheelwright and his wife and daughter. This was the first time we had ever been intimate with *gorgio* people and I liked them. The Grays brought some *kini*, wine made in the old Romany way like a golden still champagne from the petals of the dandelion. The policeman had a bottle of whisky. The wheelwright had a big bottle of some home-made wine, rhubarb I think it was. My mother had made the cakes, the real *Zingari manrickli*, and a sweet jam called *petari* which we used to eat with a spoon in the manner of the Roumanian *boro*. Rudy and Adolphus were the *bosh*-killers (we spoke English Romany now) ; I played the melodeon ; Zena Gray the castanets ; the elder Gray had his harp ; and the wheelwright, as soon as he got frisky with the policeman, began to sing. I liked policemen after that. I had always thought they were paid to harry us, but after knowing this one things looked different. As a matter of fact he was rather different, and afterwards we often went poaching together. Many a time we had a fine covey of partridges caught by the Romany and the *plastramengro* ! Our singing and music lasted well into the night, the fire and wine lighting our happy faces, and when we had sung, danced, and drunk our fill we said good-bye, swore undying friendship, and praised and toasted our *vardo* till one would have thought it the first of its kind ever made and a carpentering feat as astounding as the Ark !

Rudy and Lorenza were too excited to sleep, anxious for the dawn and the road after so many months stationary in tents. At dawn the *gryes* were brought from the *puv* and even they were frisky after their long rest. Shining and beautiful in its many-coloured paintwork our caravan seemed to smile on us, as though aware of the contentment that had come to us again. For me it was as though I had put aside all thoughts of childhood and was proudly and seriously a man, head male of our family, a man who could use his fists as well as most *gorgios* and his head better than many Romanys, a man who could outbargain and outwit, had his living at the end of his tongue and finger-tips, eager for whatever test was now to come his way. Only my mother looked at the future calmly, knowing that for her it held a round of days without companionship or hope, but of this she said nothing and the young are not over-imaginative.

At last we were ready to start, but not before my mother had said good-bye to a little mound of earth, had poured a little wine on it, and buried a crust of bread at its side. Then away we went, hearts full of hope. We had paid our wheelwright. We were once again *bilovem*.

XXXIV

FORTUNATELY for me my second attempt at education was to be happier and more successful than my first.

Ever since my first try and first rebuff I had known that to read and to write were the most desirable and worthwhile things in my world. I cannot explain even to myself how this ambition came to me, for books and book-learning have no meaning for the Romany, and had I mentioned it to the youths of my own age or to my elders I would soon have been laughed or *coored* out of it. I only know that I had always a strong desire for knowledge of any kind, and have it still. Nothing has ever seemed to me too unimportant to learn, and to the slightest new accomplishment I brought a curiosity and a stubbornness partly inborn and partly the memory of Mascka's versatility which I was to remember and envy all my life. Much as I despised the *gorgio*, finding him even at his best lazy and *bilaco* compared with ourselves, I had always felt that he had certain things to teach me. One was to use my fists intelligently, and that test I had passed with honours. The next was to read and write, for in this alone it seemed to me lay his vaunted superiority. Until I could do these things I would be inferior to him, though my wits taught me a thousand ways of earning a living and I knew the name and properties of every herb that grew.

My chance was to come sooner than I would have dared imagine. We had been *trekking* with our new wagon a few weeks and had come to the village of S—— in Norfolk and decided to camp on the outskirts. The very first morning I was out *tatting* in the neighbourhood, I was to knock on the door which led me to the fulfilment of my life's ambition. It was the house of a naval captain, later to become Admiral Sir A. K. Wilson, who had won the V.C. at Tel-el-Kebir by

fighting the Arabs with a broken sword in hand and then
routing them with his fists. He was evidently pleased to see
me, perhaps because, as a pure-bred Berber Romany, I had
much in common with the country he knew so well and the
Arabs he had fought so gallantly. He was very friendly and
took me inside the house, showing me his collection of swords
and strange weapons, including the broken sword which had
won him his decoration, and his wonderful collection of
fighting ships through the ages. He was very interested in
herbs, another thing he must have acquired in the East, and
wild flowers, and began to swop Arabic with me for some
Romany. He was delighted at the progress he made in the
Romany *chib* I taught him and was always thinking up something to amuse or please me by way of a reward. The captain
was a bachelor who lived with his sister, and she also was
interested in herbs and our language. She was also extremely
religious and a keen worker for the temperance movement and
ran a local Band of Hope. One of her first questions to me
was : Had I signed the pledge ? And when she had explained
to me what it all meant I assured her that whatever name we
Romanys might have made for ourselves as fighters or
drunkards we only took a drink when we wanted one and
never went on boozes like the *gorgio*. I assured her that the
only drink I knew was the home-made wine of my people.
The next time I knocked I was welcomed with more than usual
kindness and was given tea on the lawn with the captain and
his sister. The talk turned on music, which both of them
loved. I admitted to playing the melodeon and the fiddle and
sang them some of our Romany *gillies*. His sister decided
that I was to join her band, it being a great novelty to have a
gipsy boy among the other *chavis*. I soon found I was made a
hero of in my little uniform with my melodeon and I joined in
the fun. Then it was that the captain suggested to me one day
that I should have a better education than I had. I could not
conceal my joy and gratitude and he arranged that as I worked

all day I was to go in the evenings to an old lady who kept a night-school in the village. I was a big boy of seventeen, full of pride and a sense of my own importance as man and wage-earner, yet I was only too happy to be sitting on the benches with little tiny children who, many of them, knew far more than I did. I developed very quickly indeed and the old lady was soon giving me special lessons which the captain paid for. The old lady now started teaching me Latin and Greek, though why I bothered with this I cannot say, for it has never been of the slightest use to me. All the winter I led my double life, working by day, learning by night. I was becoming quite a scholar and I loved it. Once I had got my foothold and could read and write there was no stopping me ! I must at this time have got myself into more trouble than any Romany youth in the world, for I was always neglecting my work in my enthusiasm, and passing over opportunities for bargains and money-making. I used to run away for days at a time, and even when they took the stick to me and threatened me with a more severe milling, I used to tell them contemptuously that I was going to be a scholar now and not a common lad.

XXXV

ONE day I bought my first book. It is not so much that I remember it as that it would not be possible for me to forget it. I remember also wondering what Mascka and Lavanya would say if they could see me now. I who till now had bought nothing for pleasure or for myself, but only to press home a bargain or for use ! Though they would have perhaps a contempt for such unnecessary things, I know that secretly they would have been proud of me, for just as the Romany venerates old age so he honours experience and

knowledge. Besides, I must have been the first—and last—
Romany ever to learn to read and write. First, I am sure.
Last, I am prepared to swear, for the recent drive against
gipsies and the putting of them in tin shacks and sending the
chavis to the local schools, has little to do with the one-time
Romany. Not only are they not pure-bred but they have
become so slack and inbred with *gorgios* that these *diddikai*
children might just as well give up the pretence of gipsy life
and fit themselves for the indoor existence with a weekly wage
tacked on to it which is their new heritage. The only result of
all this education I have ever heard is the *diddikai* boy's ' howler '
description of the Armada : ' And Drake said : " The Spaniards can wait—but my bowels can't ! " '

My first book was on history, and as I read it I got quite a
respect for the *gorgio*, who seemed once to have been able to
scheme and fight as a Romany could. It had illustrations and
I was amazed and delighted at meeting with the ancient
Britons and their coracles and wicker baskets. I too could
make baskets for catching fish in exactly the same way, and I
could not rest till I had tried my hand at a coracle. Boadicea
was a revelation to me. She is the one queen in history I have
ever been able to admire, for she seemed to me a glorious
scrapper and more like a Romany woman than a *gorgio racklo*.
Boadicea with scythes tied to her chariot wheels charging down
on the Romans was, I thought, a woman any man would be
proud to follow to battle, and I still am never able to pass her
statue on Westminster Bridge without giving her a nod and
the Romany secret sign.

My mother at this time had a bad accident ; she ricked her
ankle in a cart ruck and wrenched the bone. This was a
terrible experience for one who had never known sickness and
who never in her life had been idle through ill health or any
other reason. She made up an oil of wintergreen, onion juice,
a small piece of camphor and some succini oil and I massaged it
into her ankle for her. But it was a slow and painful business.

Then I hit on the idea of reading to her. I read her the story of the ancient Britons and she was as astonished as I at Boadicea, fierce as a Romany, even to taking the poison rather than surrender. And how astonished she was at me ! No one had ever read to her before, nor had she imagined such a thing could be possible, nor how exciting books could be. She would watch me proudly as I would rub her leg and *rokker* the *lil* while she worked away at her crochet or knitting. In those days you used to be able to buy little books for a penny ; they came out each Wednesday and you waited till the following Wednesday for the serial to get along. My mother's ankle was not healing as quickly as it should, and I used to tease her, saying that the oil did not seem to be as strong as usual ! I think it was the reading that delayed it, for in the end I just used to read away and practically not rub the leg at all and she never noticed the difference ! I used to read to her of the Hindu fakir, Anga Singh, who abducted the pretty white girl, and of Rachel Pendella, the Cornish witch, and of a police sergeant's daughter, Nina Bucket, pursued by Spring-heeled Jack, and of the vampires who sucked her blood. They were all Romany legends to her ! And when we took to buying a weekly newspaper, life was really worth living for her at last. When her ankle healed enough to let her get about again, many 's the time she would knock off peddling an hour earlier to get home to be read to. She thought me a marvellous fellow, for she was so great a scholar herself that she didn't know which you had to read, the black or the white !

XXXVI

MOST wonderful of all to us then was that now we could get letters and I could read them. Up till then, illiterate people who wanted news sent would find the nearest scribe and get it written for a penny, or alternately get it read for a penny. Now we could write and read our own letters and the *gorgios* need no longer know our business, where we got our wares, or who were the London wholesalers with whom we dealt. Now when we wanted swag, the buttons, tapes, linen, and all the things the Romany woman carries in her *kipsie*, we did our own ordering. Besides, I could read catalogues now, and that was to make a great difference to our pockets. Just about this time I made my first trip to London to buy at the wholesalers'. They had never had a 100 per cent Romany dealing with them and for me it was the first of many trips. I got myself a name as a keen bargainer and soon was not only buying my mother our swag, but was accepting commissions from other Romanys to come and do their buying for them. I applied myself so well to the job that I even got to know and work out the ciphers, and could tell the prices before they told them to me. This knowledge has since come in very useful to me, and I have never taken much more than a week to learn the secret marks my rivals used.

I was also able to do my people a good turn. We Romanys are not jealous or unkind to one another when we meet on the road ; we share information and knowledge gladly enough. Unless to an enemy of one's clan or family we never refuse help and advice, and trade secrets are unselfishly passed on. It was on my buying expeditions to London that I was to find that many Romanys paid far too much for their swag and were being fleeced by certain *gorgio* traders. I told them of this on my return and of how I had found a place where prices were reasonable and extremely low. It was in Houndsditch, belonging to people called Weil, a dingy blue shop, with blue shelves inside, blue walls, and the woman who served us had a blue apron. So we christened it the Blue House, the *bleu kair*. It also became a rendezvous for those of us who had no regular meeting-place. Whenever there was anything to discuss and negotiate we would say : ' On the first of the moon let us meet at the swag shop.' I went back there recently for old time's sake and found that even to-day the descendants of the Romanys I introduced there, although half-*gorgio* now, muster on the first of the moon at the *bleu kair*, and their grandchildren still buy their swag at the little shop I found for them so many years ago.

It was during one of these buying expeditions that I saw for the first time Petticoat Lane and all the kaleidoscopic fascination of its movement and charm. I decided I would try Petticoat Lane with some Romany novelties. On my return I told my mother of the wonders of the Lane, persuaded her of its possibilities, and eventually we worked down to London and got a pitch at Battersea, right against the Grammar School wall. Here, incidentally, I made friends with one of the prefects and in exchange for some Romany tricks and words he taught me arithmetic and I got a sort of elementary education ' buckshee.' I could do sums in my head, but I could not work them out on paper. He was astonished what ready answers I could give him as far as money was concerned. All Romanys can calculate like steam, and no matter how involved the sum, once you have mentioned it you could not twist them for a fraction of a penny. I don't know what the added advantage of being able to do the sum on paper is, but I know that I was very pleased with myself now that I was learning decimals and fractions and was growing ever more proficient in the little sums he was setting me. I told him an old Romany catch, which I have never known a *gorgio* able to solve. I told it to him nearly forty years ago and am, I think, the only gipsy to tell it to a *gorgio*, yet since it seems to have gone the rounds and I have heard it again myself several times.

I give it here for the fun of the thing. An old Romany died and left seventeen horses. He left them to be divided among his three sons. The first son was to have half the horses. The second son a third. The third son a ninth. He left strict instructions that each was to have his share. He was to have more than his share if possible, but certainly not less.

Can you solve it ? Work it out a few minutes before you read the solution. I thought you couldn't ! Well, along came a wise old Romany uncle who saw the dilemma the boys were in, and so he added to the seventeen horses his own horse. That made eighteen. So the son who should have had half, eight and a half, took nine. The son who should have had a third, five and three-quarters, took six. The son who should have had a ninth, one and seven-eighths, took two. And the old uncle took his own horse back again. They all had had more than their share, and not one had had less. This story is told by us to show how we can always get out of difficulties.

In Petticoat Lane I was a surprise to the Jewish traders, seeing a gipsy roll up. But they were exceedingly kind and friendly, and seeing that I was new to the game set out to help me all they could. They treated me like a brother and one man even made a place for me on the corner of his barrow. We seemed to have a lot in common and they seemed to me more like Romanys than anybody I had seen. I was delighted with their cleanliness, and the purity of their food. It appealed to me particularly how ruthless they were about the cleanliness of their meat and fish, and I used to go to their synagogues because they actually played our Romany tunes there by way of hymns. I once went to one of their slaughter-houses and was astounded at the precautions they took to ensure that only the best meat was eaten. There were none of the insanitary haphazard methods of other slaughter-houses I had been in about the country, and I was told how, if there is the slightest trace of a defective kidney or lung, the meat is pronounced unfit for consumption. Since that day I have always bought my meat at Jewish butchers, and understand why Jews and Romanys have the smallest percentage of cancer or internal tumours to-day.

XXXVII

My first venture down the Lane was selling a novelty which I called the Magic Windmill. It was an old dodge of Mascka's, who had taught me how to make it, and it looked very mystifying and effective. I sold it at a penny with a printed slip of instructions. It had sails made of two pieces of tin, painted red, and attached to an ordinary butcher's skewer, which was notched. We used to rub a penny up and down the notches and the sails would spin round. At the word ' Stop ! ' the sails would stop and start revolving in the opposite direction. These used to sell just as quickly as I could make them. One day an old professor came along. He stood around with a contemptuous smile on his face and then came and bought one from me. But he refused the printed instructions slip. No thank you, he knew all about it ! He held up my show with a long lecture on physical laws, mechanical science, mathematical abstractions, and scathingly put my windmill's magic all down to some high-sounding technical name like the high possoboloty of the patchican-oodulum. But he was soon sneaking back to buy another toy, and with clearly printed instructions on it this time ! Actually it was very simple to work, and did not need a quarter of the professor's marked erudition to solve its mystery. All you had to do, physical, scientific, and mathematical laws apart, was to hold the thumb against the wood when rubbing the penny and the sails would revolve to the right. Still keeping rubbing but remove the thumb from the wood, and the vibration would turn them in the opposite direction. Mascka taught me that, though I do not know if he invented it, and we used to work it with the *Beng*. I would back Mascka against every scientific institute in the country when it comes to magic and common sense.

129

I was taking six shillings a day, a lot of money at that time, and I was enjoying myself. The life around delighted me, and the noise and the colour of all the markets I frequented made me feel that I was in a much more lively and vivid land. Roumanians, Arabs, Spaniards used to pass by and I would speak to them in their own language and ask news of distant countries and relatives. I was only working Petticoat Lane market on Sundays. On Monday I would make more swag and pitch in the North End Road where there was always a Monday night market. Tuesdays and Wednesdays I was down Farringdon Street. Thursdays and Fridays down Leather Lane. And Shepherd's Bush on a Saturday. I added other tricks to my windmill. The Cigarette Lit without a Match, another trick of Mascka's, which used to mystify the crowds in their hundreds. This was a preparation made from a secret formula in which the end of the cigarette was dipped or the top of the tobacco smeared—then puffed and it lit itself. This substance, by the way, is what is mostly used in the firing of warehouses and factories. The Calyx-eyed Needle which I would put behind my back and thread while the women gaped was another seller. I would go through the pantomime of the usual needle-threader licking the cotton, screwing up my eyes, bringing the needle near to my nose, and *spieling* to them about how much easier it would be to get the poor old camel through. And then, presto ! with a shrug and a smile I would thread it behind my back and have the crowd of women falling over itself for fear I should sell out ! I sold millions of those needles, the first person to sell them in England, and would saunter out in the morning with the whole of my swag in my waistcoat pocket. Another gadget with which I had fun and success was an American tin-opener which I later demonstrated in several places abroad, including the International Exhibition in Liege where, without knowing more than ten words of French, I came away with a small fortune. All I knew was, *Voilà !* as I produced the tin-opener. *Comme* ça ! as I stuck it in the tin. And *Tournez !* as I turned it round and the lid came off. And then I would exclaim, *Trois francs !* I became the catchword of Liege, and the children would follow me laughing and saying : ' *Voilà ! Comme ça ! Tournez ! Trois francs !* ' All good advertisement. I even sold one to old King Leopold who was as pleased with me as were the children !

XXXVIII

DURING these winter months of my first days in London I got to know its streets so well that even to-day by shutting my eyes I can tell by the smell of the street what district I am in. I know the smell of pepper and spices round the Minories, tea in Mincing Lane, leather in Bermondsey, vinegar in Hammersmith, the wood in Old Street and Curtain Road, the smells of the polishing shops around Clerkenwell. My mother was astonished at my success and at the easy way I adapted myself to the busy life of London. She herself was having no small success with *dukkerin*. She used to work round the suburbs with her *kipsie* in the daytime and thoroughly enjoy herself. So many doors to call at and all placed so conveniently near to one another, and all with money to spend ! She would work Wandsworth, Tooting, Balham, Battersea, Wimbledon, and Roehampton Village, which actually was a village in those days, just as the other suburbs were far more rural than anything they could imagine to-day. Most of the inhabitants were delighted to have a Romany come to their doors, and my mother became so famous as a fortune-teller that when she returned home to the *vardo* at night many a *boro-rani* would drive up in her tandem to have her *duk* read. Money was plentiful and life was easy and we were amazed at our good fortune.

131

Walking about London I kept my eyes as wide open as in
the country lanes and very little escaped me. The variety of
the shops staggered me and the opportunities they presented
for money-making seemed endless. But it was when I saw
the chemists' shops that I knew that the opportunity I was
looking for had come. They were not chemists' shops as
London knows them to-day, but dingy little places called
apothecaries' shops. The apothecary himself used to wear a
high silk hat and a long black frock-coat. They were always
old, or no importance would have been attached to their words
and prescriptions. In their dark dust-covered windows were a
few bottles of coloured water and some leeches and whatever
new remedy he had to offer at the moment. Here I was quick
to find that herbs were being sold at anything from twopence
to a shilling an ounce, and that the very roots or leaves which
we were telling the country folk where to get or were giving
them free with the *dukkerin*, were being offered at eightpence a
few leaves, and heaven alone knows how much more was
being asked for the advice on how to use them. Not only
were the apothecaries charging what seemed to me pieces of
gold for a few leaves, but so were the herb shops, and there
were plenty of herb shops in London in those days. I made
inquiries and soon came to know the names of the wholesalers.
I went to see them, explained that I could supply them with
cart-loads of herbs which I would gather during our spring and
summer *trek*, that there was no root or herb I did not know,
and that I would dry and prepare them and send them to
London in the autumn. They were as pleased about it as I was,
and all I had to do was to return to our *vardo* in Battersea and
explain to my astonished mother how the *gorgio* had agreed to
pay large sums for what we had been handling free of charge,
and that instead of wearing ourselves out with *tatting* and dealing, we could spend the following months pleasantly gathering
and drying the plants which grew so profusely about us in the
fields and on which we were to make a handsome profit.

No wonder my mother thought I was born with the wits of a hundred monkeys and chuckled each time she looked at me !

XXXIX

JUST as my wits had taught me that the enlightened *gorgio* would pay for our herbs, so they were to teach me that the unenlightened *gorgio* would gather them for us. And this they did, sublimely unaware of their own ignorance and gazing at us with open mouths as we followed their trail of destruction. For we were soon to find that what was hours of labour to us, the farmer and his *joskins* would make quick work of and throw contemptuously in heaps on the banks.

Why, then, should we overwork when a stupid farmer paid half a dozen labourers to do the work for us ? Nettles, docks, twitch grass, all were pulled up and laid on the banks to die. There was no end to our supply of herbs and roots fresh daily. By just passing the fields where the destruction was going on we gathered sackfuls. The *joskins* would watch us with amusement and surprise and ask us what we intended doing with the junk, and we would say : ' Puddings and pet mice ! ' and they were more than ever sure that gipsies were mad creatures. Yet how foolish they looked to us and still do, for the folly goes on daily throughout the countryside. The farmers paying good money to have their fields rid of dratted weeds as they call the dandelion, and at the first touch of damp or frost complaining of the rheumatics or sciatica pains, going off to the doctor, paying anything from ten shillings to two guineas for examination and a prescription, then paying the chemist five more shillings to have his prescription made up. And what are the magic words, scrawled indecipherably on the paper he hands over the counter ? *Decotium Taraxaci.*

Dandelion root, plain and simple, boiled up in water ! The finest tonic for the liver, blood, and all rheumatic complaints known to man. He does the same with nettles, showing traces of apoplexy each time he passes down his fields and sees the wicked things waving to him. But he will pay any fancy price for fancy medicines with *Urtica dioica* among the ingredients. And *Urtica dioica* is only the vulgar stinging nettle with a price on its head.

Only the other day in a Lancashire paper I read that the St. Helens Council was warning farmers that if they did not pull up ragwort, yellow dock, and southistle, they would be heavily fined. Heaven help these destructive folk ! Ragwort is splendid for sciatica and blood complaints ; southistle is unequalled for internal complaints and stomach sickness ; and yellow dock is the foundation for some of our finest herbal medicines, and once saved my life as a *chavi*. I had crawled through some barbed wire to steal some apples from an orchard. Coming away from orchards is almost always a hasty thing for boys ; this time it was a dash before a large farmer and a large dog, and with my pockets full of apples I threw myself through the barbed wire to get into the road, and ripped my shirt and stomach very badly. I took no notice of the tear at first, thinking it would heal, and, as *chavis* will, I scratched it when it was itching and getting well. It grew worse, and yet the worse it grew the less I dared say about it for I would have had to explain that I was stealing and that would have meant a *cooring*, and I didn't see why I should get a milling as well as a sore. Within a week my stomach was a terrifying sight and the sores were spreading nearly to my chest. Still I dared not say a word. My mother had noticed me scratching myself and seen the blood on my shirts where they had stuck to the sores, and asked me what was the matter, but I had always managed to put her off with a vague answer. I was really in a very serious condition of blood-poisoning and spreading irritation when, fortunately for me, she got suspicious, and while I was asleep she pulled up my shirt to see for herself what the trouble was. She gave a cry of horror that woke me up, but she wasted no time in chiding me, for the damage was too far gone for reproaches. She made up a special ointment, including as its principal ingredient the yellow dock stewed in the purified fat of the *baulo*. Later my mother told me that this was a centuries-old Romany healing ointment which the Romans also had used and had named The Balm of Gilead. In a few weeks all trace of my dreadful sore, pus, scabs, and blood-poisoning, had vanished, and I was told how, had she not looked me over that night, I would not have lived another few days.

We Romanys call the doctor the *mullah-moosh-engro*, the dead-man-maker, and the chemist the *drab-engro*, the poison-maker. I can give no reason for this nor its origin. Those are the names I learnt as a child, so the wisdom is older than mine. I only know that we gipsies have no need of either. We can bring ourselves into the world and take ourselves out of it at a good old age without any one else's help, and as I have never in my life seen or heard of a deaf and dumb or a blind or a mad Romany I can only think we manage our problems of health better than the *gorgio* manages his. Among the *gorgio* every thousandth is *dindilo*, and those who are not shut away are neurasthenic and epileptic in its various forms. And who would dare count the *corora* and the *nanichib* met in a morning's walk ? My mother used to tell me that there was one truth about sickness I must never forget. Nature makes the ailments and Nature makes the cure. And the cure is practically always side by side with the complaint. Where there is a nettle to sting you, there just beside grows a dock leaf with which to rub the sting away. Where there is much damp and water, there beside it grows the willow with its bark to cure rheumatic fevers.

Other lessons my mother was to teach me as we gathered the herbs were that each country grows the herbs and roots necessary to its climate and needs ; such as that the alder tree bark resembles cascara bark which the *gorgio* imports from abroad, yet the properties of the home-grown variety have never yet been noticed. So, too, the rhubarb root as against the variety known as Turkey rhubarb. Also that many herbs and roots by their very names point to the parts of the body which they cure. Chestnut leaves for chest complaints and bronchitis ; gravel root for stone and gravel ; liver-wort for the liver ; lung-wort for lungs ; heartsease for weak hearts ; and even the herb called rupture-wort will ease rupture. All these we used to pluck, uproot and dry, and I would label them. As we picked, my mother would explain their properties to me. Periwinkle for diabetes ; marigold, scarlet pimpernel, and cowslip flowers for sleep and nervous insomnia ; solomon seal for female complaints ; woodsage as a blood purifier ; rosemary for weak and falling hair and dandruff ; rue for female internal complaints and, mixed with elder water, good for cleaning up the bladder ; lily-of-the-valley root for heart trouble ; the white violet leaf for certain stages of cancer ; arum lily root for heart disease and fits ; red clover for coughs, and made with honey invaluable for all throat troubles ; male fern good for worms ; galangal root for stomach nervousness and weakness ; agrimony for indigestion and bowel complaints ; plantain for piles, internal and external ; soap-wort for pimples and acne ; mouse-ear for indigestion and gastritis ; red dock and yellow dock, innumerable ills and for sores and skin eruptions ; bladderwrack for obesity ; and clary, unrivalled as an eye lotion, clears, strengthens and even restores failing sight, a fine internal medicine and also good for varicose veins. Another lesson was never to spoil a tree for its bark. For this, when we wanted oak bark, etc., we would go to the timber yards, where they willingly gave us the unwanted bark by the ton, and where we did no damage.

Here again it was to be my brains that saved our backs. Following where his men destroyed we would gather the

nettles and I would then go to the farm-house and explain to
the farmer that we had all these unwanted nettles and had
gathered them for hospitals and how they purified the blood
and cured sciatica and kindred complaints and might we use
his hand chaff-cutter to cut them up on ?   Never once have I
known a farmer say no, and we would take our oak bark and
nettles, and whatever we wished to cut in convenient sizes,
and do in an hour what we could not have done in a day.   We
took our turns at the handle, and we used often to laugh when
we thought how first of all we had taken the farmer's herbs and
then borrowed his machine and would be selling them for
fourpence an ounce or more.   Actually, cut nettles brought us
in four shillings a hundredweight more than delivered uncut,
and with the hand chaff-cutter at our disposal we gaily earned
many an extra four shillings at his expense.

XL

MY mother could never resist offering her help if, as we went
along the lanes or villages, we saw a sick child.   I remember
most vividly her curing of the blind boy, and though it may
not seem a very nice story to *gorgio* readers I must tell it, for,
who knows, it may again help some hopeless mother with a
blind child.   We had *puvved* the *grye* in the Petersfield district
while we went about our herbing.   We knew the country
well and the country folk knew us.   One day, passing through
some villages, we saw two *gorgio chavis* both blind, and on my
mother asking why she was told they had been blind from
birth.

Now at that time there was a serious epidemic all over
the country of children born blind through neglect at their
birth, some pus or infection getting in their eyes and not being

attended to by the midwife. To-day, of course, the first
thing midwives or nurses do is to bathe eyes of the new-born
infant to avoid any danger of such blindness through infection.
But then, such measures of hygiene had not been adopted and
perfectly healthy parents were often, to their sorrow, presented
with blind babies for no understandable reason. My mother
examined the children well and gave the mothers something
with which to bathe the little glued-up eyes. Then she gave
them a curious piece of advice. She said that only a mother
would care to do such an unpleasant thing but that it was the
only way to make the lids open. First, she said, bathe the eyes
well with lotion she had prepared, then dry them, and the
mother must then lick the child's eyelids carefully and thoroughly. My mother explained that there was a property
about the human tongue, rough and supple, which no sponge
or rag could achieve, and that as the eyesight was not affected
but only the eyelids glued up, the only way was for the
women to do exactly what the mother cat and all animals did
to their young—lick the eyelids to open the eyes. How right
she was was to be seen within a few months. In the one
village the mother who had taken her advice had the joy of
seeing her child open its eyes, its sight restored to it, and all the
village blessed my mother and looked on her as a miracle-
worker.

In the other village the woman had not done as my
mother told her and it was too late. Years afterwards I
remember seeing her boy, grown a man, being led down the
street by a dog. My mother was dead then, but it brought
once more to my mind the boundlessness of her wisdom.
How often, how often, I have wondered where she had found
time to learn all that she knew and how so much goodness and
so much knowledge could be stored in such a neat, compact,
quiet space. A look and she knew, a nod and it was enough,
a sentence now and then and they were words to be remembered all one's days. She had no majestic height or flow of

eloquence with which to impress, but the mere sight of her wise, quiet face, her calm movements, her reassuring silences, were enough to hold all who came in contact with her in awe. People loved her, her broken English, her foreign looks, her way of making them feel that in her dark quiet look lay the wisdom of all time. Even vulgar people felt this spell, I would notice with pride. My mother had only one weakness, and that was that if you praised me she would go out of her way to reach down the moon for you, but that if you said one word against me (and I don't mind admitting that I was a holy terror for mischief and practical jokes) she would take an immediate dislike to you which nothing you could do later would ever alter.

XLI

I was herbing with her one afternoon when a chance meeting with a Romany girl took place which was to alter my life, and from a contented youth with no thoughts beyond *tatting* and dealing in lanes and country towns I was to wander restlessly and attach myself to fairs and work with *gorgios*. My mother and I were both hunting for a somewhat rare and expensive herb we had been asked to find, when we heard footsteps approaching. We thought it was some local *racklo* and did not trouble to look up, when I heard a Romany greeting and saw before me a strikingly handsome *juvval* of about seventeen. I was naturally pleased to hear her *rokker* Romany and more than pleased when she rested her *kipsie* and began to talk to me. My mother came across to us and as is usual we asked questions of a nature similar to those the *gorgio* would call introductions. She told me her name was Lovell, that she had only one sister, a girl of nineteen, that her father was dead, and her mother seriously ill. She said there was little hope of her mother living and that while her elder sister nursed her, she was earning by peddling and *dukkerin*. My mother questioned her as to where the *vardo* was standing and she named a place about four miles distant. My mother was silent a while and then she turned to me and said, in pure *chib*, one of her deep Zingari sayings : ' The life of the poorest Romany is worth all Sheba's jewels.'

The *juvval* could not understand but her expression showed that she knew my mother would help her. She was very interested in the broken English of my mother and of our pure speech and I could also see that she was weighing me up. I had already made my plans, but I did not want to seem too keen to my mother. I thought that if she knew that I was thinking more of the *juvval* than of the sick woman I would not be taken at all. So I said off-hand : ' Shall I stay and get the herbs while you both go along ? ' My mother was not to be taken in, however. She said : ' You have already made up your mind what you will do. Don't try to look *dindilo* ; besides, we have no time to waste.' She asked the *juvval* to give up the calling for the day and to show us the short cut to the *vardo*. She took us through the little paths and lanes and while we were walking she explained her mother's illness to my mother. My mother then told me to keep an eye out for herbs she would need to treat her with. It did not seem many minutes before we had walked the four miles. I was wishing we had sixteen to go ! We saw the smoke coming over the top of a high hedge and the *juvval* said : ' I will call the *juggals* so that they will know you are friends.' She made a peculiar call with her mouth and her hands and two huge lurchers came bursting through the thick hedge. They looked very savage at first, but she said : ' *Nanti, kooshti jugs, eida pralas,*' and the dogs crouched down and with bodies nearly touching the ground crept towards me and licked my hand, then crept towards my mother and gave her a great welcome as though they sensed she had come to help their old mistress. The other sister had by this time looked over a gap to see what the dogs had moved for and as she was not expecting the other one home so soon was more than surprised to see two strange Romanys with her sister. 'How is she?' the younger one asked. '*Wafodi, wafodi*,' the elder said; 'she'll be *mulled* before the morning.'

My mother went into the *vardo* where the sick woman lay, and after about three minutes came to the *stiga* and called for me. She told me to go to the nearest place and get some olive oil. The village was about two miles away and the *juvval* was to accompany me. What delight! I did not then have a thought for the sick woman, or if I did it was to think how her illness had brought me a new friend. Here was a chance to ingratiate myself with the *juvval* and make all the headway I lost when my mother was with us. We had walked about a quarter of a mile when we passed a fine mansion set back in its grounds from the road, and in a flash I saw my chance to impress the *juvval* at my side. I suggested that these big people always had olive oil about the house and that they would let me buy some if I told them about the dying woman. It would save the other three and a half miles there and back and a hundred to one they would *give* it to me as well. So away I went alone to the *boro-ker*. I told the butler all about my mission and how the village was far away and how the help was needed urgently. 'That's a good one!' he said with heavy humour. 'That's the best Hi've hever heard,' and he smiled and winked at another man. 'Give him some food,' he said majestically, 'and here's sixpence for you, me lad.' I told him I did not need his sixpence and begged him to believe me. I went over my story again and felt that no one could possibly doubt my sincerity. But the fat fool did and he was beginning to think me a bit too much of a nuisance I was getting so excited, when a lady came to the door and asked what was happening. The butler explained in his patronizing way his version of my impertinence. She asked me kindly to tell her the story myself and when I had done so she gave an order to the second man, told the butler to get me a large bottle of olive oil and get it quickly, and ordered a horse to be put in the trap and brought round at once. She insisted on driving us back herself and in a few minutes the three of us were at the caravan.

My mother was astonished when she saw the *rani* and she guessed at once what I had done. She gave me a smile and said : ' Mascka couldn't have done better himself, and that is just what he would have thought of ! ' She knew I could ask no higher praise. She was proud of me for saving time and getting the oil for nothing. Any evidence of brain-work always pleased my mother. She explained to the lady the details of the illness, and the cure. The *rani* was full of interest in us all, just another of those romantic *gorgios* who are always wondering how gipsies can possibly get along without brick houses and a banking system. She had things sent down to the *vardo* for the *juvvals* and told my mother, much to my mother's surprise, that she thought the spirit of the Romanys in helping one another was wonderful. She said no *gorgio* people would help each other like that and go out of their way to save the lives of people they had never seen before. She took out a little book and wrote down a lot of what I now know to be shorthand, asking me many questions on our words and customs. I always think of this lady as a writer and have often wondered if the scene in the caravan that evening ever appeared in a book of memoirs or romantically as the setting for a novel.

Meanwhile, my mother was doing her work in the *vardo*. I know since that the woman was suffering from acute inflammation of the bowels, called to-day appendicitis and said to be curable only with a knife and large fee. My mother spent a great deal of time placing bags of hot salt on the affected parts. She gave the woman the oil and then with herbs made a strong concoction which she said would soon relieve the pain and pressure. Each day for over a week my mother walked the eight miles to and fro to the other *vardo* while I busied myself with our herb gathering. Only once did I see the *juvval*. She came over to our *vardo* for some calico she had been sent to fetch, and in spite of my great desire to tempt her to stay and talk with me, I had to let her go for the thought of my mother sacrificing her time trying to cure the woman reproved my selfishness, and much as I disliked to I let the *juvval* go. She gave me a grip on my finger—a sign of gratitude—and a look I could not forget. I thought I could divine her thoughts, though no word had been spoken between us. I saw her running like a fawn across the bridle-path and I knew she could easily cover the distance in half an hour. I worked hard and made the *yag* and prepared a meal of sweet picked bacon, boiled potatoes, and some button mushrooms cooked in hedge-hog fat, and soon had roused a smell to tempt the dead to set to. And that night my mother told me that old Alvira Lovell was up, the daughters could now carry on the cure and that in a week all would be bright and rosy as they were coming to pitch near us. My mother then told me that other Romanys were coming too, the Bishtons, the Penfolds, the Lloyds, the Smalls, the Greys, and, of course, the Boswells, for they were all gathering for the *rommerin* ceremony with Stella Lovell as the bride and Harry Bishton as the groom. Such news always travels quickly and at a wedding or a funeral there is always a reunion of any casual caravan that happens to be anywhere within reach. It is a rest to a Romany, a good excuse for a little idleness and chin-wagging and the exchanging of confidences and news. 'You shall see some real happiness now,' my mother said. 'Get out your *bosh* and practise !' I was never a good musician, but I could always keep them alive with an accordion, and with that I practised for the big *rommerin*.

One by one the *vardos* gathered in. And one by one their inhabitants came to thank my mother for what she had done for old Alvira Lovell. They were almost as astonished as the *gorgios* at her healing powers, and although the smallest of them all she was the most held in respect. They seemed instinctively to understand that she had powers they could never attain. These Romanys had forgotten the names and values of the herbs, and even though my mother took pains to show them the different kinds and explain their properties, I doubt if many remembered the lesson. I can only recall one group who showed keen interest and that was the Sachs family, and I think they sold herbs to the herbalists many years after they had been taught to do so by my mother. I believe their descendants to this day keep up the good work.

XLII

YET how should they have remembered the ancient art of her brewing when they could not even remember the origins of their own names, nor how they came by them. There has always been a query as to where the names of the English gipsy came from. I have heard many an explanation, romantic and plausible, but I have gone into the matter myself since growing up and I feel that my theory is correct and my explanation final. I remember my father telling me that in the eighteenth century it was decided to take a census of all the Romany in England and that the Government men, unable to understand what the gipsies were saying, took down their occupations. In any case, gipsies had very few names. The investigators were sent out to the *vardos* and *tans* and wrote in their books what they thought the names should be. And the Romany names thereafter became Harris or Cooper or Grey or Lloyd. The name Harris comes from a family of three brothers, all married and with many children, who were goldbeaters, making rings and brooches from gold and silver coins in much the same way as Mascka used to do. The real Zingari word for gold is *ari* and the gold-workers are called *aris*. When the Government men came round and asked them who and what they were, they said they were *trin aris*, three gold-workers. This was set down as Trinny Harris, and to this day I know members of the Harris tribe who are christened Trinny with no idea how this name got into their family beyond that it is the name of a father or uncle.

The same thing happened with the *grye-kupers*, the horse-dealers. The *kopers* became the Coopers, and many a good old Romany is travelling England to-day with that name. Others are called Grey for the *grye* or *grast* as the true Zingari word should be, and when the Greys travelled to Wales they became Lloyds, which is the Welsh word for the colour grey. The Bishops came from a stock of Hungarian Romany called Bizop and the Bishtons also from the same source, their name being formerly Bishtan. There are the Lees and I believe them to have been formerly a tribe called Ylis, for I know a family of Romanys at Asnieres, near Paris, and their name was written thus and pronounced *E-lees*. Over a caravan near Marseilles I saw the name Lavel—surely Lovells ? There are still pure-bred Romanys on the Continent who bear an uncanny like-ness to myself in face and figure, and strange to say their own name is Boselli. I met one such two years ago abroad and we could have been twins for we noticed the resemblance at once and asked each other's name. Their name was Boselli. My family name is Boswell and Smith. I am sure this is where we Boswells come from. Smith, of course, we get from our earliest occupation and trade at the time of the census. *Petul* is a horseshoe, and *engro* added to a word always means, maker of. Maker of horseshoes : a smith. Many people must be surprised at the Romany name Stanley, thinking that they had snobbishly adopted the name in honour of Lord Derby and the famous race-course. Not a bit of it, Stanley comes from

Stanelli and many a Romany of that name will you meet abroad. But rarely a British Romany will you meet who can tell you where his name came from nor one who has ever thought it worth while to find out.

XLIII

The *boro divvas* arrived for the *rommerin*. The men-folk, as is usual at a Romany wedding, were more elated than the women. The women had the work to do. The men were there to enjoy themselves. Their most serious work was gossiping together over the merits of the bride, putting to each other questions of whether the two would make a good match, expatiating on the not-to-be-reckoned-in-gold value of a good wife, weighing up the temper and disposition of the couple, and generally forecasting what the future would bring. I mixed with the men and learned quite a lot about women that I had never suspected, assuming, however, an air of complete sophistication.

The bride had insisted on a *dui-rommerin*, a church ceremony and the marriage according to Romany ritual. The church was a very small one and besides the Romanys who went sheepishly to the ceremony there were quite a lot of *gorgio* women and they and the clergyman who conducted the service were pleased to think that the Romany were at last getting into the decent respectable way of marrying, as they called it. Then, for me, came the great moment. The words ' I will ' were spoken and the couple were asked to sign their names in the register. But neither of them could read or write ! They had to make a cross behind the names the clergyman wrote, accompanied by the humiliating words His and Her mark. That made me smile inwardly. Never before had I realized how widely separated an educated person is from an uneducated, and I blessed my captain in Norfolk, his sister's Boys' Brigade, and my own thirst for knowledge. If ever I was *rommered* to a *juvval* and they asked me to sign I could write my own name and that of my bride. I thought, too, that neither had read the paper they were signing and heaven alone knew what they would put their cross to during the rest of their lives, and again I thanked the *kooshti-Duval* for putting opportunity in my way, and above all for giving me the brains to enable me to seize the chance which had been offered me.

The wedding was over as far as the church service was over. Now for the *habben*. Now for the roast pig. Not a *drabbed* one which all writers of Romany novels have written about. These were English Romanys and they had no Mascka to catch and kill a pig that belonged to some one else. This was one that had been obtained in a fair deal with a little farmer on the outskirts of Petersfield. The local *baulo-moosh* had slaughtered and dressed it and now for the *baulo-cirol*, the pig-roasting. The *chavis* of the various families were smiling and happy. I'm afraid they took as much delight in believing the pig could feel as in the thought of helping to eat it ; *chavis* are like that. Three hours of the gentle roasting with the necessary basting, pouring the hot fat at the top of the pig and letting it run down his *truppo* to make it crisp, and all was ready for the *boro-maunje*, the big eating. The men had been to the *levner-ker* and had procured a big supply of beer. The womenfolk had brought out what *kini* they had in their *vardos*. The lovely coltsfoot wine which my mother made was all given up to the party. And then the merriment started. The men chaffed the bride and bridegroom and both must have felt embarrassed even if they concealed it. The bridegroom was jokingly refused a drink of the heady coltsfoot wine, being told he would have to keep a clear head and a steady hand, for he had taken on a difficult task. The vulgar jokes that were cracked were still a little too deep for me at the time, but the roars of laughter greeting each *sallie* made me realize that something subtle and worth knowing was being hinted at. From what I remember, however, I was surprised to see that the bridegroom evidently did not worry about his bride and his difficult job, for whether out of bravado or deeper reason, he drank more wine than any one else, and I am afraid he underestimated the power of ' Anyeta's coltsfoot,' for he was soon waving his arms about and trying to sing, and quickly left the gathering, to fall sound asleep under a tree. Then was the time for the old Romany joke of *parneying* the bridegroom. They carefully undid his clothing and emptied the contents of a copper jug of beer on his body, and what a yell of delight from them all as they watched him wake up and saw his expression !

Every one was dressed in his or her best and there was much velvet in evidence. Romanys love velvet, particularly black and a deep russet brown. The women love a corded velvet, which the men use also for their trousers. There is a black velvet skirt or trousers, a cream silk blouse, a bolero of velvet embroidered in gold or with a fringe or silver buttons, and a gaudy kinsmen necktie for the men and a shawl for the women. I can recall my mother's shawls vividly and the way she put them over her head and slung them with one movement over her shoulders, making a strange head-dress, such as is seen in the old Roman and Greek statues. I recall that she wore a shawl to the day of her death, and that by that time her shawls were sombre and restrained ; they had lost their gipsy brilliance of colouring, and were of two shades of light and deep grey. Every Romany, man and woman, has a new pair of shoes in reserve for just such an occasion, to be worn only with his festive clothes, and the *bosa-veno* can be picked out at a glance from his three-cornered piece of velvet let into the sides of his bell-bottomed trousers. This gives him distinction, proclaims his superiority, and shows that he is no mere idle guest.

Needless to say that the musicians of the party had brought

their instruments and were being begged to play. At first they were gently tuning up and then they got wilder and wilder. The women were not at all intoxicated, but the men mostly were, and the fiddles were screeching all out of tune with each other, and the singing was one screechy-rough tune of some song that was at that time very popular at Romany gatherings, and told of a girl who became infatuated with a *boro-rye* who rode a beautiful piebald horse and who eventually gave her a *chavi* and then *scarpered* to another country. It told how the girl begged her mother to let her remain in the tent, but the mother replied, in the third verse, that her sin is for ever unforgiven. A Romany *chal* would not have been so bad and might have been forgiven, but to be *cambri* with a *boro-rye* who *kustered* a *pellengro-grye* was beyond the power of any self-respecting Romany family to endure. The fourth verse informed us all that the poor girl had to leave the *tan* and look out for herself and her *chavi*. While the men were singing this their eyes kept meeting the eyes of the *juvvals*, their daughters, and the moral of the song was clearly : Now then, *ma kooshti juvvals*, you see what happened to a Romany *chi* who was made *cambri* with a *gorgio rye*. Mind yourselves and see that you never come home here *cambri*, or out you go the same day. Actually the girls needed no such public warning ; from childhood they had heard the horrors awaiting the one foolish enough to so much as glance at a *gorgio rye*, or even a Romany *rye*, for that matter. Marriage was the market and they knew it, but that did not prevent them from making great play of modesty and blushes as the elder men fixed them with piercing eyes and scraped away at their fiddles in solemn warning.

The feasting and drinking finished early that night. The men took their fiddles to their tents and caravans and soon the camp was all silence. Only the dogs gave an occasional bark when some inquisitive person's footsteps were heard too near the camp. All must be in good trim for to-morrow, when

would take place the real marriage, the Romany ritual of
the mingling of the blood.

XLIV

EVERY one was about very early next day in spite of the
carousal. The men looked rough and tousled. Their faces
showed that they had drunk too well of the beer from the
levnerker. Good pure Romany wine does not leave such
aftermaths. Some of them had a drink of the liquid of the
santekash, a brew made by boiling a few pieces of willow bark
in a pan of water, and after a good swig at this they seemed
brighter. This willow-bark lotion is extremely good for
headache, but for the clearing off of the effects of alcohol it is
said to be without equal. I write ' it is said ' because I have
myself never had cause to drink it for any reason but mild
headaches caused through sun and heat. I have been told that
the wood is the principal ingredient of the tablets called
aspirin. So you will see that once again the Romany who has
known of the *santekash* for centuries goes direct to Nature for
his salycilic acid and not to the *drab-engro*. None of the men
seemed too keen on their breakfast and one could hear the
womenfolk calling again and again for them. Only the
chavis seemed hungry and the most interested of the crowd,
and chattered like a flock of starlings round a kitchen window.

While the morning was at its height the bride and bridegroom appeared from their *tan* and it was time for the Zingari
ritual, which has since about died out in this country.

A circle was formed. The *chavis* in front. The *chals* and
chis in the row behind them. The elders at the back. Standing in the middle of the circle of their people the bride and
bridegroom held out their hands towards each other, palm

upward. A member of the tribe would take their out-stretched hands and make an incision on the fleshy part at the base, the left hand of the groom, the right hand of the bride. The two hands, bleeding from the small wounds, were then pressed together so that the blood from the one mingled with the other, and a skein of red silk, in which seven young virgins of the tribe had each tied a knot, was bound tightly around their hands and wrists, keeping the two hands firmly together. (There is another charm in which seven knots are tied in a skein of silk to arrest nose-bleeding. I was once subject to continu-ous nose-bleeding as a young man and tried this charm. I wore the knotted skein day and night until it wore away, and never from that day did my nose bleed again. I have also told this charm to other sufferers and always with the same success. So whether there is a deep, mystic significance in the number of the seven knots tied at the blood-mingling ceremony or whether it is just associated with the preventing of too much blood flowing, I cannot say.) Now the final *Chumidav* was given. The Romany kiss which means : *You are for ever mine and for ever more I am yours.*

The little *gillie*, the bridal song, was then chanted and the silken cord cut away, and the two joined hands and ran quickly to a heap of wood and hand-in-hand jumped over the *kash*. Romanys say that if the man or woman is unable to jump the *kash* no luck will come to them. It is also a sign of sterility. Too old to jump the *kash*, too old to hold your man or woman. This time the bride and bridegroom leapt well into the air. The young couple intended to show the critically watching grown-ups just what they were going to do. Their clean, true jump said as clearly as words to the onlookers : ' We are young, strong, and healthy. There will be more Romanys and *chals* to uphold the traditions of our race through such a marriage as ours.'

The couple returned to the circle and the eldest member of the crowd then handed them a loaf of bread, the sign of a wish for plenty all through life. Then the wedding gifts were handed to the groom. Silver or copper ornaments for the *vardo* are usually the most coveted wedding presents. Continental gipsies take great pride in evolving original gifts which they have made themselves and could be found nowhere else. I remember Mascka once making, as a wedding gift, a heavy candle-stick in wood and copper, in the bowl of which was a spring catch which opened and disclosed a hollow hiding-place in the stem for the bride's rings and jewels, so that the diamonds could be kept in the caravan without fear of their being stolen. But this was not abroad and the gifts were goods made in the local shops. I remember that the first gift was a half-pint beer mug filled with sovereigns. After the handing of the gifts the bride and groom were pelted with yellow ochre and flour, they having to run down between the two lines formed by the crowd three times. They were well and truly covered with luck by the end of the third run, and not only were they covered, but the *chavis* were as yellow as mustard-pots, as, being in front of the grown-ups, all the falling ochre blew back on them. But they enjoyed it and even rubbed the ochre into their little faces, for this was the kind of wedding the Romany *chavis* liked. Blood and plenty of ochre.

Actually, the blood-mingling ceremony was not as I had seen it done before. On the Continent quite a deep and long gash was cut and the blood flowed copiously, but at this ceremony only a tiny scratch was made, just enough to make it bleed momentarily. Yet they all thought it grand. Now came the fiddles, but first came the old harper. This was a venerable old man, well known at the time, and who came from Wales, for his name was Griffin or Griffiths, and Harry the Harper, as he was called, was known to all. He had been especially asked to the *rommeren*. No luck would come if there were no harp, for we say that it is the chief instrument of heaven. And Harry certainly could play the harp. There is a certain melancholy and strangeness which the Welsh gipsy has and the English gipsy has not got. He is more foreign and like his brothers roving the Continent. Harry played faint and sad music at first, which soon grew faster and faster and more lively, and the women joined in a little *gillie*, and one by one the fiddles added their accompaniment, and as the *kini* was again brought in the ceremony, the tunes grew wilder and more incoherent. Soon, again, all were playing out of tune and the singing became just a brawl.

My mother looked at me, and the look on her face told me just what she was thinking. Not like our people, eh ? I could see she was wishing for the whole thing to end quickly. It had little of the charm and gaiety which she knew so well and which I could still remember. The music of the British Romanys, even when they are sober, is not what could be called music from a Continental Romany's standard of melody and rhythm. Scarcely any of the *bosh* players know a note of music and play monotonous, short tunes by ear over and over again. Abroad they seem to know all the wild and all the classical music and play it with fire and genius, delighting in their verve and virtuosity. But here the tunes of break-down dances and four-note jigs seem to be all they know ; la-di-da-di-da, and back again. The old harpists are the only ones who have any idea of what true music can be. I have relatives named Wood (a name originating as I have explained : gipsies who lived in or near a wood and sold firewood), who still live in Wales and who, although they have settled down to the dreary *gorgio* way of living, are still fine harpists. The younger folk have even taken honours at a Welsh university recently, but music lessons were not given to the older Romany harpists. They had to learn for themselves and as they did their busking so they got practice and knowledge. The Romany has a quick ear for tunes and can usually hum a tune over after hearing it once. The music and singing went on till it was time for dinner, then the remains of the roasted *baulo* were served up with many additions and spices and cakes and *kini,* and after dinner the *juvvals* sang and danced. This time only to the music of the harp and one violin. The men were sleeping it off ! I played my melodeon to the *juvvals,* mostly good old-fashioned polkas and barn-dance tunes, which are still the only ones I can play.

And now for the send-off. The bride and bridegroom came up and received a pat on the head from each member of the tribe, and away they went in their new home with the strict injunction to travel at least ten miles away to an unknown destination and trust to luck where they would pitch their *vardo* that night. So away they went into the world, a bright and happy couple.

XLV

I REMEMBER how I looked after them with envy in my heart. A thought came to me : Why should not I do the same and set out on my own in the world with a *juvval* for whom to care and work with side by side ? She had a sister, who, I thought, had looked at me kindly from the first moment she had hailed me as we picked our herbs in the field. We had been but a few times alone together, yet always there had been a warmth in our looks and a hidden note in our voices which we alone knew the meaning of. That night when the festivities were at their height, under cover of the noise and drinking, I went across to Alvara and told her I would like to walk with her alone. We walked a few paces away from the others and I made my proposal.

I said : ' Alvara, I wish it was you and I.'

She looked at me with her big, deep eyes, like a deer, and said : ' Yes, I, too. But you have come too late. I gave the *chummidav* before I met you.'

She then told me that she had been keeping it a secret from

all but a few relatives, and asked of me not to give her away. I promised. I bade her good-bye and told her that we should never meet again. I knew that in spite of her refusal she was warm at heart for me, as we say, but a Romany girl does not jilt a man with whom she has given the betrothal kiss. Nevertheless, I felt hurt and angry at the way in which she had given no sign of being anything but free, and had answered my looks with equal warmth and put inflections in her voice which had well matched mine for meaning. I felt that however fair she might be to the other man, she had not been fair to me. The shock of my rebuff and her duplicity hurt me more than I wished to show, and without waiting for the celebrations to end I went to our *vardo*, away from the din and the drinking and the dull strummed-out song, and *chals* and *juvvals* eyeing each other and furtively touching a hand, as I had dared to do with Alvara.

When it was all over my mother came back to the caravan. I did not hear her soft footstep till she was at the door. I had been sitting thinking of many things which seemed to have no explanation, however wearily one tried to find an answer. I had also, without knowing it, come to a decision which was to alter the even routine of my days as just another contented Romany wandering the quiet lanes and by-ways, for I had thought of my youth. Just as when one is starving one thinks of food, so, I suppose, when one is unhappy, one thinks longingly of the time and the place where most one was at peace. True, I had not so long to look back, yet all at once a great desire came to me to hide from all these people and leave behind me this spot where I now felt humiliated and hurt. I saw myself again as a care-free lad of fourteen, fifteen, even eighteen, and my early escapades and ventures in the way of money-making, and the kindliness of the people in the counties I loved best of all, the Fenland, Lincolnshire, Norfolk, Suffolk, and the hundreds of miles around that part, dear and familiar to me, every inch of them. If it were possible for a

Romany ever to feel at home in one spot, I was content to find mine in that direction.

I was aware of my mother watching me, and I asked her to *trek* again early in the morning. I said : ' I understood, mother, the sign you gave me. These are not of us. Let us go back to Northamptonshire and the eastern coast. It is better there,' I said.

She did not reply to my request, but said : ' Is Alvara, then, already betrothed ? '

I nodded. I wondered how she knew what had taken place without a word from either of us. Had all women this form of intuition, or had she alone this power of knowing without words ? She knew my secrets as though she could read them written on my forehead. There was nothing to do but admit that Alvara had made me look foolish and feel bitter.

' I am always unlucky,' I said in a voice that was both hard and despairing. ' Something tells me that love and companionship will never be for me. I shall never have a *rovel*.'

' What does it matter if you never do ? ' said my mother with a slight smile as though to dismiss my hurt pride and my pessimism as of no very serious account. ' The Best Man who ever lived did not have a *rovel*, but his women friends were true.'

XLVI

As a matter of fact, whenever, later in life, I have seen again the women I might have married I have always realized how well *Pelagus*, my lucky star, has looked after me.

A Romany's pride is that he does not boast of his love affairs, so I will only say that all the women I have wanted I have had.

I must, however, also say that many is the *gorgio* girl I have turned away from my caravan, and only two Romanys have I ever been able to lure inside, and one of these girls was working independently on her own, a rare occurrence in gipsy life. And very reluctant these girls were and a very one-sided business it was altogether.

I say this not to disparage *gorgio* girls and laud the Romany (indeed, it is a tribute to the deeply romantic nature of the *gorgio*), but to make known the truth about Romany women which I have long wished the world to know. I can only hope that the poor romantic world will believe me!

But how can it believe me with its *gorgio* women writers concocting fantastic tales of passion and moonlight and hot-blooded gipsy women and vengeful, handsome gipsy men. There is not much harm done here, except to stir up the neglected hearts of lady readers and schoolgirls at the dreaming stage. How can it believe me with its *gorgio* men writers boasting how they can walk across Hungary or Roumania, enter any gipsy encampment, and by playing the fiddle and giving off half a dozen sentences in faulty Romany be invited to the tents of all the wives and virgins. I read such a book recently in which a man was supposed to wander in a Hungarian encampment and just by striking up two notes on his fiddle had more invitations from the women than one would have thought it possible for one man to accept. This sounds very tempting and pleasant to people who do not know differently, but to me it is just Grimm's fairy tales retold for grown-ups. Admittedly, there are many wandering tramps and wandering street-walkers in Roumania as there are in the streets and by-ways of Dublin, but that does not make everything one finds encamped on a roadside a Romany. I have not spent a week or a holiday with the gipsies, but my whole life.

These people who delude themselves that they have only to play a note on a tin-whistle to charm the heart out of a Romany girl should try their luck even among the modern commonplace Romanys of the New Forest, where they are all inbred *diddikais*. Try with these first before you let yourself

loose among the true-bred Zingari. Those of you who believe
the fantastic tales of glamour and tinsel brought back from
Continental holidays by thrill-seeking writers of romance and
adventure, try taking a fiddle to the New Forest and ingratiate
yourselves into the good graces of the men and the *tans* of the
women. You would sleep all right, but it would be the sleep
of unconsciousness from the pain of Romany *mauleys* or a
big *kash*, because a *diddikai* does not even bother to learn the
true Romany song about not *cooring* a *gorgio* with a *kash*, so
they are not so particular what they use in self-defence. If a
Romany has had so little luck in a lifetime, how would a
gorgio fare for a week-end ?

The truth is, and it is a harsh truth, that there is no romance
among the Romany as the *gorgio* knows it. The *gorgio* is the
girl who dreams. The Romany is the girl whose pride lies in
creating an atmosphere of chilliness that will freeze the most
ardent suitor, unless his intentions are so strictly honourable
that the most exacting parent would find him above reproach.
True, when she has got her man she will fight like a tigress to
keep him from any marauding woman, but these rare outbursts of passionate fury are the only times she ever behaves
something a little like the *gorgio* novelists describe as her daily
temperament. These outbursts are rare indeed, for the
Romany is by nature a calm woman, with the patience and
evenness of temper of a people used to living in the open air,
working too hard, unused to worry, and having the freedom
and good manners of the birds and beasts around them.

It is only when you have lived among them for years that
you know how cold the Romany women are. They have
charming smiles and light, graceful ways, and these they use as
they go along the lanes and doors to tempt the *gorgio* to buy
their wares. A light pressure of the hand, a pretty look sideways from gipsy eyes for the *bilaco gorgio*, and it means no
more than when the pretty girl over the perfume counter
tries to persuade the young man opposite her to buy the most

expensive scent she can sell him with a smile and a flattering word for his beloved. But let the *gorgio* take advantage of that polite friendly smile and it will be a different story. I once saw this happen to my mother, and I have never forgotten it.

I was about eleven years old at the time. My young brother was doing china mending ; my little sister was with me looking after the *gryes* and the *habben*. My father had gone to a farm to buy a horse and he had taken my mother with him as far as the next village, and she was working her way home, calling at the cottages with her wares. Now my mother was an attractive woman, dark as an olive, and with a face classic and startling as a siren. A *gorgio*, seeing her alone, gave her a smile. A smile to a Romany woman is a sign of peace and welcome. I suppose she smiled back in recognition. The *gorgio* evidently took her smile to have a deeper meaning. He followed her, and as she quickened her pace, so did he. She was within three hundred yards of the *vardo* when he caught up with her and asked her if she would kiss him. In her best English my mother told him what she thought of him, but he was a persistent Don Juan and caught her round the waist and tried to kiss her. Down went her basket and then began one of the liveliest scraps I have ever seen. My sister and I each got a large stone from a heap by the wayside. We could not throw one at the *gorgio* for fear of hitting our mother, but she shouted to us in Romany : ' Stand away. I'll see to this ! ' She fought wonderfully ; she punched, she scratched, she bit, she clung to his ears like a leech. He did not try to stop any longer and was intent on getting away, but evidently my mother was roused and thought she would have her fight out. They both fell together. I ran up and hit him a bash on the nose with my stone and the blood trickled out. He made a wild lunge away from us and was off down the road like a streak of lightning. My mother stood up with a handful of hair in each hand and said something that was the Roumanian equivalent of ' That'll larn him ! ' This is not the sort of scene a *gorgio* novelist would care to put among the glamorous scenes of beautiful gipsy women, but how proud I was of her ! We never saw the *gorgio* again. It was also fortunate that my father never found him out, as for a long time he did keep an eye out for a man with a cracked nose and a bald patch while we were in that district. We used to wonder what he told his wife, if he had one, and what sort of an accident he could have invented to explain his extraordinary appearance when we had finished with him !

XLVII

To return to Romance v. Reality, the Romany *juvval* wants to be married. They do not wait long. They like being married and tied up to one man. They do not believe in being old maids till the age of thirty. There is seldom a Romany girl who gets past the ages of eighteen or twenty without being *rommered*. For after twenty, in any case, the love thermometer goes down rapidly. The men themselves think there must be something very wrong if the girl is not married by that time. They begin to look for the snag, and what has apparently no value for others soon has no value for them. You can pluck the rose in the bud without waiting till it is faded. Let it bloom for you, we say. Physically, another reason for early marriage is the bearing of children. The younger a woman bears her children the better, we Romanys believe. The better for herself, the better for her child. It is nothing short of barbarous, to our way of thinking, to see the English *gorgio* woman bearing her first child between the ages of twenty-six and the late thirties. By this time a woman's bones have hardened to iron and it must be a grave strain on her with hardened muscles and set bones. A woman can bear a child more easily and healthily at seventeen than she can at

twenty-seven, and all this *gorgio* talk of marrying later in life
goes to show how little they know of marriage and its true
function. Incidentally a Romany woman never lays up
when she is to bear a child and puts on fat. She is out with her
kipsie often to the last day, and all the better for it. And when
at last she is up again every one makes it an excuse to forgather
and drink—but they toast the husband !

While on the subject of children, I suppose few people know
of the Romany way with the new-born child. It is plunged at
once into cold water. It gives a great yell, naturally, and every
one is happy. They know then that it will have no complaints, and its health and strength are assured, for its lungs have
been given a fine start in life. A *gorgio* midwife I knew who
used to come round the caravans helping the women at birth
was very surprised and shocked the first time she was told to do
this, but later she found that Romany children gave no trouble
whatsoever after this immersion and had none of the ailments
common to *gorgio* children. Romanys have done this for
centuries and it might be interesting to pass it on to any *gorgio*
doctor or lady who has the welfare of children at heart. I once
asked my mother why this was done and she told me that to
plunge the new-born infant into cold water immediately on its
arrival in the world is to give it a good shock to the lungs. It
then takes a mighty breath, cries, has taken in with that cry all
the air it needs to start living, and will be strong-lunged and
healthy from that moment onward. I think I have said else-
where that never have I seen a Romany who was a *nanechib*
or *corora* or *dindilo*. I put this down to the fact that among
pure-bred Romanys there is no inbreeding. Cousins do not
marry cousins and pass on bad family strains just to keep money
in the family. A Romany girl always looks for a man outside
her own family, and a Romany man chooses always a girl not
of his own tribe. They believe in fresh blood and fresh ideas.
The man can strut like a peacock in new surroundings and the
woman is glad to get away from the circle she knows. I

always put down any brains that I may have to my mixed
parentage : my Berber mother, my Welsh Romany father.
Naturally, my father, living in England, had not the brains of
my mother. The *boro-rye* may have made his name world-
famous by putting his father in his *lil* (or, as I am often tempted
to think, my grandfather, Tinker Jasper Petulengro, may have
made George Borrow famous by giving him a fine sentence to
put on *gorgio* calendars and Christmas cards . . . if he ever
did !), and my father was certainly a good steady man and a
first-class horse-dealer. But for intelligence and knowledge
he could not touch my mother's little finger-joint—and he
knew it. Every one knew it who met her, and he was proud
and jealous and adoring of her from the first day he saw her to
the day he said good-bye-till-the-evening, never to return. I
have always found that children of mixed parentage are the
keenest and most intelligent. It is like a true-bred dog, over-
bred till it is practically brainless, refined till it is hysterical and
unfitted for whatever it first set out to be, whereas a good
mongrel will tackle anything and everything and be the delight
of whoever owns it.

XLVIII

ONCE and for all, and as kindly as I can, I would like to release
gorgio ladies and girls from their dreams of gipsy love. Sheiks
may be all they believe them to be and all that the romantic
novelists whisper ; I have never met one. But I do know the
Zingari. I also know the *gorgio* girl. I have had them come
to me for advice so often. I have had their confidences ;
father confessor and doctor in one. I have heard their
stories of how they are leaving the shop or the office or whatever their work, and how much easier life will be now that
they have decided to take on such-and-such a man, the best

162

they can do, as they dare not risk waiting longer, and how much
better it will all be than the grind at the office or shop. And I
realize that all it means is that marriage to them is an easy way
of getting one man to work for two, and when she gets bored
and dissatisfied at her humdrum life she will treat him on his
return at night to good nagging and bad cooking, and a lecture
on the petty importance of the neighbours and their own
inferiority.

A Romany husband, you know, does not bring his wife a
cup of tea in bed each morning, as the nice hardworking
gorgio husband does. If he brought his wife a cup of tea, it
would be to throw it over her face and ask her what she thinks
she is doing in bed with the sun high an hour since. Romany
caravan life sounds one long lazy kiss when written by a *gorgio*,
especially by those ladies who spend a little time among
glamorous circus tights and spangles and have picked up
cockney Romany *kant* (as though everything that led a wandering life was a gipsy !). I have had some *gorgio* women come to
the caravan while I was cooking in the open air, and the ash
fire and the sweet-smelling food has seemed all too good to be
believed. 'How good it smells !' they have sighed grace-
fully. 'How quiet, how free, how romantic it all is here !'
or words twisted to mean the same thing. Aye ! but how
good would it be to catch and prepare it ? How good would
it be to lead the life a Romany expects of his woman ? For
he will not tolerate laziness. A lazy woman is of no use to a
man as hard-working as a gipsy. A Romany woman takes
on a man for three things : to be a mate to him, to bring him
into the world bonny children—and she doesn't mind how
many she bears—and to help him in their work. Her life
begins at dawn and ends when she has tucked the last *chavi*
in his *kip* and sung him a Romany *gillie*. According to *gorgio*
standards these women lead a life of hardship and care, and
their lives, if truthfully put to a little woman in a suburban
villa, would seem very dull indeed. But one thing such a life

can never be (and perhaps here lies its romance after all) and that is sordid. And sordid, whether hard-working and poor or middle-class and idle, is what the *gorgio* woman's life is bound to be by our standards, as it is entirely based on money-making and the impressing of neighbours, relations, and strangers. We Romanys, fortunately, have to impress no one, which has always seemed to me quite the most difficult to bear of all civilization's burdens. I am wrong when I say that the Romany woman is not wild. She is wild in spirit but not in temper. In fact, she is far more wild than the men and far more of a wanderer. Rarely will a Romany woman recon-cile herself to settling down. She will be out with her *kipsie* to her dying day, if they will let her. I knew a dear old gipsy couple, Toby Grey and his wife. They finally decided to settle down, but never in a house. Toby was dead set on finishing with the hard old workaday life and felt they had earned a little peace and rest. They drew the caravan in a tiny piece of ground which they had bought. It had a little front garden and a little orchard, and they settled. Toby was eighty-nine, his wife Sara was ninety-one. And Toby con-fided to me sadly that he had the very devil of a job to keep Sara from wandering again. She wanted to be back on the road each day as it dawned and was never really happy with the new life in one spot.

There is one thing for which I honour the Romany woman and place her high above most *gorgio* women I have met or who have brought their troubles to me. She will always place her husband before her children in the scheme of her life. This will seem a strange reason for honouring a woman, for *gorgio* education is almost entirely sentimental. A true-bred Romany man and woman take each other by the ears and give the betrothal kiss and mingle their blood in the marriage ceremony. For them there is no divorce. They do not need it, they work too hard to be dissatisfied with each other, they have no subtle mental problems to bring to their married lives.

He does not go off to work at nine o'clock in the morning and leave her alone all day and then trust to a fortnight or three weeks' holiday as a reward for the year's work. A Romany and her man go out together and when one works the other works, and they have real companionships. Among *gorgios* artists live like this, and they, too, are free and happy by comparison with other folk and professions. Romany women never quarrel or nag their men, they not only never have anything to nag about but they are too drattedly tired of a night. She doesn't have to toss and take aspirin or drug to sleep, and he needs no rounds of golf, dragging over a green with heavy boots and a sackful of old iron like any gipsy *tatter* ! The *gorgio* doctor's pet prescription, which never fails, ' two rounds of golf a day, old man,' and (to make the cure certain !) ' some of these little pills taken after each meal.' I once found one of these golf enthusiasts taking some expensive pills which he showed me proudly and assured me they had done him a whole world of good. On the box was written *mica panis.* I said : ' I had three slices of those pills with bacon for breakfast this morning.' When his indignation had cooled he was hurt to the quick to find that he had been taking breadcrumbs in Latin ! All to make them sleep and eat their breakfasts of a morning ! With us when breakfast is being prepared in the fresh early air every one has a hand in it. All who wish to eat and drink must help prepare the food, and all enjoy it better, and sit down to it with a zest that would mortify all Harley Street. Nor need the women fear to be seen at their best at so early an hour. Romany wives use their own faces. They keep them as smooth and as soft as they can with balms and unguents for as long as they can, but when the years are too many they need have no fear of being slighted because of a few wrinkles. That is again where our women score over civilized women. As they cannot read, they know nothing of advertisements telling them that unless they are an eternal twenty-one their husbands and all men who gaze on them will turn away in disgust, such as haunt the *gorgio* woman and make her birthdays a nightmare as the years advance. The Romany woman does not know her age, she only knows approximately how old she should be by physical signs and the sizes of her children. When wrinkles come she does not have to break her heart or fret for her man's affections. They have grown together in work and companionship and mutual interest, and as their days have been full so have their hearts been loyal. Wrinkles to Romanys are a sign for respect and admiration. We like the wrinkles on our elderly women's faces, and have no foolish craving for girls with faces of fifteen moons only. Poor *gorgio* women brought up with such unreal achings for Romance, only to find that it all centres on a face that never shows a wrinkle and finger-nails which must be painted up like their lips before some dolt with his hair plastered down by the latest super-product can be induced to look at them ! How curious a conception of life on which to base the happiness of one's people !

XLIX

I ONCE nearly married a *gorgio* girl, but I lost her in a game of dominoes. I was desperately serious about Annie (I still have that face of hers tattooed on my arm), whom I met at a Romany gathering. She was the local publican's daughter and extremely pretty, with large blue eyes, masses of chestnut hair hanging down her back, and a mouth like a cherry at its most luscious. Annie courted me, though I needed no courting for I was crazy about her, *gorgio* though she might be, and would have married her any minute she said the word. I was madly jealous and set out to tame Annie, handing her out my cave-man tactics. She had, however, another suitor, a *gorgio* boy, timid and small, called Jack. We used to go for walks—all three, Annie in the middle—and we used to fight to tie up her shoe-lace as it came undone, which was frequently. Annie had also leanings towards Jack, because he was gentle and slow, and not fiery and untamed as I was then, always threatening Annie with death or unconsciousness if she as much as spoke to another fellow. Jack was devoted and cowed, and contented himself with adoring her silently with pleading eyes. One night, in a temper, I told Annie all this must stop and that she must choose between Jack and myself. Annie said that she was thrilled by me, who was the romantic one, but that she was also greatly attracted by Jack, who was the gentle one. She could not make up her mind. I said I would fight Jack for her, but that was so manifestly unfair, he being such a thin weedy fellow, that I had to take the challenge back and we decided we would play a game of dominoes for her. The stake to be the girl and the loser to have a pint. We walked to her father's public-house and Annie watched us play. Jack won and I had the pint, and went back to the *vardo* and prepared everything for the *trek* away the next day. (Women were always making me pack up and *trek* into other counties, somehow, in those days, it seems to me now.) Years afterwards I was round in that district again, photographing tradesmen before their doors, and other local beauty spots, and doing exceedingly well on it. I was photographing an imposing butcher with his knives and staff arranged outside in front of the artistic distribution of pigs heads and corpses, when a woman with a perambulator and several children made as if to pass. I said, without looking her way, a warning : 'One moment, please, madam, one moment,' and waved her back till the photograph was taken. To my surprise, after taking the picture, I heard myself called in a whining voice, and—heaven forbid !—it was Annie. Annie, frowsy and down at heel, two infants in the perambulator, and the rest in steps clinging to her skirts, unkempt and squealing all at once. My only thought was that, indeed, my *kooshti cherino* had been over me that night, years ago, on which I had lost that game of dominoes. She looked me over, my new suit and peaked cap which gave me a neat official air and reassured the local shopkeepers that I was indeed a desirable and experienced camera-man, and said in a sort of joyless whine: '*You* seem to've done well for yer-self!' and then was off in a tirade of complaints against life and the way it had treated her. I pulled a golden half-sovereign from my pocket and said : 'Here, Annie, keep this for old time's sake.'   She took it eagerly and said in a low voice : 'If you like to meet me in the churchyard to-night, I could meet you there!' I declined the invitation and hurried away. I do not know a Romany who could have said that, or have taken the gold.

L

STRANGELY enough, Annie was the only *gorgio* girl I ever wished to marry. Many a romantic *gorgio* girl comes hanging around our caravans, and I have often thought that although we are only Romanys many a *gorgio* youth has had a heartache when he has seen the top of the old caravan coming down the lane again. This has happened to me frequently, some girls being very persistent and difficult to get away from our *vardos*, especially the Suffolk girls who seem extremely fond of Romanys.   One of the most romantic and charming *gorgio* girls who ever came to my *vardo* on such pretexts as to see how gipsies lived and cooked their food and so on, was a schoolmistress at a school near the Suffolk coast. She used to come around about tea-time fishing for a cup of tea and wondering if I would be there to offer it to her. She was a beautiful girl, very lady-like and very well-bred. She had a quiet manner, a deadly pale skin, and deep auburn hair. At a word from me, I know, she would have packed up her school-teaching and come with me about the country, living as she imagined the gipsies lived. I was sorry for her, she was so gentle and refined. I remember the afternoon she came to tea (it used to give her such a thrill of adventure having tea in a real Romany wagon, poor simple girl for all her learning !) and I told her I was *trekking* on the morrow. She looked at me with her pale pretty face slightly flushed, and the tears fell slowly down her cheeks and into her cup, held forgotten on her lap. But what is the use of having a toy around you ? That is for the *gorgio* man to afford, who asks of women to be playthings. A Romany wants something more tangible, and no woman is of use if she cannot work. So I did not take her with me, in spite of her tears and entreaties when I *jalled* to the next *gavaste*.

My first *juvval* had told me as she read my *duk* that I was to hold more women's hands than any man in the country. I doubt if there is another man living who has held the women's hands that I have held and looked into their lives and characters. Practically every day of my life has brought me a crowd of women eager to be told of the future and their stars. I have learned some strange things about women through this constant reading of their fate. I have found their chief characteristics to be selfishness and greed. And their two desires summed up in the unvaried question : Is there a lover ? and will money always be plentiful ? Money and a lover. A lover and more money. I have also found that women value themselves too highly. Eighty per cent of them think they could have done better, and their idea is that they have been very badly treated by fate. It does not matter how hard their little worm of a husband slogs for them, they still have been sent from heaven to be worked for and to cause somebody some trouble. Men, I have found more simple and more kind. The man will want to know if he is going to be

more successful and perhaps move into a bigger house and
have a bigger income. He wants power and wealth, always
to please some woman. He wants success, a partnership, to be
somebody among the Freemasons, or in the limelight at
Councils and Board Meetings. But he does not want money
for its own sake as a woman does, and once married, even when
married to the dreariest harpy, never asks questions about
romance or love. Perhaps, poor man, he has had his dose.

Never have I known a man to ask me for some charm to do
away with a nagging or elderly or sick wife. And many has
been the woman who has come to me with her mock-innocent
query of how one could rid oneself of a husband who bores one,
or is too old, or is sick. Women are utterly unscrupulous in
this matter, and I do not wonder that all the poisoners on a
grand scale in all lands throughout the ages have been women.
With these women I refuse to have anything to do. In any
case, my sympathy is entirely with the husband. Also these
dangerous and stupid women should always be avoided by
decent-thinking people. I see no glamour in the potential
murderess or in these hundreds of thousands of women who
urge me to tell them that a new lover is coming into their lives.
I suppose I have been brought up like a poor dull Romany,
whose idea is that a man and a woman shall give their lives to
one another and walk the earth together at peace, their hearts
and spirits satisfied, and the strict moral code of the people
among whom they live making all the civilized nonsense of
dissatisfaction and infidelity taboo.

LI

I DID, however, once give way to temptation and advise a
woman how she could lay a curse on her husband and kill him

without the police being any the wiser or the circumstances of his death looking in any way suspicious. She had come to me and told me a tale of how she hated her man and she had prayed for him to die, but no one seemed particularly interested in her prayers as they had been going on for some time, and there he was as alive as ever. As a Romany, she was sure I had a spell or a charm. She was a heavy grenadier of a woman, stern to look at, and terrifying to be near. I had seen the husband she loathed so much, a thin small man with a melancholy face and aimless moustaches, pottering about in the front garden. I told her that there was one spell which could not fail. But then she, too, must play her part. She promised and she begged and she listened, all ears. I then told her that the Romany's best curses were always worked on food. I told her that as her husband was a thin little man the best thing was to feed him up. I told her that she must give him a beef-steak pudding every day, help him to a good portion of it, and see that he ate every mouthful. I told her that this would give him the most appalling pains and eventually kill him through causing the heart to cease to work through its rolls of encircling fat, to say nothing of the spell I would cast over his plate. I said that on the beef-steak and kidney-pie curse he could not last out the year and that, lest he suspected her design, the dish was to be varied but the portions to remain the same. I said that the curses Romanys cast work much more quickly if the women using them speak less than usual. I said that while the curse was taking effect she should speak as little to her husband as she could manage, and that as spells work always by contraries she must be as polite to him as possible. She promised to carry out my instructions to the letter, thanked me profusely, and offered me five shillings as the price of her husband's death, which I gallantly refused. A month later, when I passed that way, I saw the first part of the curse taking effect. The husband seemed to be finding life surprisingly pleasant. He had brightened up and put on flesh, and was moving about his

171

little garden almost with a swagger.   Poor man, he was having his first decent-sized meals in years and eating those in their first decent silence, too.   I ached to know what he thought of his wife's lavish cooking and how he liked her new treatment of him, compared with the starvation diet and nagging that had been his lot till a month ago.   I am not ashamed of saying that I like doing a little good whenever I can and seeing people happy, but I certainly marvelled at the stupidity of women, and thought again how viciousness so often goes with lack of brains.

Many is the woman who marries a man for his money and confides to me that he seems to be living longer than she anticipated.   Though women, from what I have seen of the majority, would just as soon put away a man because he bores them as that he is too old or unfaithful.   One woman, however, I have never forgotten : she was such a happy contrast. She was a girl in her twenties who had married a man in his sixties, and she came to tell me how dearly she loved him. She said he was the most wonderful person it was possible to imagine : gentle, considerate, and deeply in love with her. She had suddenly woken up to the thought that he was considerably older than herself, and the idea of life without him, she assured me, was more than she could bear.   She begged me to help her and to give her herbs or charms or medicines to prolong his life so that he did not die before she did.   Actually, I was so exceedingly touched that I did give this virtuous and charming young woman a jelly recipe that is a marvel for prolonging life and vitality and which should have added an easy fifteen years on to his life for her.   She is a woman I have never forgotten, as she had, to me, with her rare request, brought something of the touching quality of a real heroine.

LII

But with the thousands who are disappointed with love there
are the thousands who seek for it. Will he love me ? Shall
I meet my love ? *When* shall I meet him ? How does he
look ? Tell us, gipsy, for surely you know ! Love philtres
are as eagerly sought to-day as in mankind's earliest stories of
love and passion. To a Romany the feather of a swan means
love, eagerly given and eagerly reciprocated. But it must be
found floating on a stream, then you shall keep the ardour and
affection of your lover for life. Many true Romanys sell these
feathers to love-stricken girls, and never has one been sold that
did not come to them floating on the water, for all Romanys
are respecters of superstition in whatever form it is met.

Then there is the love charm of the Love Bag for maidens,
by which the Romany *chi* dreams who her *chal* shall be. For
this they must have the front left foot of a rabbit, three pebbles,
a piece of rosemary, a piece of rue, four different kinds of straw,
wheat, oats, barley, rye, anything dipped in the blood of a
pigeon, all these placed in a bag and never opened and never
undone. Then they sleep on it, if on a certain night of the
year, say March 21st, the new astrological year, romantically
equivalent to your midsummer's night, and the face of their
lover is revealed to them.

Our *juvvals* also practise the old Egyptian charm by which
they make a man love them though he has scorned them
previously. The ingredients of this charm, which is as old as
the Nile itself, are the blood of a white pigeon, the yoke of an
egg, pimento, taken and mixed together and put in a phial.
The phial is sewn in a bag and sunk in the sea. The love-lorn
one must then say *yanaheim*, which is supposed to be repeated thirty-three times. She must then say the three mystic
words of the Romany : Y.O.D. After that, we may be sure,

the man cannot help but find them irresistible. Another variation for the girl who loses her lover our *juvvals* practise is casting the petals of flowers, *only* the petals, on a running stream on the night of the full moon, chanting the magic words *yanaheim*.

Then there is the love charm of the cherry-stones, which used to be sold some years ago here. I do not know if English Romanys still practise it but I do know that they are still peddled by gipsies everywhere on the Continent. This charm is worked on what has been called the Lucky Gipsy Cherry Stones, and are the stones of the White Heart cherries, the stones shaped something like a heart. The Romanys say that these represent the white heart of the man who is not red-blooded enough to ask for what he wants (or must be made to want). The *juvvals* make the charm themselves, and quite a troublesome one it is. They gather together as many stones as would make their age, say eighteen, and drill a hole through one each night, starting with the new moon. But they must not drill one after the *chuna* is full, so that that makes a hole through, roughly, fourteen stones a month. It will then take her two months to do this. When all have been drilled she must wait until the next new moon to thread them on a piece of elastic. Then she must sleep with them for fourteen nights round the left knee. This will get a spinster a husband, they say, and will make the man of her choice aware of her. Roumanian women keep these charms for life. Many were the cherry-stone beads I saw hanging on the walls of cottages, which the old women had kept from their youth, that I saw in Roumanian villages a year or two ago.

The gipsy maidens also look on the ground for a stone with a hole in it—through this they will tie a shoe-lace. This they fling up into a tree and if the stone drops down to earth again it is a disappointment in love, but if it hangs to a branch then there will be a marriage for them before ten moons go by.

The wishbone is, of course, of Romany origin. The

gipsies brought it with them about the early fifteenth century. We used to sell the wishbones of all killed birds, when I was a boy. The idea is that the man who has killed the bird must not keep the wishbone or it will bring him ill luck. Once the Romanys used to give them to the old *ari* workers and have them covered with silver or gold. The Romany would put a spell for luck, closing his finger over the opening, and incanting to the new moon. It would then be sold as a charm by whoever bought it, either for love, for wealth, or for happiness. English Romanys no longer do this, but in middle Europe a Romany wishbone is still much sought after. The really, really lucky ones are the bones of the cock bird, we say, but the reason for this I have never known.

The Worm Charm—to know the month of your betrothal —is not one that will appeal to the *gorgio juvval*, but the Romany maidens practise it to this day. They will go out and dig up six worms by moonlight and then cut them in half, making twelve ; one for each month of the year. They must then thread them on a piece of worsted and hang them up in the evening. They must then watch which worm is the last to die, and on that month they will be married or betrothed. Say the third worm dies last, they will be married in March, the ninth in September, and so on.

My mother used to believe completely in the Nutmeg Spell, and many a love-sick maiden or woman has she brought joy to by this charm. I used to help her cut up the nutmeg in equal parts, and she was pleased with me for discovering a trick by which each part was sawn equal with not a hair's difference between them. The Romany girl works the spell this way. She will take a nutmeg and break it into four equal parts. One part is then buried in the earth ; one part is buried in water ; one part is buried in fire ; and the last part is boiled and the water drunk. She then takes the nut from the water and carries it about with her and sleeps with it under her pillow ; and she will vow to you that with this charm no one will ever be able to take your lover from you. Many a charmed nutmeg did my mother sell. She used to swear by them and nothing you could say would alter her belief. She had had proof beyond counting, she would tell me, and as never in my life had I ever known her to tell a lie I believed her. Personally I think the success of the Love Charm is much a matter of faith and will-power. It makes the timid bold, and the foreknowledge of success makes the eye sparkle and the carriage alluring. A *juvval* who on the turn of *chuna* finds by whatever charm she used that she is to meet her man within a month and be *rommered* before the year is out, has a confidence and a tilt to her head that are of themselves a potent charm and an assurance that she will not be overlooked, as one who is too shy to gaze a man in the eyes and is secretly sure no one will ever marry one as graceless as she seems to be.

LIII

I KNOW a charm that would bring love and happiness to many a *gorgio*, man and woman, only their strange manners treat it as taboo and as a subject for laughter. *The gorgio woman should be allowed to propose.* I think the world would be fifty per cent happier in its marriages if the woman could have a more definite say in the matter. Unpleasant as many of the women's traits which I have mentioned may be, much of it, I am sure, is due to their having to take the last or the first or the only choice that comes their way. Their lives are soured and third rate, however outwardly successful, and they are not deceived as to what the loss of true love has meant in their lives. Much of their impatience and bitterness is really only that a woman never gives up hope, whereas a man is nearly always a fatalist and will accept what the marriage lottery has brought him with as much grace and intelligence as he can muster. But a woman is a fighter. If she cannot fight *for* a thing, she will give her life to fighting against it. Of the two she is always the more hurt and the more unhappy, so perhaps one should leave her her less pleasing characteristics, for only love that is perfect can make a woman a perfect being, and that is rare enough on this sad earth. If only the *gorgios* would realize that it is not only the man who feels the urge of love they would be less amused at the idea of a woman proposing marriage. Marriage is for the woman, in any case. Man can get along more than happily without it. It does not harm love to bring a little common sense to bear on it ; on the contrary, if it cannot bear the light of common sense it is doomed from the start.

I get scores of proposals after every B.B.C. talk I give and among the thousands of letters following my horoscope articles in a Sunday paper. It is wrong to dismiss these as the outpourings of silly women. They are women of all ages and classes, and although I wish they would not do it (for I am in no need of a wife and have every intention of finishing my days wifeless and in peace) I have been greatly struck by the reasons women give for wanting to marry me. They want, of course, romantically (their word), to marry a Romany. They want, biologically (for a husband to a woman is always the father of her children), to marry a man who to them seems free. Free, they assure me, to get a living wherever he finds himself, free of spirit, free from the petty restrictions of the *gorgio* man, tied up in his collar and under the shadows of his employer and constant fear of losing his job. When you read these letters you begin to wonder what are the great benefits civilization has conferred on the Englishwoman, who shares less in her man's life than any woman living.

A curious letter, full of intelligence and pathos, came from a girl of sixteen and a half. She told me that after having heard me on the wireless and having seen my photograph in the

paper (a very flattering one, I regret to say) she would like to
marry me. I must not mind her being so young, she said, for
she had always wanted to marry a man much older than herself. She told me with great simplicity that her own mother
had married a man older than herself and had been very happy
indeed. She said her mother had told her not to bother about
the young men for they were fools and knew nothing of
women or life and therefore made poor companions for a
woman of sense. She assured me that this was true, as she had
seen many young men in the place where she worked and
sometimes had been out with them, but they were much sillier
even than you would expect a man to be. She told me that
having heard me speak on the wireless she knew I was the man
she had been looking for, and added, as final bait, that she was
a hard-working girl and earning thirty shillings a week. She
wrote that she had no fear of work, would love to live in a
caravan, and if I wished it would willingly go on working and
bring the thirty shillings to me for our living expenses. I had
to refuse all these fair inducements in as kind a letter as I could
manage. But that did not prevent me from being very
touched at the simplicity of heart of such a young girl, loving
and sensible, and sitting down to write of her life's dream to a
man unknown to her. I hope she will meet some kind middle-
aged man who will appreciate her and that she will be as
happy as her mother was. The folly here is that possibly even
if she met such a man and he was attracted to her he would
put away the thought of marrying her, thinking of that
sentimental saying : ' Youth calls to youth.' That is nonsense.
Man calls to woman, or if you prefer it, woman calls to man,
and that is the only thing you can say about love that admits of
no argument. Women know this, as this young girl knows
it, and that is why they should be allowed to propose. Yet
although marriage and children are the most important things
in their lives, they are not allowed to do this for fear of ridicule,
and because the *gorgio* man who has no free will left in his

organized mechanic life needs this last sad pretence of free will and manliness left to him.   That is why there is so little of love in a *gorgio* man's hand and so much of defeat in the hands of the women.   That also is why, when I take the hands of these women in mine and hear their melancholy requests for lovers, no matter what their ages or situation, and read on their palms so much that is tawdry, I try to bring them as much hope as I can by making them more contented with their lives, and to remember my mother's words to me when first she taught me *dukkerin* : that what lies deep in the human heart is not for man to pass judgement on.

LIV

STILL, it seems a Romany can know all the charms and yet be crossed in love.   Alvara had played me false and I was not to have a wife after all.   She was to set me off the next morning on a *trek* which was to lead me as far from her as I could go, and, although she never knew this, was to land me in America before the year was out.

My mother, seeing how things were, was willing to *trek* wherever I wished.   She, too, loved the fen country.   She felt less an exile there, for there she had been happy side by side with my father, and there he lay buried beside a wood.   From my earliest memories of England I have thought of the Fens with especial warmth.   The dikes full of eels, herbs in abundance, and kindly people with good sense who loved their gipsy herbalists.

There was a fair on in the Northampton district when we arrived, and I naturally strolled along to see the *fakirs*.   That stroll was to end in Philadelphia.   As I was wandering about the ground I thought I heard a word of Romany in a *spiel* that a *fakir* was putting over. I turned and found myself before a medicine stand at which a *crocus*, a quack doctor, was demonstrating a magic herb with the usual hyperbole and guarantees of eternal life here below. There was no ill his elixir of life would not cure : scrofula, eczema, pains in the back, throbbing in the head, splinters in a wooden leg. Cripples could be made to walk, the deaf to hear, and those with one foot in the grave were winning 250-yard flat races after the third dose. I stayed till the end and gave him the Romany greeting. I found he was a *diddikai* whose name was Professor Copsie and who was sick to death of his elixir and the life it was leading him. He was a tallish fellow, bandy-legged, his hair was strawy-ginger and there were two thick bunches of freckles on his nose. He looked as though he had been tarred with treacle and dipped in a bran-tub. When first I saw him he had a little drip of water under his nose and when I saw the last of him he had it too. Later I used to look at him sideways and sing, 'I have seen the dew-drop clinging to the rosebud freshly born,' and he would automatically rub his nose on his sleeve. Later still, I had but to hum the first three notes. Otherwise it would always have hung there, one drop of clear crystal water, balanced like a seal with a ball, and never dropped. Professor Copsie had already introduced himself in his *spieling* : 'I am not a phrenologist, a biologist, or a theologist. I'm a coptologist. I cop all I can !'

I asked him what herbs were in his brew. He said : 'God bless my soul, I don't know one brew from another, so don't ask me !' I told him that I did, and why not give people the proper cures while he was about it ? Why should we not get together and go shares, sell pills and brews that we could make up at no cost to ourselves as they were all about us in the lanes and hedges ? But Professor Copsie saw no point in giving away good herbs with a lot of bother when he could go on selling his own nameless concoction without it doing them any more harm than the usual messes they were swallowing. He had no feelings for the crowd. His feelings were all for himself. And they were very sore. He hated the work. He hated the crowds. He hated his native land. There was one land of golden opportunity in this world and one only. There you picked up sovereigns for the whistling, where here you couldn't earn a tanner without cutting yourselves in pieces and handing it to them with a knife and fork thrown in. And that place was America ! 'This b—— country is knackered !' he kept repeating, banging his fists till his medicine bottles danced. Nothing doing. Nothing under their hats. Nothing in their pockets. Nothing for a man of brains but to starve and make shift on pence, whereas navvies over the other side became millionaires in a day. America ! Land of the Free, Eldorado, heaven on earth, where beggars were as rich as Crœsus and where all you had to do was ask and it was given you free. Food, drink, home and gold !

That *crocus* could not have impressed me more if he had been trying to sell me a ticket on the spot. I'd have bought it with my last penny. He himself had been to America several times, he told me. It never occurred to me to notice that he had not come back as rich as every American beggar, nor to ask why he had come back at all. I was under the spell of a new word : America. It never needed gold to make me want to *trek* to a new place. It had simply to be new and another place. Always another place from the one I was in at the moment. To move, to chop and change, to see what was around the next corner ; new sights, new voices, new experiences. Any excuse was good enough for me, even being a millionaire. My own enthusiasm seemed to add more fuel, if that were possible, to the professor's fire. Very well, we would go there together. He and I would *trek* to America and, loaded with gold, were to return the envy of every mug who couldn't see farther than his own nose and remained in this isle of starvation wages and ticking his forelock to the squire. We forgot that we had met but half an hour ago.

We shook hands on it and I went home to explain its brightest side to my mother.

I could see without words, for as usual she said very little, that my mother was not too pleased at my news. Yet she raised no objections nor did she try to persuade me to stay with her. I repeated all that the professor had told me, enhanced by my own glowing enthusiasm. Money! I told her. Beggars were millionaires there, and when I returned we would have a special *vardo* built just to carry our gold! I said that if it was so easy to earn a living in these lanes, imagine what I could do in a land where people used silver as these used pence. My mother watched me as I spoke with that long inscrutable dark look of hers that revealed so little of what she might be thinking. She listened to my plea of great wealth, went on with her work of preparing our evening meal, and as though knowing that wisdom would be entirely lost on me at such a moment, quietly threw at me over her shoulder : '*Money is not everything. A soldier will die on the battlefield for honour. A lover will die by his own hand for love. But no miser living will die for his gold.*'

LV

Nevertheless, three days later Copsie and I went to London and haunted the docks to find out how to get to America as cheaply as possible. Fate took a hand again. We were having a drink and a sandwich at a little coffee-stall built in a recess in the wall of the West India Docks, when a man joined us. ''Mornin', Tom,' said the stallholder. ''Ave a good trip back ?' 'Pretty fair,' said the man, and called for his coffee. 'When 's the old boat going back ?' asked the coffee-stall man. 'Sunday,' said Tom laconically. 'Got any one to go with 'er ?' ' I ain't 'eard of any one, I must siy,' said the coffee-stall owner, 'but if I do I'll letcher know.' I nudged Copsie and whispered to him to 'tap the fellow,' get into conversation with him and find out where he was going. Copsie did not seem to feel like doing it and said he would wait a bit till he was gone and then find out from the coffee man who he was. But I was never one for letting a chance slip past me and this one seemed sent straight in my lap, so I took the lead. The stranger's cup was empty by then. 'How about having a cup of tea, sailor ?' I said. He looked at me and I could guess his thoughts. Had he more money than I had or was I the more flush of the two ? He decided that he was the richer, for he said : 'No, you'll have one with me.' 'No,' said I, 'I've got the money all right, and I asked you. Fill these three up, boss.' And when the coffee-stall man put down three freshly filled cups, Tom moved nearer to us, which was what I had wanted. ' 'Luck,' said Tom, raising his cup, and added : 'It's 'andy for us chaps having these stalls to come and get a drink at.' I asked innocently : 'Just back from a trip, sailor ?' And in a sentence he gave us all the information I wanted. 'Just home on the *Eagle Point*. One of the Point boats. Port o' London and Philadelphia. I often go across. Works me passage like, y'know.' At that the *crocus's* ears seemed to stand out like rhubarb leaves. He, who knew so much, had paid to go when he went and to get there buckshee was going to be more exciting. 'Any chance of our getting across ?' I came back. 'It's just what we are set on doing.' 'Easy !' said Tom. 'Would you like to go on Sunday ? I can work it for you now.'

Within ten minutes of ordering that coffee, Tom had told us the ropes and how easy it was to work. These boats took out cargo of every kind and brought back everything from bullocks to oysters. We would be given work to do and when we arrived at Philadelphia we should get ten shillings if we had been satisfactory. We would have to go to the office, so the sooner the better, said Tom, as there might be a dozen or more waiting to go. But Tom also said that he was in with the cargo skipper and could always get a preference for his pals over others, so we went to the office and signed on. The fellow who gave us the card was no more alarmed than if we'd asked for a bus ticket to Whitechapel Road and asked no other questions than ' British ? ' My friend the *crocus* flashed out a ' Rather ! ' and looked apprehensively at me. He looked at me and I nodded confidently. Of course I was British. My father's ancestors had been here since A.D. 1400 and my mother's nationality did not count on official certificates. ' Name ? ' he said. ' Copsie,' said the *crocus*. ' Wood,' said I, and the two adventurers, Copsie and Wood, walked out of the office holding their tickets as if they were passports to heaven.

Tom followed us. I was the first to speak. Something was worrying me badly. ' Wood isn't my real name,' I said at last, ' but I always use it.' ' Well,' said Tom, ' Brown isn't mine.' ' Lord love us,' said the *crocus*, ' Copsie isn't mine ! ' Delighted to find we were all in the same boat, we then confided in each other. Tom told us his father was a respectable little chemist in the small country town of G——. Tom had got himself in a bit of a muddle and the only thing was to clear out. He'd been working in a place where some females were employed and he ' had been a bit fresh with them,' he said. And that was all Tom would say. The *crocus* had come from Romany stock on his mother's side. She had married a showman, had died, and his father had then married a young woman, little older than Copsie himself. They had got on too well together and the old man had smelt a rat, said Copsie mournfully. I said aghast : ' But surely you didn't fall for your step-mother ? ' ' No, I didn't,' he said, ' but she fell for me and with these women, what can you do ? ' I thought : what a strange couple I had fallen in with ! I also thought that women seem to cause all the trouble, and was now no longer surprised when I thought of the recruiting-sergeant's words : ' Love or murder ? ' It was my turn to tell my life and I thought they would find it very dull indeed, but instead they were enthralled with my descriptions of our *vardo* and how we worked the lanes. For many weeks after we had joined together I would amuse them in spare moments with stories of gipsy life. We were exceptionally good pals, there was never a cross word between the three of us, and as I had seen a good bit of fighting on and off in my time I was only too pleased to jog along without fists and tempers.

We left the West India Docks on the Sunday night at the stroke of twelve. Sirens were shrieking away and singing and shouting was heard. We had been so interested in our new venture that we had forgotten time and dates. It was New Year's Eve. ' What a time to start a new venture ! ' I thought as we all bid each other a happy New Year with a great deal of noise and heartiness. The *Eagle Point* moved down the Thames and we were off, but little did we realize what a rough time we were in for. We had got to the Lizard when a propeller broke and instead of getting to Philadelphia in ten days, as scheduled, it took us twenty. I am quite sure that that ten bob we were promised at the end of the trip was the hardest money ever earned, though the hardships were not very noticeable to us. The trip certainly seemed a bit rough, but we did not know that the propeller was off—we just thought it was a rough passage and that all was well. Actually, the captain and seamen had a frantic time. But we were below looking after the cargo, swopping yarns, getting trip and food buckshee, and it hardly mattered to us when we landed so long as we were going in the right direction. As a matter of fact, we had been listed as missing, and there had been some concern for us in the papers, so that when we arrived at last in Philadelphia all the newspapers bore streamer headlines : ' Missing Ship Returns.' We were made a great fuss of by the newspaper men and treated like heroes, and though we down below had known nothing of all these heroisms we shared in the glory and we gave the friendly newspaper men unblushing stories of death staring us in the face hourly and the remarkable feats we had done to stop it staring. They filled us up with beer and food, and I'd have had anything happen to be made a fuss of like this. Only the captain suffered from that trip. A cable awaited him that his wife had died the very night we sailed and as the propeller broke near the Lizard. There was no wireless in those days and among all the congratulations and beer-drinking he was a lonely figure, seeming not to care that we had made port after the struggle.

We may have landed in America in a blaze of undeserved glory but we were very soon told that we were not wanted there and could not stay. We replied at once that we did not want to, thanks. England for us every time ! We wouldn't stay a moment in such a country as this, we told them contemptuously. All we dreamed of was to get straight back home the moment the boat was repaired. Tom had put us up to that wrinkle. ' Tell them what a rotten place this is,' he had warned us when the officials came along. ' Say you hated it before you came out and the sight of it has been enough. Be very British,' said Tom. We took his tip and disarmed any suspicion the officials might have that we wanted to stay in their country, so they left us alone as we would need no watching. We were supposed to sleep on board till the departure of the ship or go back on another. The *Eagle Point* had to go to the repair dock and that suited us down to the ground. That night we slipped ashore for a couple of hours and went back on board to sleep. The next day we were going to *scarper*, as the *crocus* called it. And *scarper* we did.

And here it was from our first hour on American shore that I began to realize that the professor knew as little about America as he knew about herbs. I found myself even beginning to doubt whether he had ever been there at all. In fact, I found myself doubting many things in his past enthusiastic descriptions of this land of golden opportunity. He certainly was not as confident about our prospects as he had been when he thumped the table at the Northamptonshire fair. The fixing up of things was left entirely to me, just as it had been left me to take the initiative and approach Tom. All we knew was that we had to get out of Philadelphia for fear the officials would put us under observation. I sat in my bunk wondering how my wits would get us away and where were the *vardos* filled with gold that I had promised my mother jokingly. I knew now that Copsie knew just about as much of America as I did, yet I bore him no grudge. Indeed, I have been grateful all my life, for though I made no fortune I did make several more trips to the States, out of which I was to have enormous fun and invaluable lessons on how to get across worlds and continents buckshee.

LVI

On the following day we packed up our few oddments and came ashore, determined to put the city as far behind us as we could. As always happens when one is keyed up to expect difficulties, nothing at all happened, and we just walked away unnoticed and unsuspected. We had made no plans, for we knew plans to be useless. You have to know your ground before you can plan, and we knew nothing except that we wanted to stay here and earn our living as lavishly as possible. We seemed to walk for hours before putting the last house behind us and being at last in real country. As we walked through the open countryside we saw, here and there, a policeman ; we had the newspapers and our return tickets to prove our story and we were going to say that till the *Eagle Point* was ready we were passing the time walking in the country. But it was not necessary, for unlike their behaviour on the films to-day their police never came up and barked at us, but left us courteously alone and unnoticed.

I have never forgotten my first night's sleep on American soil. Our inquiries in the first little town had led us to a lodging-house owned by a man called Joe, the Swede. He 'ban got one room,' but unfortunately for us it only 'ban empty to-morrow.' We must have looked very crestfallen and Joe must have been more than usually kind-hearted or in need of cash, for he couldn't bear to see us go so sadly away. He called us back and said that he had a room, but he would have to clean it a bit and if we would come back as late as we could we might have it. When we got back Joe still seemed loth to show us the room and he kept on talking his Swedish-American till long after midnight. At last he could postpone our going to bed no longer as we were getting decidedly querulous and he took us upstairs. He showed us into the usual lodging-house with a large bed at one end and a screen at the other. Joe said anxiously : 'You folks won't meddle or touch no t'ing in dis room ah guess?' and we assured him we were too worn out for anything but sleep.

Early training has made me a light sleeper, for we Romanys sleep like our *juggals* with one ear cocked and half-an-eye open, and I woke about an hour later to the sound of a low gurgling. Copsie was obviously a heavy sleeper and he was well away. I heard the low gurgle again. I shook Copsie awake and told him that there was some one else in the room. We sat up in bed and listened, but not a sound broke the silence. I was just beginning to think I might have been mistaken and Copsie was almost off again, when I heard the sound of the gurgling even louder than before. I dug him in the ribs again and put on the light and we sat up again listening. This time it gave an extra loud gurgle, like the last of the bathwater rushing down the drain. Even Copsie heard it this time, and said : 'It's there, Pet, behind that screen !'

We ran to the screen and looked behind it and there was a

dead woman lying all laid out for burial, hands crossed, and stretched between two chairs. Now if there is one thing a Romany loathes above all else on earth it is to see a coffin or a dead *gorgio* ! After one appalled look I rushed for my clothes and I do not think I have ever dressed in such a hurry in my life. I shot downstairs at a great rate, to be met by Joe the Swede, who had been sleeping by his safe with a revolver in his hand. ' My God ! there's a dead woman in our room ! ' I panted. ' Did you no say no looka behin' da screen ? ' said Joe who seemed as aggrieved at my betrayal as God was at Adam. Joe told me to go back to bed, it would be all right and she would be buried in the morning, but I sat the night out in the kitchen, none too pleased at having to be in a house where there was a corpse. Copsie, though, had more pluck than imagination and he stuck it. He said no woman, dead or alive, was going to do him out of his night's rest, and he covered his head up and forgot about her. We did not stop a second night at Joe's though he thought us very unreasonable, seeing that the corpse had left that morning. Joe might be a very obliging landlord, but how did we know what he still had up his cupboard for us !

We walked about the little town wondering how we could earn some money and found that stalls were being placed ready for the next day on a piece of ground which formed the market. I saw my chance. If I were only allowed to book a piece of ground I could start *grafting* to-morrow. The *crocus* suggested that we should buy some pills from local chemists and that we should both work with them, but when I had spoken with the men who were rigging up the stalls and found out that the majority of the folk who came were women, I decided to work alone. So the Professor bought instead a bar of green soap, cut it into little squares, and wrapped them neatly up, and there was Professor Copsie's infallible corn cure. I bought a dozen or two wax candles, took out the wicks, and made them up into little oblong

tablets and I had 'The Greatest Scientific Novelty the World
has Ever Seen.'

We were early on the market the next morning and laid
out our wares. The Professor soon broke the ice as he called
taking the first dime. I felt really ashamed of the *crocus*, but
he said soap is not bad for what they call corns, it is really hard
skin through the old chumps wearing shoes too small for
them. The soap softens the skin and it comes off. 'Anyway,' said Copsie, 'they won't miss a dime. And women
love spending other people's money.' I had laid out my
stock which consisted of the pieces of wax wrapped in
shining blue paper, a few newspapers with prints on them, a
packet of cream-laid note-paper, and a large metal spoon which
I had borrowed from our landlady.

I started *spieling*. 'Now, ladies, don't fail to see this wonderful novelty! I have travelled 3,000 miles to show it to you.
The wonderful Photo-and-Print-Reproducer! With this
wonderful preparation you can copy a print from any newspaper or periodical into your album or scrap book. Perhaps
you possess an old faded photograph of some dear departed
friend that you value. Here is the chance to make certain
that you will always have a copy even when the original has
faded completely away. Now, ladies, watch how easily and
simply it is done! I rub a little of the Magic Reproducer
on a sheet of this paper, then I apply the print face downwards
on the prepared portion and with the handle of this spoon I
gently rub over the back of the print, and here we have an
exact reproduction taking, as you see, less than sixty seconds
to make. What a joy for your little ones at home to be able to
fill their scrap books with all these topical pictures! What
fun for YOU, for the Magic Reproducer works equally well
with coloured prints as it does with black and white. They
are only five cents each. Or a packet of three tablets, enough,
ladies, to reproduce FIVE THOUSAND copies, can be
bought for a dime . . . AND DON'T FORGET, I HAVE

ONLY A FEW DOZEN LEFT!' I cleared out my stock within an hour and when I counted up I had earned a clear *bunce* of one dollar seventy-five cents, equivalent at that time to seven and sixpence in our money.

The Professor had done none too well. 'I knew I wouldn't,' he said disgustedly, 'if I started off too early with a sale.' However, we were quite happy for between the two of us we had cleared ten shillings. 'That's a good fake of yours,' said the Professor enviously. 'I've never seen it worked before. I'll work it in England when I get back.' He never asked me if he might take my fake, which was a trick Mascka worked on the fairs when I was a child, and I believe he would have started back for home immediately had I not told him I had some far finer fakes than that one. I then told him of a wonderful stain remover that would take out ink from either cloth or paper, remove fruit stains, and would even prevent wrinkles on old women's faces. I told him of how my Uncle Mascka had sold it in every town on the Continent and never once drew a blank.

The Professor decided to sell off his stock of corn cure and then I would hand over the Magic Reproducer to him and I would work my Stain Remover. We got a little book from a stationer which gave us all the information we wanted as to the markets and fairs at the various towns. It was now February and only the markets were available. And the conditions were awful. I had long since put out of my head such words as Eldorado. My fingers were so cold that the metal spoon used to feel like fire on them, but we stuck it out, and if there was no rain or snow we went out and grafted, and on wet days we would get into a saloon and have a drink and play a game, incidentally getting a cheap feed off the free sandwiches which used to be on the counters.

We had been working for about seven weeks when the Professor decided that he would return to England. He wanted to get back home and work my candle-fat fake. I tried to persuade him not to go back till we had made all those fortunes he was so sure we would make in England. He was a spineless creature, a man absolutely without guts. You had to be father and mother and all the other parts of the family to him, and I was not so sorry to lose him. He had picked my brains and shared my money and now was eager to return to the knackered country which was so down and out when he was in it and so full of golden promise when he was away. Years later I saw him at a small fair still working my Magic Reproducer. He was taking a few pence, but he still did not know that it is the personality you put into your *spieling* that carries the crowd. I need hardly say that I did not make myself known to him, for I had had enough by that time of people who stole my ideas and sponged on my silly good nature.

I was left alone, and I wandered around every town in Pennsylvania selling my Magic Stain Remover and my Magic Reproducer. I made all the money that there was to be made at the fair game, which is hard work and constant work, had jumped every train like a native-born, and had memorized every trick known to man of how to get a meal buckshee, and decided, at the end of May, to go home. I jumped a train to Philadelphia, walked round to the docks and found that the *kooshti cherinos* were with me. The *Eagle Point* was in and would be leaving in a few days. My first inquiries in England were, of course, where my mother was last heard of, and I made my way to Epsom Downs where the Romanys were gathering for the Derby. I had not done too badly in America. I had paid my way and I had 200 greenbacks, as we used to call the one-dollar notes. Not bad savings for four months' wandering and train jumping, especially as in those pre-war days money *was* money. I had also learnt the ropes over there, found out that America was an easy enough country to work if you had something good to sell, and that if you could make pence without experience you could most certainly make silver once you knew where to go for it. I was, however, very unsettled and kept asking myself if I had done wrong in returning and wondering what had drawn me back home again. I consoled myself with the thought that I could get back any time I wanted to, and I made up my mind that I would return and give them herbs that would cure and not fake cures such as my *crocus* friend put across unsuspecting fair crowds.

LVII

I FOUND my mother among the *tans* and *vardos* and the noise and the colour. It did my heart good to see again the *tans* of my people, for though the English Romany may be half-*diddikai* and few are pure bred, a tent or a caravan with Romany *chavis* playing around the wheels and the placid old women smoking their clay pipes on the steps and the Romany greeting given with the hand and smile, all warms up the heart as no sight on earth can do by its sense of friendliness and freedom. My mother greeted me with joy, surprised at seeing me back so soon. She made no reference to the *vardos* filled with gold I should have come dragging behind me, but congratulated me on the sum I had made in so short a time. She had not worried for me, she said, for she never had any doubts about me. ' *You* will never want, son,' she had said to me many a time. All she ever asked of me was to play straight. ' A conscience cannot be cleansed by dirty *dloova*,' she would say in her quiet voice that used so few words yet used them always in such a way that I was never to forget them.

The lanes and the little towns and the old familiar villages seemed to me tiny indeed after my taste of America. Distances were short day *treks* where they had meant train jumping for hundreds of miles all spiced with danger and filled with the

glow of adventure. Every time the wagons came to a stand-
still you lay low and held your breath and peered out from
beneath the tarpaulin and wondered where you were. It was
always somewhere new, something unfamiliar, and all your
wits were needed to decide what to do next. I was restless
and unsettled in England at the good old round of *chopping*
and horse-dealing, *trekking* the small cut-up distances from one
country to another which had once seemed to me quite imposing distances. I went off for trips abroad, through Spain,
France, and Belgium for months at a time, working off the
edge of my restlessness that way ; home again, and back across
the Channel, adding to my smattering of the languages and
my never-ending pleasure at the freedom and life of the
Continent.

But a day came when I knew I must *trek* for America again
and that I had no more excuses to offer myself for keeping
away. My mother took my decision as calmly as she took all
my decisions and sudden departures for abroad. She asked
me only to write to her this time and let her know each week
the new things I did and the new places in which I found myself. She said she would get a *gorgio* to read it for her and that
she would answer me, though she added sadly that her news
would hardly be called new.

Philadelphia seemed like home to me now that I knew the
ropes and had no difficulty in getting just where I wanted to
go. I had seen nothing of America yet, for when people in
England asked me had I seen San Francisco, Los Angeles,
Chicago, Boston, I had had to say no and feel small and out of
it. My previous four months had been spent in little market
towns selling magic remedies, but I was going to *see* America
this time and it would be with something good. I had underestimated my knowledge of herbs. I had been suffering from
an inferiority complex. I thought every one I met better
than myself. But I gradually woke up to the fact that even
people who had been well educated did not know as much as

I did. (I still marvel at this to-day, meeting people with every 'advantage' of expensive educations who know absolutely nothing that is worth knowing when it comes to observation, common sense, or getting themselves the simplest of livings.) They seemed to get along well in peacock's feathers, I noticed. Very well, I would do the same. My mother used to say to me : 'Never mind your clothes. Clothes do not make the man. Remember that a peacock in all his glory cannot whistle like a thrush in its drab feathers.' I thought it out. She was right, but I could whistle and I'd whistle still better with peacock's feathers. The careless gipsy wardrobe was discarded. I became Dr. Thompson-Thompson, world re-nowned herbalist. I assumed, as feathers for this rare bird, an elegant black vicuna suit, an opera-hat that shut down if you sat on it, black patent leather shoes, a pair of spotless white spats, a stiff collar, and fawn wash-leather gloves. Also a hoighty-toighty voice. I was a good mimic ever since child-hood. We used to take off the toffs at the fairs and among ourselves imitating the manner of the *boro-ryes* when you went up to a house and they said : 'Haw. What-a are you-a selling-ah ?' 'Pegs, sir.' 'Haw-haw. Indeed-ah. Pegs-ah. I do not think-ah we need any pegs-ah.'

I soon found a firm that could make up pills for me to my own recipe. I had them nicely boxed and labelled and I worked as I had never worked before. I worked up and down the country as the great Dr. Thompson-Thompson, with my top-hat, spats, voice, and pills, and a good time was had by all. This time money was plentiful and at last it was silver instead of pence. I remembered my father's advice never to be afraid of a big 'un, and did some of my best work round the stock-yards of Chicago. This time I had the 'lime trick' helping me, which Mascka had taught us as *chavis* and which he had always found the quickest money-maker ever invented by the wits of man.

I would make my way to the slaughter-yards as the luncheon-hour broke and the men were coming out for their midday break. The pig-stickers were not particular as to their appearance : blood soaked their sleeves and trousers, their knives were stuck in their jack-boots, blood and hair were all over them in nauseating profusion. Dagos, German toughs, Swedes, great big hulking fellows with huge blond moustaches—a terrifying crowd to the average man ; but I have always found that the larger the man looks and the bigger bully he seems to be the simpler he is to get along with, and a little man can lead them with a word. They were so simple that they had, apart from my wares, a great admiration for me, for they really believed that I had pluck to come and tackle such great fine chaps as themselves, and that if my pills had not been all I claimed for them I would not have dared do so !

At this time my method was to hire a buggy or a wagonette and 'pitch' from it. When the pig-stickers saw me directing the buggy-puller (the man I had hired to help me) to pull the buggy towards them they stopped eating their dinners and looked at me in wonderment. It was the lunch-hour and these men came out for a breather and used to eat their lunch outside on a piece of waste ground. We made a strange contrast, I in my black clothes, dazzling collar and cravat, they in their butchers' blouses, their corduroy trousers stuck in their huge blood-soaked jack-boots, ornamented with the knives they used in their hideous work. I smiled at them, the broadest smile I could put up. Some of them thought me a missionary or a follower of Brigham Young from Salt Lake City and I heard their wise-cracking comments as I busied myself getting my gear ready. Some of the more inquisitive ones came closer and with mouths full of bread and cheese asked me in a sideways drawl who I thought I was ? 'I will tell you who I AM!' I shouted in my best la-di-da English. 'That is what I am here for, gentlemen, TO TELL YOU WHO I AM !' I would then get up on my little stand facing the blood-covered crowd, my top-hat at an elegant angle, my snowy cuffs as I held up my little boxes a truly impressive sight, and I would begin my *spiel*.

'GENTLEMEN!' I would shout, starting with a flourish that always brought the men around me, 'I have come three thousand miles to cure you of your ailments. You have heard of me. DR. THOMPSON. THOMPSON-THOMPSON. Son of PROFESSOR THEODORE SYLVANUS THOMPSON, the celebrated British scientist, who thirty years ago visited Montana and came across an aged Indian chief. The old man was one hundred and seventeen years of age. My father asked him to what he attributed his longevity. The old man gazed heavenwards and smiled, and mentioned a wonderful herb that grew on the mountain-top, three thousand, three hundred and forty feet above the level of the sea.' Here I would pause impressively. 'On the following day, with the assistance of a couple of guides, my father climbed to the mountain-top and he secured some of these wonderful herbs which, as objects of great value, were then dispatched to the Continent of Europe. Some, gentlemen, are growing in His Imperial Highness the German Emperor's private garden at Potsdam. The others are at Kew Gardens, but by a special arrangement with the authorities, my father has the sole right of gathering these leaves when they reach their maturity. After being powdered and pulverized in a scientific manner known only to ourselves, they are made in the form of pills. AND EVERY PILL I AM SELLING YOU TO-DAY CONTAINS TWO GRAINS OF THIS SPE-CIFIC HERB. If you are suffering from flatulence, dyspepsia, pains in the back of the body, lumbago, sciatica, and that throbbing feeling at the temples when you rise in the morning and again at night when you get to bed, and feel you are falling through it, and your heart palpitates, THESE are the pills which in a brace of shakes will get away that cursed feeling, the bogy of every living man.' Here again would come an impressive pause. 'Owing to the limited number of these pills, gentlemen, we have to restrict you to one box only. No living person can be supplied with more than ONE box. PLEASE do not ask me for two, for I do not like to refuse you. These pills are worth their weight in gold, because gold cannot buy LIFE and these pills give it! But I am offering you to-day this Elixir of Life which will put TEN YEARS on to any man standing around here, FOR ONE DOLLAR A BOX.'

Then pointing to the most weedy specimen in the crowd, I would point him out and gaze at him with a fearful hypnotic glare : ' THERE is a man in the throes of life,' I would cry like an angry prophet, ' who does not know that DEATH is near to him. Do you know, sir, that if you go on as you are going you will not be killing pigs but killing yourself ? Death awaits you almost on your doorstep. Step up here, sir, please. I would like to prove to these gentlemen that what I say is correct.' The poor weedy specimen, already much greener than when I had singled him out, would come furtively to the platform and his buddies would crowd round in great excitement. This is where Mascka's trick came to my aid. I had got under the table two bottles of water. In one I had placed a piece of unslaked lime and then decanted it off again. To blow on this water, though it looks clear enough, turns it a milky blue from the action of carbonic acid gas on the lime. In the other was pure water. I would take a glass and pour it full of the doctored water, handing the man a straw with much slow ceremony, and ask him if he would kindly blow down the straw into the water. Immediately the water would turn a cloudy milk colour, and I would snatch the glass, hold it above my head, and address myself gravely to my audience. ' YOU SEE, gentlemen, what your friend has on his lungs ! ' There was always a murmur of consternation at this pitch. I would time my effect, the weedy friend looking as though death really were around the corner from him, and handing him a glass of pure water and a pill I would say : 'NOW I AM GOING TO SHOW YOU, GENTLEMEN . . .' The man would gulp the water and the pill and I would wait a second as though to give the pill its proper time to work the miracle. Then I would pour him in another glass another dose of pure water and hand him another straw with an airy wave of the hand. 'NOW take the straw and blow, sir. . . .' I would say, while a hush fell over the big husky slaughterman, their eyes round as *chavis* at a Punch and Judy show and their mouths well open. The weedy one took the straw and the glass, blew, and of course the water was crystal clear. 'WHAT DID I TELL YOU, GENTLEMEN . . . ? '

I never lost this great moment for the final impression. Raising my voice loud and commanding above the awed silence I would begin pointing to heads in the crowd. 'This is not the only man suffering from this complaint,' I would say hypnotizing them with my glare. 'THERE is one ! . . . and THERE . . . THERE . . . THERE ! . . . *You*, sir, and YOU . . . and YOU. . . . You are alive to-day and where do you think you will be to-morrow ? I dare not tell you, gentlemen, but I know that I have come just in time. . . .' They evidently thought that life was worth a dollar for the whole stock-yard used to clammer for a box and some even sneaked back for another, thinking they were not noticed.

When they had bought their box and paid their dollar I would tell them how to take them. Very solemnly I would say : 'Take a pill every night upon retiring to bed. Drink a pint of pure cold water. AND ON NO ACCOUNT MUST ANY ALCOHOLIC DRINK BE TAKEN WHILE YOU ARE TAKING THESE PILLS OR IT MEANS INSTANT DEATH. And watch the difference, gentlemen, in a week ! ' And the difference in a week was astonishing. Back I would go at the end of the seven days and see what the crowd of blood-covered huskies was looking like. They would welcome me back with grins and waves of the hand, swearing they felt new men. Of course they felt new men ! Not only were the pills very good pills but for one whole week the men had kept off the booze. They had been off the drink (and they certainly knew how to drink, that lot !) and had given their kidneys a clean flush out with pure cold water each day. They all asked for a repeat order in case I did not come back for some time. These great muck-covered fellows wrung my hand and called me the saver of their lives. They could hardly believe their luck that I had been sent all the way from England to Chicago to snatch dying pig-stickers from the edge of the grave. Time after time I went back and time after time I was welcomed with dollars and open arms. I could go back to-day and still get a fat living there if the folk still come outside and eat their lunches.

LVIII

I WAS getting letters from my mother and was sending her money that must have totalled no mean sum, at this time. I was also saying money myself, for I was determined to have a handsome caravan and a beautiful *pellengro grye*. I had always wanted a piebald or a dappled-grey horse, for they clean up so well and look so smart with the wagon. But though the money was so plentiful I felt that Chicago and its blood and screaming pigs was not for me. Also I wanted to see America. I have always had the feeling that I could always be able to get a meal however old I grew, so I have never hung on in one spot just for the sake of the money. I was going to travel and travel in style. I was a doctor and doctors did not *ped* the *boro-drom*. So I bought a pony and buggy and went on *trek* in style, visiting many towns, working the markets, the fêtes and galas, of which there were always a surfeit. The money was more than good and continued to be lavish enough both to send home and to save.

It was at a large fair in Ohio that I met with two American *diddikais* whom I have never forgotten. They were an old couple, the old woman being a delightful old soul who used to make home-made rock and a kind of flat gingerbread resembling honeycomb, which she called Maryland Honey-cake. She told me she had a little home in Maryland, for American Romanys live in houses in the winter not *tans*, but she worked the fêtes and fairs in the summer and lived on her little business in the winter. She was as round as an apple with a heart as large as herself. She was for ever pressing on me glasses of lime-juice and her gingerbread, for she liked my voice and used to tell me : ' Gee ! but haven't you got a tongue ! ' I think it was her flattery that made me like her even more than before, for I had never been flattered as yet and what man can resist it ? Her husband was a thin plaintive little man, rather delicate, with a good nature and no ambition. His wife used to sing his praises all day long. There was no man in the world like Dave. I certainly thought there was no one so lucky. To have a wife who was giving him perpetual praise while he left all the work to her and to simply stand and moan about home and Maryland instead of working every minute of the day did not seem bad luck at all. Yet Dave was a good fellow, and I think he had got down-hearted with adversity and wanted to get home and die there.

The end of the fêtes were coming and she had got boxes of this honey-cake made up. Whatever were she and Dave to do ? If only she could sell it out and get back to Maryland she'd be happy. But it certainly did not look likely. What with a moaning husband to support and her work to do the poor old soul was in despair. I could not bear to see two people so harmless and so helpless, and I made her an offer. It was only in the daytime that I could graft my pills for that was

when the serious business of the day was done. In the evening
when the young people came along only to squirt water in
each others ears and to puff wind into long paper tubes called
blow-outs, and tickle the maidens with feathers on the end of
a piece of cane, I would be free and would give her a hand.
'But they don't seem to want to buy these days,' she would say
sadly. 'Why, I used to sell a hundredweight in a day once!'
'Leave it to me,' I told her confidently, 'you will soon be sold
out and in Maryland again.' I became the first Romany
Jekyll and Hyde. I was Dr. Thompson-Thompson from the
moment the fair opened to 5 p.m., and Petulengro, the Seer,
from 8 p.m. to midnight. I had decided to give every
customer who paid a dime (5d.) for a four cent (2d.) ginger-
bread, a short *dukkerin*. I set about my *spieling* and how they
rolled up. Abigail wanted to give me the extra six cents, but
I was helping her and help her I meant to without being paid
for it. 'Now then, boys and girls,' my voice would ring out,
no longer hoighty-toighty but companionable. 'Your future
told, good luck given you, and a cake of Abigail's renowned
Maryland Honey-cake for a dime!' The boys and girls were
waiting in rows for the *dukkerin* and the ginger-bread. I never
saw such a transformation in a man as I saw in poor drooping
Dave. He actually smiled once. In a week the entire stock
was gone. Then I cleared up the rock for her. I had taken
over three hundred dollars for them and the profits were, of
course, three times more than if they had sold out in the
ordinary way. I went to the *vardo* of Abigail and Dave the
night before they started to *trek* to their dear Maryland and
they were both in tears. 'If only we had you for a son!'
they wept. 'Come to us whenever you like.' Dave gave
me a present of a little gilt watch, which I have kept to this
day. He wanted to give me money but the satisfaction of
knowing that I had brought such unexpected happiness in
their lives was more than money could have bought for
me. I never saw either Abigail or Dave again, though

years afterwards, passing through Maryland, I was to see their names on a tombstone.

LIX

LONELINESS is not a complaint from which I have ever suffered, as solitude comes naturally to the Romany, but parting from Abigail and Dave saddened me, for I realized how alone one can be and, perhaps also, how far away I had come from the only being who had my life and interest at heart. But the remembering the Tarot Fool I did not put off to-day's work until to-morrow but did my usual pitching at another little *gavaste*. I was heading south to Kentucky. The negro population was getting thick at each move. But they were fairly good ' punters ' for my pills, and somehow a negro has that instinctiveness about him that ' nature's way is the right way,' and I found that the negroes were in many ways superior to white folk. They usually listened to an explanation without sarcasm and heckling, as is usual with a white crowd. We generally know these hecklers. They are mostly people who are in a business to which naturally the herbalist is a gentle rival, but we generally get the best of an argument by saying that the ancients of the Biblical days took herbs as medicine many years before the multiple drug store opened up a branch in their High Street.

Naturally, I have had many set-to's with people in the different places I have visited. Rarely can the village wit resist airing his superior knowledge and idea of humour, but a few years of training on the road makes a grafter capable of answering any question, however inane. But these towns-people of the southern states seemed very interested in my talks and I used to start my *spieling* with little stories, some pathetic, some to amuse them. I always find that if you can get a crowd in a happy mood they'll eagerly spend money if they've got it. To work to a crowd of niggers that you make laugh is a joy in itself. When they open their mouths and show their lovely sets of strong teeth and haw-haw heartily it puts even the worker in a good mood, and, as I have said, I was happy even if I *grafted* to all negroes. In some towns the white population had pitches where the negroes were not allowed to attend and in others the negroes had their little market which the whites avoided. I think the negroes used to spend a ' quarter' with me because I was pleased to be among them. I always remembered a sentence of my mother's to the effect that the same *kooshti-Duval* who made the negro made me and saw no difference in us. So I bore no colour malice.

It was while I was in one of these southern state towns that I made the acquaintance of a man who was to put me in the way of my one vivid and important memory of America, often as I visited it later. I was *pitching* to a mixed crowd and had just finished serving when a tall ginger-bearded son of Scotland approached me. He told me he was extremely interested in my lecture and had a proposal to make to me. A typical Scotsman he went the long way round to bring his point out and kept the sugary part of the story till the last. ' Coom and hae a drink when ye've packed awa ye guids,' he said, ' I hae a prroposeetion that will mak' ye reel glad and happy." I'm always particularly on my guard when any folk want to do me a good turn. In helping me they generally have both eyes on themselves, and I thought as I went over to the saloon : ' I wonder where this one leads to !' Jock called for the drinks. He had a fire-water rinsed down with a beer. I had a soft drink, not that I was teetotal but that I wanted to keep my head clear while it listened to the prroposeetion.

It seemed a week to me before he started and finally I egged him on by saying ' Better spit it out now, Jock, I die at ninety-two.' So Jock ordered two more drinks and then told me all about the great idea by which I was to be made glad and reech. He disclosed that he was the manager of a medium-sized tobaccy and cotton plantation. It was a lonely spot but in beautiful surroundings. There were sixty negroes in all, men, women, and children. But there was no doctor handy. Would I like to come down with him where I could sub-manager, doctor, and handyman combined. He told me that among his crowd were some of the most beautiful half-breed girls a man had ever seen. That when he was away no work would be done as the ' charge hand ' was as bad as the others. And that I'd be doing him a real favour and at the same time find myself in a paradise on earth. I pondered it over another soft drink. What about my horse and buggy ? What about my stock of pills ? Sell the horse and buggy, said he, and the pills we should want by the millions. Every dusky maiden would want pills supplied by a man of my stamp, said Jock adding the deft butterfly touch of flattery. Why, that was the reason he had picked me out. There would be no malingering. They knew now that there was no one there to tell them whether they were ill or not. One had to take their word for it. Besides, there was a law against using the ' thong ' now. So there it all was. He would bring down a distinguished English doctor and I would make a great impression and get exceedingly good pay for knowing who was ill and who was malingering. There was to be everything I wanted in the way of food and drink, and as a special allurement I was to have the pick of the *juvvals* as house-keeper. ' There's one called Rosalie, and nearly as white as yesel' ! ' enthused Jock and with the air of a man who need say no more. He was right. Like another strong man, Samson, I fell, but unlike him I had not even seen my dusky Delilah. Poor old Dobbin, my *grye*, must have a new master because I was to have a new mistress. I was very upset at parting with Dobbin because a Romany does not willingly part with his horse, particularly for bait he has never seen. But a fat round little baker bought him and I was consoled, for a fat man is kind to horses. They are too contented usually, and even a slow horse will not make them cruel. So it looked as though Dobbin would be in clover.

Jock took me for a meal at a haunt where he laid in his stocks of spirits and tobacco. This brought from me the query : why buy tobacco when you have a plantation of it ? Jock explained that you could not make it as he grew it. It had to be cured and faked with liquorice and all kinds of stuff I have forgotten. I thought it strange that even the pure things have to be faked to make them palatable and how the *gorgio* likes things only when they have been doctored ! We began our journey and we had over thirty miles to go. He assured me that his horse was a good one and would do it easily in four hours. It soon seemed as if I had known Jock from the day he was born at a little place near Ayr in Scotland. He described Glasgow and Edinburgh with all the detail and eloquence he could muster, but there still was no place in the world like the little place near Ayr. Here was another man who 'didn't do exactly right' at his home but made good thousands of miles away. Strange how many men do wrong at home and right when away from it.

It was a memorably beautiful night, with scarcely a breath of air, and the bees and insects humming along the last lap of the day. The sun took its slow time to go to rest, leaving on the sky its most harmonious colours which seemed unwilling to fade, and by the time we reached our destination the moon was shining as bright almost as the day. At the entrance to the plantation we were met by five or six of the younger members who took charge of the horse. Jock used to bring them simple little trinkets for presents. The men wanted tobacco, and, if very lucky, a bottle of fire-water. The others wanted handkerchiefs and bandannas. Jock was a psychologist and knew how to manage them—as he had managed me. The boy ran like a deer to the hut where they all gathered after work to sing their simple plaintive spirituals, and shouted out like a town crier : ' Dere's a new lovely white boss come heah ! '

They came tumbling out and falling over each other to get a good view of me. But they were very shy when I got near them. And then Jock called them up like a pack of hounds. Pete, Abe, Mose, Tubb, Eb, Tonk, Millie, Rosalie, Mame, Doll, Chloe, Dinah, Lil, Tannie, and they all took up the position he pointed out to them. I thought how much like the real Romany they were in these things, they were sized out, and then when all was quiet Jock addressed them. Here was a doctor who had come from much distance away. He will be boss when I'm gone to town. They must all obey me. Heap big punishment for any who dare question my authority. He talked to them for an hour, frequently telling them of accomplishments of mine which I never knew I had myself till then. He also convinced them that I could work magic and make any one of them have big pains, if they annoyed me. I was surprised to hear this one, but I had shown Jock some tricks in the saloon and he had thought them marvellous. I had also told him of my power to charm away warts and growths, and obviously he was twisting this simple information into something startlingly like witch-doctoring. Each one then made obeisance to me and grinned their shy child-like grins of welcome.

My first job of doctoring already awaited me. One of the girls, ' Bud,' had not turned out. She had slipped down an incline and had sprained her ankle. I made up an embrocation, a temporary one of vinegar, turpentine, and the whites of eggs, and with this I massaged the already swollen ankle. I noticed that Bud was exceedingly pleased with herself and most glad to have had the accident, and by the grin as I did the massaging I decided she must be either very stoical or indifferent to all but the thrill of being my first patient. I realized I would have to have many unguents and restoratives with me now that I was doctor to such a large family, and I made up a list there and then so that when Jock made his next journey to town I would have enough herbs and incidentals to do practically any job but an amputation.   It was early in the morning before I finally got to bed.   Jock had had a bed prepared for me in his hut, but my hut would be all prepared for me on the following day he promised me.   ' See if you can pick out Rosalie in the morning,' said Jock, ' and tell her you want her to do your work.'   I explained as tactfully as I could that I would manage all right on my own and rather liked the idea of doing my own work, but Jock said it was good for discipline, as all the girls would do their best to supplant Rosalie in the honour of doing my work.   I understood that Jock was going to offer the honour to the best girl as a prize !

LX

It was late when I awoke the next morning.   Jock had been up long since, but I had been too tired out to stir.   I was lying half asleep and half awake, thinking that I must feed Dobbin and vaguely wondering where I was going to pitch that day and what luck I should have, when I remembered Jock, and the new job, and my new home.   I rubbed my eyes, sat up, had my tub and dressed, and asked myself what had possessed me, a Romany ever on the move, to take a stationary job, fixing me in one spot for who knew how long ?   Hadn't I come here to see the country, and here I was behaving as cautiously as a *gorgio* !   Still, I decided it was worth trying for a month or two and then I would pack my herbs and take to the road again.

Jock had not waited for me to pick out Rosalie.   He had

sent her with a jug of hot coffee in which, as an extra, was a liberal sprinkling of Jamaica rum. Rosalie soon introduced herself. When Jock had called them up the night before I had not taken notice of which one answered to the names. But Jock was evidently a good judge of a comely *juvval*. Rosalie would have made Cleopatra look like Nellie Wallace. Tall, narrow, lithe as an eel, and brown as a *kuklo*. Her brown cheeks had a flush of red beneath them, making them an even dusky pink. Her lips were like a glass of wine and she had a set of teeth that would make a Duchess's pearls muddy by comparison. She said : ' Ah'm Rosalie. Mr. Mac toll me come heah. He say if you dohn lahke Rosalie you say no an' Ah come away. Ah hope you lahke Rosalie. Rosalie work oll der day if boss say.'

I had not compared the others with Rosalie, but she certainly looked as if few could beat her, and I did not want to seem ungrateful to Jock for picking me out the handsomest and best servant he could find. So I said : ' All right, Rosalie. You shall be my housekeeper.' And simple Rosalie fell down at my feet in gratitude. Poor Rosalie took to idolizing me and from her treatment of me I might have been king of some vast continent. Her deference was embarrassing. All she could say to explain her attitude was that I was different from the other white men she had ever known. Often I would ask her who her parents were. She told me of her mother and said her father had been a big white boss himself once, but had gone away when she was a *bubbo* and she had never seen him. Her mother was dead now, but Eb, her uncle, had charge of her. Rosalie would let me ask her any question, but she did not like me asking about her childhood, and she always tried to avoid discussing her parents.

There was nothing that was too much trouble for Rosalie to do. Personally I had been used to doing things for myself and could not even ask for things to be done for me. I found it so much quicker that way. But Jock insisted that

every bit of work in my hut must be done by Rosalie. ' Hoots,
mon ! ' he would say. ' Prestige is what matters here. Lose
it and yer done like a dinner.' So I had to conform to custom
and even if I had a bath Rosalie had to have a hand in it, and
although I am not bashful I insisted that I preferred to bath
alone. But Rosalie was not to be put off. She had been sent
to serve the white boss and one of the things she called serving
was to pour jugfuls of water over me as I sat in the bath, as
though she were doing me a rare favour, as when the negroes
bathe in the river and help each other in their ablutions.

Alas, in a week jealousy was rife in the camp. Another
pretty half-breed girl decided she would apply for Rosalie's
job of housekeeper and to achieve this she did everything
possible to win my favour. I used to tease poor Rosalie and
say I liked Bud, whose ankle I had massaged. But I had to
stop this teasing, as I began to live in fear of Rosalie manufac-
turing an accident so that I must cure her. To avoid this I
had to tell her that if ever she were ill I should have to have
another housekeeper and Rosalie would never be able to
cook my meals again. This had such an effect that once when
she was really ill the poor child stuck to work till I had to force
her to go to bed and lay up for several days. Rosalie, however, was not going to bed without issuing her ultimatum,
and she told me that if Bud or Tibbie or some other dusky
belle came to work for me while she was ill she would take the
berry. On inquiring what taking the berry meant, she
showed me a plant of little berries which she said would make
Rosalie die. I had to go very canny with her after that and
I never did anything that could possibly annoy her, if I could
avoid it. It saddened me that so much affection should be
lavished on me, who had no desire for it. She was so helpless
and sincere. She was absolutely selfless and asked only to
serve others and yet I would think how her devotion would be
taken for granted all her life just because they could call her
a half-breed. I am glad to think that I hurt Rosalie as little

as possible and never played on her intense jealousy which must have been agony to bear. I think it was this consideration which she understood I was showing her that made her so loyal to me, and was probably why my self-appointed task of teaching Rosalie that she must not like the boss too much was not too successful.

I naturally had to mix with all of them. I bound up their cuts, I treated the old men for rheumatism and sciatica and every form of ill they thought fit to contract now that a real doctor was on the spot. The youngsters were the most difficult problem ; I suppose I was too kind to them and if I drew out one of their first teeth I always gave them sweets afterwards. I'm afraid I must have taken out many a good tooth because some little Topsy got a pocketful of sweets as a soother. The old girls too would come running if they had the least tinge of pain and tell me they were nearly dead, but a glass of burdock medicine would make them come alive very quickly. I have never seen such faith as these poor folk had in me. Things were very tame after working hours, so I set out to make it a bit livelier for them. No one had ever bothered what they did for themselves before and they were surprised and delighted at my interest. I spoke to them of music and how lively a band is with several of them playing different instruments and they were enraptured with the idea. They agreed to put a little sum aside weekly and then I was to go to the burg, as they called the town, and buy some instruments for them all. Rosalie pouted her lips at that suggestion. She was one of the only two people in the camp who could play any instrument and she was proud of her guitar. She used to play only to me, and was not pleased that I was willing to teach the other negroes to make music and rob her of her accomplishment and the envy it brought her. Eb, her uncle and the only other musician on the lot, could play the whistle, banjo, and the fiddle. I got a melodeon from the burg when Jock went down and I made them sets of wooden castanets, a kettledrum from an old round zinc bath, some mouth-organs for the *chavis*, and a kind of xylophone which I rigged up with pieces of wood in different lengths and wooden hammers with which to hit them. The youngsters had such great mouths that at the first rehearsal I began to doubt the success of my plan, feeling sure they would swallow them before we were half-way through the tune. The first thing I taught them to play was the easiest tune I knew, 'D'ye ken John Peel ?' and soon they were vamping with the mouth-organs, hitting the drum, clapping the castanets, and the whole place rang with music and laughter. Negroes love laughter ? left alone they are a happy people, and the very thought that anybody could be doing all this to please them sent them wild with delight, and the noise helped too. Then I made a bargain with them. Each day that they worked well we would have a musical night. And how they worked after that ! Thongs and lashings had been replaced by fines and other petty restrictions, but fines, lashings, and stopping their pay altogether could not have had the effect on them that the thought of a happy evening banging the clappers had on their diligence and output. Jock thought I was working black magic on them, but I have always found that gentleness instead of fear is the only kind of magic you need work to get the best out of people. For love they will give you all they have and more ; for fear, everything they do is half done or done grumblingly and in dislike of you. By day my negroes worked willingly and practically without supervision so that at night we could be a large happy family singing and laughing like a lot of children. They taught me their melancholy spirituals, which seem to repeat themselves, the same line, the same beat, for hours on end, and I would teach them Romany lilts without telling them where the music came from, for they thought me the Great White Boss Doctor !

LXI

ONE fine day without any warning the directors of the plantation came down to see the camp. It was the first time I had seen any of them. They were men with the crude stamp of the hard business world on them, and Jock warned me they would be hard to please. I warned him that I should be hard to please, too, for if there is one form of irritation I dislike most it is directors and managers and heads of this, that and the other, with their pompous manners and complete lack of knowledge of the difficulties and human problems involved when a crowd of people work together. Also, they have always seemed to me an idle lot compared to the underling with his nose to the grindstone from this hour of the morning to that hour of the night, all for one quick drink on Friday night before he turns his wages over to his wife.

These turned up with the usual amount of bluff, but they had to admit they were astonished and pleased. Even they sensed the difference in the attitude of the blacks working for them. Work had been made almost a game and a competition as to who should take the floor with the best songs that night, for the best work done during the day. But they would not let well alone, and, with much peremptoriness, began questioning me as to the place of my birth, my parents, my former employment, why I had come to America, and a hundred and one questions which I had never dreamed I would be asked or expected to answer. I turned the subject by saying I did not trouble much about home and parents, that I was a wanderer who wanted to see life in all its aspects and who took it as it came. But they were not to be fobbed off with indirect answers to their stupid and inquisitive questions. One of them became really angry at my refusal to talk with them, and said that it was an unheard-of thing to have some one working as a sub-manager who had no credentials. I retorted that there was no place in the world where I would stay if I was not wanted and I was willing to leave that night. Here Jock took a hand. 'We've never had sich a season for fine worrk,' he told them, ' and if Doc goes I go too. An' I go richt noo.' The directors drew in their horns and decided it was no use worrying over my suspicious past and parentage. Before he left, the director who had bluffed the most sent for me and said : ' I know you are not a bad feller and I want you to know that I admire the way you stuck to your principles. I suppose we were a bit inquisitive. Here's a ten-dollar bill to show you there's no ill-feeling.' It was then that I let my tongue slip for the first time. 'I'm a Romany,' I said. ' You'll have to take me for what I am.' ' A *Romany* ? ' he said, pleased as a schoolboy. ' I've heard of these kinda guys. You read hands and fortunes, don't cha ? ' I said I did and I would do it for them, and I did and I collected fifty dollars, and the men who had arrived all authority and high-hat left as though we had been bosom friends for years and were as happy as sand-boys.

But not I. *Dukkerin* had brought back memories of the road and freedom. What was I doing here, after all, I began asking myself ? Which is always a sign that a change is coming soon and that one has found the first excuse to pick fault with one's surroundings. I tried hard to break this feeling down, but each week I made up my mind I must tell Jock I was going. Rosalie sobbed her heart out and made life unbearable. I stayed on and on, restless yet unable to hurt these nice people. It was over a year since I had come to the plantation through that chance meeting with Jock at the fair. Never in all my life had I stayed so long in one place. I had had good wages and sent much money home, but money I could pick up anywhere in the world. Mascka had seen to that for me ! Besides, our band was becoming an ever greater success. Eb taught the younger men to play the 'Jo' and I taught one bright young girl to play the melodeon. She was a born musician and within a month could play as well as I could play myself. We had nights that made the ordinary *diddikai* encampment look very small where music was concerned. These negroes had the same love of rhythm and instinct for music as the true-bred Romany has, and although they would never know those wild leaping melodies that race more quickly than the heart or ear can follow and which the Roumanian, Serbian, or Hungarian Zingari conjure from their fiddles, the love and the feeling for it were there and expressed in their slower, more mournful, way. I found more fun in teaching these children than ever I got out of life before. I thought of them always as children, for even those of seventy had hearts and minds filled with eagerness and surprise like a child. I made them pop-guns, catapults, wooden whistles, I taught them many of the *fakir's* tricks, even that of taking pictures off the papers which I had sold as magic reproducer, and it was no end of fun to them. I taught them things I would never teach a *gorgio*, simple tricks which look so complicated, and how to make practically a world out of oddments of wood, string, a few nails, and nimble fingers. Things which would keep them amused when I was gone, and get them a living should they ever find themselves in want of one.

Three months had passed as a week since the day of the directors' visit and still, despite my nostalgia to be gone, I had not found courage to tell them good-bye. But a thing was to happen that made up my mind for me in a lightning flash. One morning as I sat idly outside my hut I heard the croaking of a strange bird. It was not a raven, but it was an ugly black bird with a shrill croak. I shooed it away, for its ill-tempered craw-crawks, which it seemed to shrill at me as though it would attack me, made my blood cold. It may not have been a raven, but it was so obviously the next best thing that I sensed trouble. I had too much superstition in my blood not to know that this was a warning for my ears alone. There was only one person in the world whose death meant anything to me. The world could have been blotted out with plague so long as my mother was left. I knew now that there was something wrong at home and that I was going to her. In several of the last letters which the *gorgio* friend wrote me for my mother I had noticed that she spoke of ' the days when I shall see you again,' but I had not attributed much seriousness to them, thinking only that my mother was tired of being alone and thought it time I should come back. But now that the black strange bird had been sent to warn me, I knew that those sentences which I had ignored had held more than met the eye.

Rosalie could see by my manner that this time I meant what I said. She threatened to throw herself in the river and swore she would never live to work for another boss. I cheered her with promises of all the lovely things I would bring her back from across the *boro–doriav*. But I explained again and again that I must go home to my people after being away for over two years. I would be back, I said, before very few months · had passed. Rosalie was comforted and finally was made to smile and say : ' Ah'm so sorrow. Rosalie so sorrow, but she wait fo' you till she die.' Jock was very upset at my departure. I told him, too, that I would be back as soon as I had seen my people again. And truth to tell I did intend returning. I had been very happy with these simple folk, the nicest I had ever known in my life before. Here among these negroes and half-breeds I had found love and affection. Mostly in my life it had been all give and no take. But here there was nothing they would not do to make me happy and to give one of them a smile was like giving a *gorgio* a bank-note. I was as sincere in my promise to return as they in their tears and prayers to me to do so. I was deeply moved by the sight, as I sat in the drag in which Jock had put his favourite *grye* Smiler, of the sixty-six negroes around me in tears and waving branches of leaves, bits of coloured rag and their bright bandanas, calling :

' Come back soon, boss. We-all pray fo' you ! ' My last sight of them was blurred, for my own eyes were full of tears. Never had a *roy* received such a send-off. The journey to the station seemed very long, for neither Jock nor I spoke. We knew without words that we had no wish to part and that the break was bad for both of us. We had a last doch and doris together, Jock headed Smiler for home, and I set out on the long journey to Philadelphia, England, and my mother.

LXII

At the West India Docks I was off without waiting for food or drink.

I knew where I should find my mother. I also knew that I should find things greatly changed since my long absence in America. My letters from my mother had told me of how she had moved to the town where Ahny and her husband lived, and of how she had seen Waldo again, and had spent much time with them. She told me that they had treated her with much kindness. Rudy had *rommered* a *gorgio* girl and my mother had given them our *vardo* in which to live now, while she herself either had her *tan* or spent her time with Ahny in her home. My brother Waldo was at work from six o'clock mornings to six o'clock evenings and four o'clock on Saturday afternoon. Sixty hours a week was the working man's time then, and I think they got about twelve shillings in this particular town.

Rudy and his wife had *trekked* up with the *vardo*. My sister Lorenza, who also had married a *gorgio* and now had two sons, was on her way. But it was for me that my mother was waiting, and to me that the bird had come bringing ill tidings. I found my mother in bed in a neat little room, a strange thing for her. Stranger still, they had called in a doctor. They explained that it was to avoid trouble in case anything happened. If a doctor was not called there would be an inquiry as to why she had died. I understood but greatly resented it. The doctor came while I was there and I asked him what he thought of her case.

' The strangest I have ever known,' he replied. ' There is nothing physically or mentally wrong. She does not seem to be ill and she has no worries on her mind. She says that she has " had a call " but that she would live till she had seen you.'

He asked about my father and whether my mother was very fond of him. I replied that she lived for him, in the true Romany way. And then came the worst moment I have ever known in my life, before or since. I have suffered pain and sorrows, but a thousand spears in my heart could not have brought the pain of his next words.

' Perhaps she was lonely. You should not have left her.'

Ah, how in my life could I ever have imagined that my mother could be taken ill, let alone die ! Every one would die, my father, brothers, myself, friends, loves, the world, but not my mother. Without her, to me, there was no world, how then could I imagine her leaving it ? All that I had done, I had done for her in my unthinking way. All that I had learnt, all that I had won, the distances I had covered, all that I meant to do. All was, all had been, to impress her. To make her see me as a man worthy of her training, to show her that I could take knocks and meet them with a shrug as Mascka met them, to show her that I was a son after her own heart and had not gone *bilaco* and faint-hearted like the rest in this easy-going country where all Romanys were *diddikais* with whom she could have nothing in common. Why had I not taken her to America with me ? But does a grown man, restless, born without a home and without a country, making his decisions in a moment and with nothing to prevent him acting on them the next, does he hamper himself with a mother each time he decides to be off and away, though she may be more to him than all the world ? Why, then, I asked myself, had I at least not taken her back to her own country, to her brother, Mascka, and her own people, where her heart had always been.   But here again I was not altogether to blame, for her own heart was divided.   She loved her people and her home, but her heart was with my father, and she could not bring herself to leave the land in which he lay buried greatly as she would have liked to go, and no matter how long now my father had been dead.   In that, I knew, it was not for me to reproach myself, for she had gold enough to go many times. For a long time now there had been no need for her to *trek* the distance which separated her from her own people and endure the two years of hardship and wandering by which, years ago, we had come to England.

It is not want of heart, I found bitterly, it is want of thought that causes us life-long regret.   Yet even as I reproached myself I argued my own case and knew that given the time again I could not have done differently.   I was bred for wandering, and for the nomad life.   Why could I not settle down and be happy ?   Why can a bird not settle down in a cage and live on bird-seed ?   I could love some one with my heart's blood, yet I could not settle down in one spot and be near them.   Life to me meant movement.   It meant coming back from wandering in other worlds and bringing her curious things that I had picked up for her and which she treasured, knowing that there was none but me to bring her such things. Always showing off in front of her !   Showing her that I had pluck and was not afraid to face the world alone, walk over it, take its gold.   I liked earning money.   Not for anything outwardly flashy but to satisfy my one ambition, to show her that she had bred a man who could find for himself and for her if need be, by sending more money home in a week than we could have made in months.

And just this, just this vanity of mine to show my inde-

pendence and impress her with my worth, had taken her from
me. For the more I thought of it the more I could see how
all that to me was independence, was to her a sign that she was
no longer needed. My father needed her and she needed him.
But I, it seemed, needed no one. This thought was too bitter
for me, and I turned it round to my advantage. My mother,
who could see to the bottom of my heart, who could read my
innermost thoughts as she read the lines spread on my hand ;
why had she let me go ? She who was like a sphinx in her
silence, and her eyes from which nothing seemed hid, must
have known that by a sign or a word she could have kept me
with her many a time and brought me back without a
moment's hesitation. But she was so deep, so impenetrable.
That was perhaps why I went away. For who could fathom
her mind, seeing that she never spoke ? And that when she
spoke it was in riddles. *She* knew what it meant, but often
we did not. Sometimes, as a child, it had taken me hours to
think out the meaning of one of her cryptic sentences that
hinted, by their inflexion, something quite different from
what they said. From childhood she had spoken to us like
that, leaving us to puzzle it out. There was always a key if
only one sought for it. She would smile and say : ' Use your
head and wisdom will come ! ' But of what use was wisdom
to be now !

When the doctor had left they told me my mother was
asking for me. She was lying raised on several pillows, and I
sat on a small chair beside the bed and she held my hand. I
looked at her and everything I had ever done, to tease her, to
show off, out of devilment, thoughtlessly, came in front of me
and was there in my face as I gazed at her and her eyes answering mine, told me that she understood and forgave me. She
knew without words all that I had been reproaching myself
with. We looked at each other silently a long time. She
knew my reasons for being a wanderer. She knew that she
must speak to me, for she said, as though answering my

doubts : 'If an old bird shuts itself up in a cage, there is no wish to see her young in a cage too.' Then she gave a quick little laugh as though to say that she had seen enough of Waldo ever to wish for me to be like that.

I told her about America and of the fairs and the pills, and of how simple the *gorgios* were and how easily they were pleased with our little toys and tricks, and how everything that Mascka had taught me as a *chavi* had come to my aid. How we laughed over the candles and the blowing of the water ! She liked hearing about America, the country she would most have liked to see. We laughed too at how I had enjoyed myself among the nigger people and how they had taken me for a great doctor. She was happy that I had been kind to them. 'I am glad you showed them a Romany heart,' she said. I begged of her to get well. 'I am with you now, mother,' I said. 'We are going to be happy.' She smiled and said in the Romany *chib* : 'I shall soon be happier, son, than ever before. I shall be in the arms of my man, and looking to the day when you will be with us. One day I shall " call " for you and then you, too, will know why I have no desire to stay here longer.'

I knew then that my mother had gone beyond any persuasion of mine. With us it is the law that when the call comes from our dead we must answer it. Many a Romany has willed himself to die at a certain date (as I myself have done) and it never fails. She had got the idea (let science laugh itself hoarse ; I can give them a hundred incidents of things even more strange) that the beloved dead wanted her and had called to her, and when a Romany gets that call he has no wish to live on. As she said, she was tired. She had worked well. She had harmed none. Rest was for the asking and she was ready.

She then gave me some things she especially wished me to have. First of all she gave me back all the money I had sent her home from America and other countries for years past.

She had kept it all for me (all of it !) and I had thought of it as keeping her comfortably free from care. She gave me it back as a bag of gold, a thick canvas bag which she had made herself, seamless, gathered with a string at the mouth and opening in one movement. Then she gave me twenty-two shirts which she had made for me while I was away. She explained how she had made these with different size neck-bands, as I would be bound to grow fatter. They were the shirts with smocking at the wrists and breast in the true Roumanian fashion. She gave me also many valuable diamonds and jewels in which she had put her own money, which was how Romanys invested their gold in those days. She told me to use my head and sell them eventually as they would be worth far more gold than she had given for them. She told me never to part with the family charms and trinkets she gave me, but that for the diamonds and precious stones she held no brief.

LXIII

She had seen Rudy and Lorenza, and had given them a few mementos of herself and a few words of comfort. She liked Rudy and she liked Lorenza but not more than liked. I cannot explain the difference in the way she treated me and the way she treated them. From a child it had been like that. She would teach me things and she would know that what she taught would sink in. Good advice, she knew, was never wasted on me. · The others would snigger and pass it off lightly, like *gorgios*. But she and I, we would talk as though we were one. I think, also, she loved my association with Mascka and Lavanya, the last link with her home, the only one of her children she could recognize as a Romany.

It seems to me now that there was nothing in all the world

she did not know. She knew everything. The older I get, the more I know, the more I miss her. Every deal I make I think of her. I would have my arm cut off to-night to have her hear me on the wireless or read my book and have her see that even in the *gorgio* world I can make my way. She is the one person in all my life I have ever wanted to impress, and without whom all triumphs are saltless, and even bitter. Above all, she was so wise. She could sum up a person on sight. By a look, a voice, a remark, she would know a true person, a *tatcho* person, from a false. She was like a judge sent among men, but faultless in her conclusions. She was straight in all her dealings, and she would say to me : ' Always be straight, Pet. Look at the ones who are not and see what a mess they make of it. A man with an uneasy conscience is like a bee in a syrup jar. The more he flies about, the more he glues his wings up.'

It was in sentences such as those that in her quiet, inscrutable way she would mould my mind and make me see things as she saw them. She had a way of saying a thing that gave it an almost Biblical quality, as though it were now final. As though, to all that she said, there was no answer. Many an instance comes to my mind. Once when I had given money away and I thought she would reproach me for my folly, she said only : ' Give away all you can, Pet. Money given when you are alive is gold. Money given when you are dead is only lead.' And once she stopped me from apologizing to a farmer from whom I had poached, but about which I felt no remorse or ' guilt ' and couldn't see what all the fuss was about. ' Don't apologize if you are not sorry,' she said. ' Remember that a hypocrite is always worse than a rogue.' She taught me to smile and be less impatient with people by saying : ' A kind word can unlock a cold heart quicker than a golden *klizina*.' And once, when I was boasting that people who thought they could get the better of me would find me very tough, she said : ' *Duro jilos san kooshti*

ande cöouangres, bera nanti ande homus.' [Hard hearts are good
in cabbages but not in humans.] And for anything hard or
unforgiving that I would applaud she would say : ' A diamond
is hard, Pet. It can dazzle. But it cannot make a *corora dik.*'
Once I complained bitterly that I had got the blame for something I hadn't done, and added angrily that I had even done the
woman a good turn by getting her some herbs she needed and
curing her sore. ' Never mind, Pet,' she said. ' The best
Man who ever lived they crucified. And He'd raised the
dead ! '

I remember, too, her answer to the old *gorgio* women who
were superstitious about green and always made it their excuse
for not buying a thing : ' Can you think of any other colour
the good God could have made the grass and trees ? ' my
mother would ask them gently. She was never sentimental,
for my mother had nothing vulgar in her character. Many a
good *cooring* she gave me when I deserved it, and we both
would forget it afterwards. Once when I grumbled that I
had taken no money all day and was nearly knocked up, the
only sympathy I got was, ' Leather is always best when it has
had a good hammering,' and I took care not to complain
again. She never thought things sad or pathetic, as *gorgio*
people do. I remember once coming home with the tragic
story of how a Romany woman farther down the road had
lost her man and was left with a small child to keep. My
mother said coldly : ' It's a poor hen that cannot scratch the
puv for one chicken.' In such ways, sentence by sentence, she
would pass on her wisdom, hand on her experience, all of
which was mine for the taking, and because I took it eagerly
and without question, she loved me and felt close to me and
far from the others. I was, however, soon to learn that this
daily wisdom was as nothing compared with the strange and
nameless secrets she had in store for me. For my mother had
more than wisdom, she had knowledge. She had the true
knowledge, which, in what is called the modern world, is lost,

but which was known tens of thousands of years ago. It was known to those who built Stonehenge, to those who built the Pyramids and the Sphinx, to the earlier and the greater races of mankind. Above all, to the Berbers, her people, the only race living to-day that can raise its dead, make them dance, make them prophecy, cut out their tongues, bind up their mouths, and return them to the graves from whence they came.

LXIV

Two days after my return, we were all of us, Ahny and her daughter, Rudy and his *gorgio* wife, my sister Lorenza, Waldo and I, taking tea in my mother's room and laughing and talking with her. Nothing could have been less like a sick-room, for my mother complained of no pain and there were no medicines. She lay there watching us and joining in the talk. Her black hair shone like raven's feathers and her dark look was gentle and almost gay. We were happy and light-hearted, all seemed well again and the shadow had been lifted from our minds. I was telling them of my negro friends and their customs and simplicity, and imitating the monotonous sing-songs they call their spirituals. All of a sudden my mother broke into the middle of the talk and banter. She asked them all to leave the room, for she wanted, she said, to be alone with me for a little while as there were things on her mind which she must say to me alone. They did not mind, for it was known to all of us that I was my mother's favourite, and they went willingly, reminding me not to let her talk too long or tire her needlessly.

When we were alone and I was near her, my mother explained that there were things of great importance which she must tell me, and which none but I must ever know. She bound me by sacred oaths not to reveal what she was about to tell, till I too came to die and in my turn must hand it down to one near and dear to me. She then told me of charms and spells and magic signs handed down secretly by word of mouth from times so distant that they cannot now be traced. She revealed to me the secret of the Tarots, called the Bohemian Bible, and of the magic number twenty-six derived from the YOD-HE-VAU-HE, most mysterious of all words and to which she now gave me the key. She gave me also her two greatest treasures, a pack of Tarot cards and the eye-tooth of her father Zig. The Tarots were never to be used foolishly, she told me, but only in great need. Her father's tooth would enable me to charm away growths and warts, but never must I take a coin in payment of the good it did. The eye-tooth is sacred among the Zingari, and regarded as a sacred trust. We think of it as leading to the eye and to the brain and that it thus gives power of vision. A true-bred Romany in handing it over, hands over to your keeping his knowledge, his gift of prophecy, and his power over the future. He argues that all of him must vanish, his bones rot, his flesh decay, his memory be forgotten, but his tooth can neither rot nor decay and through it his wisdom shall live on and his memory be kept green.

All this my mother told me, my hands in hers. I found myself thinking how lucky it was that I had got there to see her in time, and I said so. She answered : ' If you had not come back for a year, I should have lived on.' I said : ' Live on, and I shall not go from you again.' But she smiled and made a sign I knew well. A sign in memory of my father, which she had used many a time since his death when thinking of him. I knew then that whatever her love for me, she would leave me and go to him, for there alone peace and happiness lay in wait for her.

My mother then read my *duk* and told me of all that life would hold for me, and the date of my death, 1949. We

Romanys always say that a dying woman prophesies best, and that the death-bed prophecies of the gipsy always come true, no matter what has been told. I found this hard to believe on listening to my mother, for she said one thing which was so senseless that I thought she was rambling or perhaps already delirious. She said : ' *Later in your life you will speak to millions who will never see your face.*'

My mother could neither read nor write, she had no way of knowing of such names as Marconi, in any case unknown to the world then, or of the experiments which were secretly taking place. There was no wireless when she spoke those words and no hint that such a miracle could be brought to man in his very home. Strangely enough it was only after my second broadcast that the meaning of her words came to me as I sat in the train late that night, returning to my *vardo*. My heart missed a beat and I am not ashamed to say that my eyes filled with tears.

Here I will speak of another instance of my mother's remarkable power of prophecy. Through her reading of her Tarot and under a vow of secrecy, she gave certain Egyptologists hints and clues, uncanny in their accuracy, which have since led to the finding of the Valley of the Kings and the Tomb of Tutankhamen.

A smile of great sweetness came on my mother's face when she had spoken with me. We sat for some time in silence, our hands still clasped together. I thought she was falling asleep, when she roused herself and asked me for a drink of water. I brought it to her and held it while she drank. She thanked me and smiled again. Then she said, ' Kiss me, son ' and I kissed her. She laid her head on my arm, closed her eyes, gave a little gasp, and did not stir again.

For her there was no *vardo* to be *yagged*, no leaping flames, no wild music. She had chosen the spot in which she would lie. She wished to be buried where she had died—for Romanys do not like being moved from the place of their death—in a piece of land adjoining the churchyard. There was to be no name or sign above the grave to tell who lay there. Often I have longed to put a stone above her grave and write her name on it, but always her wish has stopped me. She called tombstones the stones of mockery. She said the *gorgio* fought, quarrelled, and hated in life, and thought that all such folly could be smoothed away in death by a lying epitaph. It is on the warm hearts of those we love that our memory must be engraved, she would say, not on cold stone.

I stood at her graveside as the clergyman intoned the words so familiar to him but which I was hearing for the first time. I was thinking how peaceful it was, this spot in which she was to lie for ever, with its walls covered in ivy and beyond it a great avenue of her favourite tree, the walnut, stretching as far as the eye could follow. But I could not reconcile myself to the thought that there was no music, no wailing fiddles to set her spirit on its flight to the prince of *bosa-venos*. It filled me with such an intolerable sadness that I took no heed of the clergyman's words. I stood there looking down into the grave, thinking only of the wrong that a Romany was being buried without music, when suddenly down the road a barrel-organ struck up. An Italian organ-grinder by a row of houses on the other side of the wall was playing the Barcarole from the ' Tales of Hoffman.' Never has music sounded so sweet in my ears ! The sexton made a movement as if to go and stop him, but I told him no. I think I said that my mother would have been the last person ever to want any one prevented from earning a living. I did not care how shocked they looked because the music drowned the words I no longer listened to. I only know that it went on and on and that my heart sang with it for joy and gratitude. Anyeta had her music after all.

LXV

Aᴆᴛᴇʀ my mother's death I did not go abroad again for several years. I suppose I had no desire to show off, no curiosity strong enough to help me make the effort to leave England, and very little incentive to ambition now that there was no one I need impress.

I certainly had no plans. I only know that I had made up my mind never again to settle down in one place and I also decided I would get a *vardo* again. By a curious twist of irony it was Waldo's firm who made me my new caravan and it was my brother Waldo who helped in the making of it. As I have mentioned he was then earning twelve shillings a week, as wage for a full-grown man working sixty hours a week. I have often thought with bitterness that had I my brother Waldo's chances of being educated in the *gorgio* way, and been given what is called a start, there would have been no limit to what I could not have achieved. On the other hand, when I think of Waldo I realize that my bitterness is wasted on an idle dream ; for you cannot have Romany independence and *gorgio* docility. One or the other is bound to win and in the struggle all is lost. Anyway, there was I ordering a new caravan and there was Waldo at twelve shillings a week helping to make it.

The joy of the road is its freedom. Its complete freedom from worry and its absolute freedom of movement. The fascination of the road to my way of thinking is due to two things : (1) that your time is all your own, and (2) the people you meet on your way. The people one meets on the road are nearly always original and unusual. If this is an exaggeration, then all I can say is that you have more chance of meeting with unusual characters on the road than in any walk of life. One of the most original and interesting I

ever met was the Reverend C——, Vicar of S——
A——.

While my caravan was being built I went out with my
camera, starting appropriately enough at a place called Eye.   I
was working schools, which means taking the photographs of
children in groups, calling at all the schools for miles around.   I
also took photographs privately but worked the schools as an
advertisement and bait for the parents.   I was out one day when
I came across an old remnant of the Romany, a Welsh harp-
player, a man with a taint of the old Welsh Romany in him
and who still carried on the same game that his ancestors had
excelled in : *busking*.   He was seated on his little stool playing
the harp outside the offices of the local brewery.   Not a bad
place on a hot day, thought I, and I was not far wrong.   I
was soon to discover that there was good reason for Charlie
being there.   A good-hearted old *gorgio-rye* whose name
was, I think, Sir Thomas Tacon, used to invite Charlie in to
have a drink, and on this day when I first spoke to Charlie
and we were talking about his ancestors, we were both invited
in for a cooler.   I went and Sir Thomas showed us the curious
door to the store-room.   It was centuries old and was on a
pivot, so that the door swung round instead of opening on
hinges, and this fact got Charlie many a free drink.   He
used to take some one up every day to show them the door,
knowing that it was Sir Thomas's great weakness and the
pride of his life, and of course every time the door opened
what was more natural than an invitation from Sir Thomas
to have one.   Charlie likes his drink.   I was practically teetotal.   I liked Charlie.   He had Romany blood in him ; he
was a good harpist ; he could get his living and travel at the
same time.

I was staying at a little inn and Charlie came and stayed
there too.   We struck up a bargain.   Charlie would help
me in the daytime.   I would help him by night.   We
were *mug-fakirs* in the light, *buskers* in the dark.   I am not

going to say I was ever a good singer, but I will say that in the villages the voice doesn't matter very much. The villagers liked ' comic ' songs, so Charlie twanged the harp and I sang and did the *bottling*, which is the word for going round with the little sea-shell the *buskers* use as a collection-box. We got on well and our next move was to a place called Ipswich where we took a season ticket on the boats which ran up the Orwell river and I made *busking* a whole-time job. Our job was to go down the river on one boat, play to the trippers, come back on the next boat, and return again. This was a happy life, but as Charlie said it was a short season. The boats did not carry enough passengers to make a living the year round, so we went back to photography and music, two things the Romanys always fall back on. (The Romanys were the first people to work the old tin-type photo on the Continent, after Daguerre, the French scientist, discovered it and made it a commercial proposition.)

I had my new caravan by now and we found ourselves at a place called Debenham, working the villages around. I had an order to go and photograph the choir at one of the local villages and it was this that brought about Charlie's downfall and introduced me to the Reverend C——. He invited Charlie and myself to stay for the service, the first thing of its kind we had ever seen. But Charlie was so impressed that that night, after getting well oiled in the bar of the local inn, he developed a passion for saying his prayers. Now there is never a night goes by but that I say my prayers. Charlie was not contented with a prayer. His was a frenzy of prayer and song. He chanted most of the night, slept on the floor, and kept me awake till nearly dawn. I thought it was an overdose of malt and hops and forgave him his lapse, but when again on the Monday night Charlie repeated the performance we had it out. Charlie had developed religious mania and this was his new idea of how to spend his nights. We parted on the Tuesday, and I never saw him again.

LXVI

NOT so the Reverend C——. I was up with my caravan at a little village called Wivenhoe, when just after dawn one morning I heard a knocking on the caravan door. I got up and was astonished to see the Christ-like face of the vicar whose service had converted Charlie. It was a remarkable face, this. A replica of the popular pictures of Christ, the face long, the nose very fine, the whole thing was of a strange magnolia pallor and his beautiful black beard made his handsome face look even paler than it was. The Reverend C——was strikingly good-looking, and I have rarely met a character so fine as his. I invited him inside, got dressed and made breakfast, and then inquired how he knew where I was and what brought him. He told me that a lady to whom I had written about some photographs had told him where the letter came from. He had decided to take a tramping holiday and would I join him? He told me that he had walked through the night to find me and that he wanted a week's holiday with a gipsy. I thought he was joking, but he was deadly serious. I told him I had some work to finish and deliver but that afterwards I would willingly spend a few days with him. He then confessed to me that his great ambition was to have one week as a gipsy fiddler. I could have all the money, he said, but he must do the fiddling.

He spent his first day sketching the River Colne, the fishing smacks, the village church, and other little views, all of which he did from a sixpenny box of paints he bought at the village toyshop. Then I humoured him, closed up the van for the day, and off we went *busking*. The visitors at Walton-on-the-Naze and Frinton little thought as they put their pennies in the bag, that we two were the strangest couple in the country : a true-bred Romany and a Reverend whose wealthy mother actually owned the living of his church, and who claimed kinship with one of the most famous generals of the day. He was as happy as a truant *chavi* and he would eat his bread and butter and whelks, and drink his tea out of a mug, as I did, and love it. He told me many a time that he was a true Bohemian and that that was the life he preferred to all others and understood the best.

It is by no means unusual to meet the sons of wealthy parents tramping the roads. I do not mean tramping for the fun of it, but men who through adversity have had to *coor* the *dròm*. I met one of this kind once who was the son of the then Member of Parliament for an important Yorkshire town. He had gone off the highway of respectability and had been turned down, as he called it, by his people. I was sorry for him. He had spent the last few hundred pounds he had of his own and now he had to look out for something, he told me ruefully. He explained how difficult it was for him to get even a stray job, as, though you may be a B.A., everybody wants a reference from your last employer. To have told people truthfully who he was would have been ridiculous : they would have derided him or called him a liar. Besides, he did not want inquiries made about him at his home. What could he do ? he asked me helplessly. He told me that he could draw a face so naturally that you could even recognize the person he intended it for. He drew an old diary from his pocket and made pencil sketches of his father and mother. I was interested in him and believed him. Even the way he held his pencil had the authentic artist touch about it. ' Draw me,' I told him, and as we sat on the road he made a life-like sketch of me, even down to a scar which I still carry over my right eye, memento of a Romany scrap. I looked at the drawing and then at him. ' If you aren't the biggest and daftest *bilaco* I've ever met ! ' I exclaimed. ' You come and tell me you can't earn a living and you sit down and draw a picture like this in three minutes.' And I put up a scheme to him, which after much persuasion he decided to try. Persuasion, I say, and a great deal of persuasion it took to make him do the very thing that would make him an independent man. I do not say a man of independent means. But a man independent of his people. As I have said before about my own brother, I don't know what makes me do these things, helping lame dogs and other foolish creatures to try and do a little thinking and a little effort. I can only put it down to stubbornness, and an obstinate streak in me making me tread down obstacles.

My plan was for him to go with me to the fêtes and galas of which there are many in the little villages during the summer. It is a nice easy way of passing through the best part of the warm period. These country villages arrange that their shows never clash with each other so there are a few weeks good living to be got out of them. We would work the fêtes. I would do the *spieling* and he would do the drawing. I worked that he could do one drawing every three minutes or so and that meant twenty an hour. If we only worked a couple of hours a day when the shows got busy we should have five shillings each. We would soon have a good few pounds and I should be doing him a good turn as well as myself. I need not describe the village flower show. The big marquee for the vegetable section, a smaller one for flowers and fruits. Another one for the refreshments and a small one where the Nobs of the village who act as judges can retire when they feel like having a livener. There is also a roundabout set, some swings, the ubiquitous coco-nut shy, the fat lady and her husband the Human Skeleton, a dart board, a 'Roll 'em,' and if the local *plastramengro* and the management are good natured, the old Roulette board for the local sports and their small flutter.

It was to such fêtes as these that I took Raymond, as he told me his Christian name was. I had bought him a supply of paper and some black crayons and off we went. I told the crowd of joskins all about Raymond's famous reputation and how he had drawn all the crowned heads of Europe (and so he had—just to show me he could do it!) and we had samples of these up, including one of King Edward, the Prince of Wales (King George) and the Kings of Spain and Belgium, and some famous Edwardian beauties thrown in for the ladies. ◦ Actually Raymond made dozens of drawings of King Edward for the people who had their own drawing and in their own words would now like one of the King ' to make a pair.' Raymond and I became good friends. He taught me the educational side of life. I taught him how to get a living, which was better. Raymond confided in me and told me the real secrets of his life and why the split in his home had come. There were times when Raymond wrote to some one and would get a reply at the post restante of the town we were *trekking* to next. He told me that they were letters from the only one who had stood by him in his trouble, his sister, who wrote to him and let him know how the land lay. The reason for the secrecy over the letters was that Raymond's sister wrote to him in his correct name and he did not want everybody to know his short-comings and name, as the local village and small town postmen have a way of spreading such news like fire. Raymond liked life in my caravan. He used to say he would never go back to his old life again, even when things had cleared up. But he did. One day he came to me looking very glum. ' Pet, old boy,' he said, ' I've got to leave you. My father's dead and my mother has relented. Besides, there's a piece of entailed property that I must have in spite of everything.' He handed me the letter of his sister and it was then that I knew for the first time that he was the son of Sir ——. Raymond went home and I was on my own again. Tears welled in his eyes as he said good-bye. ' Now listen,' he said earnestly, ' if ever you come round my way, you can pitch on my land for as long as you like and I'll see that you are all right.' Raymond got married shortly afterwards to a fine lady. I never went near him although I had repeated letters from him offering me the pitch and the hospitality. I thought it might cause friction with his people, and besides I needed no assistance to live my life. Romanys are strange that way, and do not sponge on their friends.

LXVII

WE naturally meet some queer folk on our travels among the villages. One of the queerest I ever met was a man whom the villagers where I was pitching called Mad Jack the Sailor. I did not know he was *dindilo* and when he spoke to me I was very civil, as is usual with me. Jack took a great fancy to me and spent a lot of time around my *vardo* and one day when, I suppose, the moon was well up (the villagers said he was right in the head till the full moon) Jack let out what was worrying him. He asked me how I moved the caravan from one place to another. 'With a horse, of course,' I said. 'HORSE!' snorted Jack, 'I knew you'd say *horse*.' 'Well, how else do you think I could move it ?' I asked. 'You don't think I could pull it around myself, do you ?' 'I've been round the Horn in the best ships in the world,' said Jack. 'I've been in the *Cutty Sark*, the *Flying Fox*, and the fastest clippers that ever sailed the seven seas, and we never had *horses* to pull our ships, did we ?' I then realised that Jack was *bilaco* and evidently feeling the effect of *chun* and thought it wiser to humour him. 'Well, Jack, what's the idea ?' I asked. 'Can you tell me how I can get the caravan to go without a horse ?' I fully expected to hear about some little engine that could be put in a corner of the *vardo's* food cupboard, when Jack gave me some real information. 'Fit a sail to it,' he said. That would certainly be a novelty, I agreed, but how should I expect to get a sail to drive the caravan seeing that it weighed two ton. ' *Two ton* ! ' shouted Jack contemptuously : ' Why, the *Southern Maid* weighed FOUR HUNDRED AND FIFTY TON and could do eighteen knots an hour ! ' I then pointed out that the *Southern Maid* was on water. The van was on land. Jack argued that it didn't matter. With a big enough sail the *vardo* would do any journey under its own power. I pointed out obstacles like trees on the road, railway arches, and other things, but Jack said the sail could be made to lower ' mast and all ' and, better still, I could have the railway arches removed if need be. Poor Jack ! One day I returned to the caravan to find Jack sitting on the roof. He had a saw in his hand and he was going to cut a hole in the roof to fit the mast in, he said. I got my gun and said : ' Jack, if I see you here again I'm going to shoot you, so off you get before I count ten ! ' Jack scrambled down and raced round the bend like a hare. I really think he believed I would do it, for he never troubled me again. But the villagers often told me that Jack still insisted that caravans should be run by the wind and not horses !

Gorgios seem to think that all whom they meet on the road, whether showmen, peddlers, buskers, circus-people, or tramps, are gipsies. This is not so and is exceedingly unfair to the Romany. I do not protest because these people have sneaked in on our ' picturesque.' Indeed, I have shown quite bluntly in this book that we are not what the *gorgio* likes to imagine as picturesque, but an entirely different race, with ways of our own which never completely merge and secrets to which we alone have the key ; hardworking, fond of driving a bargain, honest, good at work and play, and nothing like the lady and gentlemen novelists conception of us. I protest that peddlers and tramps are mistaken for gipsies because there is not a handful of real Romanys left in England, and because the lazy riff-raff of the road gives the word gipsy (with which they have all been tarred) its undercurren of contempt and disapproval. In any case, these people are *gorgios*.

We are the kings of the *drom*. Even the tramps acknowledge that, and every tramp on the road gives the Romany ' the seal of the day ' as they call it. They envy us our caravan. We are snug and independent with our cooking apparatus. They with the discomforts of the *paddencan*, as they call their humble hotel. I have always felt very sorry inwardly at the lack of knowledge of these *gorgio* tramps. They cannot cook. They cannot catch a rabbit, a hare, or a pheasant. They are the rudderless ships of the road. Some will carry a little tin, and *mooch* a drop of hot water to make a can of tea, trusting to luck and their sorry appearance for a woman to give them a bit of sugar and a drop of milk, with a slice of bread perhaps as well. We despise these *moochers*. Why don't they use their heads and their fingers. Make something, sell something. To trade is good and honourable with us, but to take food from people who can least afford it, and perhaps eating the food some poor hardworking labourer has to earn, is very wrong to the Romany idea. Much better to poach a rabbit that runs around and that the big people *think* is theirs. We Romanys do not call that stealing. And if the *gorgio* in greed calls that theft, even so to us it is preferable to being parasites.

The *moocher* is always a *gorgio*-bred tramp. He is the fellow who scrounges. He lives free, hates the sight of work, is dirty and lazy, and the slum-dweller of the road. The *griddler* is another. He is the one who sings those hymns you heard in your church or chapel in your childhood days. Do not think he is religious and doing it to show how good he is. He thinks you are *bilaco* and cannot resist a badly-sung hymn. He is doing it to touch your hearts and pockets. He may have been an actor in his time, perhaps held a good position in a bank which has been lost through drink or stupidity. I know one who was a clergyman and got twelve months' imprisonment and was unfrocked for rape, but he still sang his little hymns. You hardly ever hear a *griddler* sing a lively song. Their good old days were in the Sankey-Moody period, the time when those heart-rending hymns were in vogue, ' When the Dewy Light was Fading,' and ' Dear Father, dear Father, come home with me now.'

There are many Romany-bred tramps, and these noticeably all work for their living. We call them *diddikais*, half-breeds, but mostly with only a fraction of Romany blood in them. They have got even this fraction well watered down now, as for years past no gipsy blood has been allowed to come into England. These fellows of the road get their living in many different and useful ways. Roaming around as they do they get to know each other and they have copied the Romany in putting signs on roads and houses, telling where good-hearted people live, and where the *wafodi*, and other information useful to the next comer. But tramp signs are not Romany signs, any more than they know spells, charms, or the Romany secrets of horse- and dog-breeding.

The *roamers*, called the *diddikais*, are workers and independent. They do not beg. The first of these is the *chiv barr-er*, the grind-stone man, the knife and scissor-grinder. He trundles his ' works ' in the form of a barrow well adorned with gaudy coloured paints and brass ornaments which have probably been taken as souvenirs from *paddencan*, lodging house, in which he has stayed and which once decorated an iron bedstead. He calls at the cottages, collects a dozen or so pairs of ' snips ' as he calls them, grinds and delivers them. If he is of the better self-respecting sort he always has a white apron tucked up half-way round to look professional when he calls to collect. In fine weather he can pick up a fairly easy living but in wet weather it is a difficult job. His ' wheels ' are mostly made by himself from a piece of circular wood and covered with a piece of leather which he ' dresses ' by covering

239

them with glue and rolling them in powdered emery. In the rainy season when the emery comes off the wheel, he gets a piece of red brick and a file as substitute, and he can knock up enough for his *kip*, and from all the philosophy that grows from many such little knock-downs, he knows there will be some sunny days coming around again.

The *taso-fakir*, the china-mender, is another one whose trade betokens erstwhile Romany blood. I have seen some real Romanys who have made a life-long business of china-faking. They use the same appliance as my Uncle Mascka used abroad, the drill being that used by the goldsmiths in the days of the Pharaohs. True Romanys make their own china-faking tools, still on the old plan. My younger brother Rudy once mended a Ming vase of great value which had been broken in more than a hundred pieces. It took him more than a fortnight and never have I seen such love put into a piece of work. I thought it looked better mended than before it was broken. He was very proud of having it entrusted to him and he thought the ten pounds given him for his incredible piece of jig-saw work more than generous. I think he would have done it for nothing. Rudy was an incomparable china-fakir. He was so fond of his trade that he never willingly did other forms of work. He was utterly unlike me, whose insatiable curiosity makes me eager to try every trade always to show the other fellow that what he can do I can do better. Rudy loved china-faking and was content with one familiar spot, one *vardo*, one wife. I have often thought it unfair and cruel that so peaceful a soul as Rudy should have met such a violent and ugly death. He was at a fair when some drunken *gorgios* set on him, kicking him violently as he lay on the floor unable to move. The kicks broke the lining of his stomach, and the fact that he had to crawl to a ditch and lie there in the rain all night unable to get any farther, developed pleurisy and he was dead within the week.

Incidentally it was my brother Rudy whose *gorgio* wife

thought she knew better than the Romany and refused to *yag* his *vardo* at his death. Rudy told her that if she did not do this he would curse her, and that in any case he would see to it himself that his *vardo* was *yagged*. She thought it nonsense to give up her nice comfortable home and merely laughed when he threatened her. We were all returning from the funeral and making across the fields to the *vardo* when before our eyes and before we could reach it fortunately, it was struck by a blinding flash of lightning and completely charred and wrecked. It taught one *gorgio* at least not to laugh at a ' silly gipsy superstition.'

Another *diddikai* worker is the *cane-fakir*, the old man or sometimes woman who mends your cane-seated chairs. Scarcely any tools are needed for this. The little sharp *chiv* and *progger* made with a piece of metal like a tapered skewer and some cane which the real chair-mender splits dexterously down with his knife to a thousandth part of an inch. These he threads backwards and forwards, over and under, from one side to the other, in a way which is far more difficult than it looks and he certainly earns his money. There is also the coco-nut matting repairer. His stock in trade consists of a needle, a knife, some coco-fibre and his brains and fingers. This also is one of the original Romany trades.

The *mush-fakirs* used to be in clover in the old days but in these days of cheap mass-production umbrellas, he finds it difficult to make anything like an adequate living. When *mush-faking* was at its height they did not have so many steel-framed umbrellas. They used to have them with the frames made of what the Romany called *pikey*, which was real whalebone. My father used to tell me of the huge gig umbrellas, six foot across which used to be used when travelling in the gigs and landaus of the day. Every old farmer had his *pikey-mush* and it was handed down as an heirloom, the frames being covered again and again. There are still some in use in remoter parts of the country. It used to be the *mush-fakir's* dream to chop a new imitation *pikey-mush* for an old one. These imitation frames were made of cane polished a greeny black to resemble the real thing. The coverings used to be made by the true Romany women at that time and dyed with a solution made of logwood chips, which would be a deep violet colour in its liquid state, but which by little secrets known only to us can turn the umbrella cover into various shades of brown, dark green, or black, and which once dyed would never run or change its colour in sun or rain. The *mush* of to-day is useful for a few weeks only, then you buy a new one for it is cheaper to throw it away than have it repaired. The machine-made umbrellas of to-day are no good when they are bought so you cannot expect them to be good after use. Your ancestors used to pay a little more but they got the right thing, and were not afraid to put up a *pikey-mush* in a thunderstorm when travelling in their gigs, as whalebone is not only a non-conductor of lightning but an actual safeguard. Whereas, you moderns, the first thing you have to do in a thunderstorm is to fling from you the one object you bought to keep you out of the wet !

LXVIII

ALL these are honest men with traditions of work and honesty behind them. They are not Romanys, yet they are not tramps. A very different person is the *shallow-runner*. He is the down-and-out you see walking around with his toes out and his coat in tatters. These scarcely ever speak to other tramps, and of course a Romany ignores them. Their method of getting a living is to excite pity and they cut their coats and trousers into rags, rip out the toes of fairly decent old boots, and beg whiningly for an old coat or an old pair of trousers. They beg from the wives of City men living in the country, and *mooch* from the wives of the middle-class folk, spinning their yarn about how they were bank clerks themselves once till bad luck or ill health brought them low, and the kind-hearted wife of the bank clerk thinks how sad it must be for any one once in a position like her dear George to fall so low as this. And the *shallow-runner* comes away with several old suits over his arm. These old clothes are often very good suits because a man in an office or a store, or in a good position, cannot wear a suit slightly frayed or showing its first signs of wear and tear. They make splendid suits for working-class folk who buy them either direct from the old clo' man or on markets where a man who works under the name of a *tog-fencer* sells them. I have seen a Birmingham labourer looking so smart in a suit bought from a *tog-fencer* that his people wanted to borrow money from him thinking he'd come into a legacy! There is quite a big business to be done in this and I once knew a man named Joe, who was a *tog-fencer* and book-maker combined, *grafting* old clothes one day and shouting the odds at a race-meeting the next. He was a good *grafter* and full of wit. Joe's descriptions of some of his suits were wonderful and he always told them the history of the previous owner. You could buy one of the suits ' the late property of the Hearl of Woxer for honly four bob! The Duke of Spontz's Dress suit three and six! Lord Stumfumkum Macgregor's Lahvly lahnge suit for 'arf a dollar,' and the waistcoats of ' hall the nobility for anything from tuppence to a bob!' ' Blimey!' Joe used to say ' Hits cheaper than getting the missus to sew the buttons on yer old 'un! 'Ere's a luvverly one! Once the property of an Indoo Prince. There may be di'monds idden in the pockets. Yer never knows and I ain't looked! THREE BOB—'oo wants it?'

These are some of the togs collected from the good-hearted wives who say to their men on their return from the day's work : ' Oh ! darling, such a poor old man came to the door to-day. I gave him one of your suits, you know, dear—the old one with the shiny knees. You didn't want it any more, *did* you darling, and he had *such* a nice sad face. He'd seen better days, too, poor old soul.' And the husband grumbles and forgets about it and the wife has done her good deed for the day or week. Lots of the *shallow-runners'* stuff get exported to Africa where there is always a ready sale for it among the niggers. The more difficult to sell varieties, top hats, dress suits, fancy waistcoats, these can be seen at the ole clo' man's, being ' bundled ' ready for export. I once in Africa saw a nigger dressed ' to kill ' in the cream of a *shallow-runner's* collection. A black dress coat with tails, a pair of striped trousers that had had an accident in the rear and had been cut into the shape of a large diamond and filled with a piece of scarlet from an infantryman's tunic. The waistcoat was canary colour, and he had on a pair of bishop's gaiters and a high hat. Yet the *shallow-runner* himself never wears anything better than the rags you see him in. If a duke were to give him his whole wardrobe he'd be just the same the next day.

LXIX

I suppose the greatest of all road events to the Romany is Derby Day, and a big gathering of the clans. The Romany men devote themselves to selling their little tricks, novelties, some old, some new; the women to fortune-telling; and the *chavis* to *mooching* and telling the kind ladies they look lovely. It is here we meet the tricksters and confidence men of all countries, all types, all creeds, all colours. There is the *thimble-rigger*, the three-card-trickster, the balls-in-the-box, the spinning jenny, the old crown-and-feather ('penny on the white, tuppence on the black, thrippence on the red, sixpence on the lucky old—colour, and a shilling on the crown and feather!') and the evergreen purse trick, and pricking the garter.

In most of the tricks the spectator hasn't a chance of doing anything but lose his money, but a few of them are fair game and worth the gamble. The *Spinning Jenny* is always faked by a footpress and manipulated so that the ball can fall only in the colour the tricksters want turned up. Same thing with the weighted dice—the Old Jenny—which has a pivot through it and is movable, the lead falling upward or downward. 'Ave a try for-ra six!' they shout—and they put the spindle so that you can only win when he wants you to . . . or when everyone around is sick of losing. 'YOU 'ave a try, g'vnor. Six to one you do it the first time!' And you *do* do it the first time and maybe the second—but he'll do it the other ninety-eight! The Finding-the-Lady *Three-card-Trick* is another game at which you cannot win. It is worked by clever fingers and optical illusion. You have as much chance of finding the lady as a celluloid mouse has of getting off chased through hell by an asbestos cat. The *purse-fakir* is another swindler who never lets you win and has things all his way. He is the fellow with the little penny dip purse who throws in the half-crowns . . . yes, throws them in the palm of his hand and clinks the pennies in the purse! This is a trick for brazen tactics and elastic palms. I have known a clever trickster hold as many as six half-crowns in the hollow of his palm without being spotted and as many as twelve coppers. This is such a popular trick with the crowd that I wonder no one has spotted it before. The trickster makes great play with a handful of half-crowns which he holds in one hand and throws, ostensibly, into a small purse held out in his other hand. Clink, *clink*, CLINK goes the money—, straight into his hollowed palm beneath the open purse.

Perhaps one gets in the purse, but mostly it is pennies. Now you are supposed to hand over your half-crown and buy the purse at your own risk. You have seen the money go in! You then find threepence instead of three half-crowns such as went into the purse, *but you never squeal.* The *purse-fakir* is a psychologist. He always knows the nervy ones and always spots a ' can.' He never dares flaunt in the face of a man who is a sportsman. Year after year the crowd gets caught at this business, and it always comes back for more. You may say you would be brave enough to protest at finding a penny in your purse instead of the silver you expected, but you would only be laughed at. There is no law against preventing people paying money of their own accord for what they think is a bargain. And all the fakir would say would be a brazen ' Well, you can't be lucky EVERY time, can you now G'vnor ? ' There are always a few *gees* around to help the fakir at his game. These are his confederates, the boys who get the big money and it is worked between them very cleverly. The gee gets his purse for which he has bid, and puts it in his pocket hurriedly. ' ARE YOU SATISFIED, sir ? ' calls the trickster, drawing everyone's attention by his impressive manner and loud voice to the *gee.* ' Don't be afraid to open it, sir. *I'll* tell you what I'll do ' as the *gee* still hesitates ' I'LL BUY IT BACK FROM YOU FOR FIVE SHILLINGS *NOW*, SIR, BEFORE YOU OPEN IT ! IS THAT A BARGAIN ? YOU REFUSE ? ALL RIGHT SIR, BUT I'D LIKE IT BACK, YOU KNOW. THAT'S A SPORTSMAN HE DOESN'T EVEN LOOK AT IT. HE'S CONTENTED ! ' Now all eyes are on the *gee,* who very reluctantly takes out four half-crowns so that every one can see them and tips them into his pocket. Then he seems to brighten up and comes up eagerly for another try. ' NOW then, sir, don't be GREEDY ! ' cries the trickster in mock alarm. ' You've 'ad your puddin'—let the others 'ave a share. We aren't here to make yer a Rothschild, yer know ! '

and so it goes on. The *gees* are usually pickpockets, too, and where you get an interested crowd there you will find the light-fingered gentry with the mackintoshes, over one arm, who gently taps your pocket and marks you with a chalk (from here derives the term : a marked man) to indicate to his friend the *tea-leaf* or *poke-lifter*, the true pickpocket, where the money lies.

The *pricking-the-garter* is the knife in the leather belt, which looks so simple and yet is one thousand chances to one against your ever finding the end of that belt until the fakir wants you to. But the *balls-in-the-box* is a good trick and very fair. It is a real game of luck and cannot be faked. The fakir has twelve pieces of wood about six inches long numbered from one to thirty-six : three numbers to a piece of wood. These are sold to the customers at threepence a piece. So you are getting three chances. In the box are thirty-six balls numbered from one to thirty-six. The boards are then handed round to twelve customers, the balls well shaken in the box, and a child is asked to pick one out. A number comes out—and you get half a crown. He gets sixpence. But when he gets a real crowd and appeals to sportsmen, the sticks go for a shilling each. The stake is thus twelve shillings, and you get ten. He gets two. This goes on hundreds of times a day. It is like backing a ten-to-one winner with three chances instead of one. And the sixpence or two shillings which he pockets every time are honestly earned, as he fakes nothing and it is a matter of your own luck. This is an honest fake with fun for all.

There are a thousand and one other fakes and swindles, and I'm left wondering why I ever started to put you on your guard against them, for the more I see of crowds and fairgrounds the more I realize that mankind loves being swindled. Only he likes it to be called sportsmanship and luck. I could expose for you every trick invented by man, and every youth reading this book will still (at the ages of seventy-five and eighty) be at the Derby of the year 2,000 handing over the same old half-crowns to the same old swindles !

LXX

MANY a time I have been asked the secret of the Romany's power over dogs and horses.

However savage a dog may be, a real Romany (not a *diddikai,* who runs away from anything on two or four legs) will walk straight up to the gate. The dog may come down at him barking and furious, but always it will be wagging its tail when it is within a few paces. How often a sentimental *gorgio* woman has said to me : ' There must be something very nice about you because our dog has let you past ! ' Dear lady, he could not have kept me back ! We are naturally possessed of a power over dogs and have been taught a secret that will render the most ferocious dog powerless without the aid of a drug. We have another secret, from making them docile to making them mad. I shall never forget the face of one vulgar woman who, treating me like a tramp said shrilly : ' If you don't go away at once, I will put my dog on you and he will bite you.' I said : ' Bring your dog here, madam, and I will make him stark staring mad and he will bite you—and God help you then ! ' That quieted her ; she went a pale green and begged me to forget what she had said. I must add that this trick, a form of dog hypnotism, is rarely if ever used, for we Romanys are too fond of animals to cause them pain.

I cannot reveal to you these secrets because one never knows into whose hands such knowledge would fall and it can be used most unscrupulously. Also I may not reveal the inner secrets of my people, jealously guarded for thousands of years. But one or two little hints I will give you which will be helpful to *gorgios,* for they know very little about dogs and breeding.

One trick which every one will be wise to remember is how to keep a dog from biting you or to make it release its hold. No dog can possibly bite if you catch hold of its front paw—either paw—and nip it tightly. Squeeze it as hard as you can, and much as the dog will try it cannot get a grip on you. This is because certain muscles of the jaw are connected with the paws and when pressed no dog can move or close his jaw. Moreover, a dog to whom you have done this will never bite you again. He will know who is master.

Another Romany trick : our dogs need no leash by which to be aggravated and half strangled. A dog on a leash is cowed at heart and loses its sense of being a dog. He is only a very much bullied walking toy. Our dogs always follow to heel. This is a matter of training and a very important matter where owning a dog is concerned. No dog should need a leash to follow its owner. Take a dog, a puppy, in the country. Naturally it will start running wild. We take them out hungry, for you will never train any animal after it has had its dinner. Take with you also some little bits of meat chopped very small. As you walk, you give him a little piece of the meat held in your hand behind your back. You walk a few yards, letting him sniff your hand. If he runs in front tap him gently on the nose and say: ' Come behind ! ' in a sharp voice, and each time give him a little piece of meat. If he doesn't, then another tap on the nose. When a puppy, very young, just a tiny pin-prick of a bit will do ; *never* feed him, just whet his appetite. Take great pains and do this twenty times in as many minutes. Next day start again, and see how long he keeps behind you. If he keeps behind you fifty yards he gets a nice little hunk of meat, so that he gets to know that there are bigger rewards to be had for longer stays. Have patience and within a week or less your dog is perfectly trained to follow always at your heels and not be a nuisance or danger as the untrained dog cannot help being.

In training your dog, and in all your dealings with him, imitate him and he will understand. Let him know by your face what your mood is, so that he will need no words but only a look to obey. When you are angry scowl at him. He will understand, because it is much the same expression as he uses himself. When you smile, show your teeth and let him see that you are smiling. If you have noticed, when a dog is pleased it always smiles, shows its teeth and breathes quickly like a laugh. Impress your dog that you are the same, and he will know that you are in a good mood. When you pat him, smile at him, and gasp a bit and he will know. This may sound foolish, but we can do anything with our dogs and we take great pains that he should know our mood on sight.

When we want a dog to go forward (say we are poaching) we train them by a scratch of the foot along the ground or pavement. If we want him back from a distance we stamp our foot a certain number of times, which sound vibrates along the ground a long way off. On such dark nights, when poaching is good, you cannot whistle, but he will listen for the vibration of your soft stamp. We also train them to bring us eggs without breaking them, but that secret I may as well keep, as it is of no use to you, I am sure !

Generally a dog will do anything for a man's spittle. If you give it something—a dog biscuit or a piece of bread—wet it first with spittle and the dog will love you. The same with bread under the armpits, an old Romany trick. The scent of your body is there and the dog will do anything in the world for you after that. If this sounds unpleasant to the more genteel *gorgio* readers, I might add that nothing is so filthy to the Romany as the *gorgio* habit of letting a dog lick the face. This is not only the dirtiest thing that could possibly happen to one, to our way of thinking, but it brings disease and almost always cysts. Large cysts that can be removed only by the surgeon's knife from faces and necks are ninety-nine times out of every hundred the result of letting your dog lick you. We recognize the need a dog has to show his affection by having something of yourself, so we give it spittle (a dog loves to be spat at in the mouth) and bread soaked in sweat. A dog will always love to eat a piece of food which has been first in your mouth. But to let it bring all the filth off its own mouth, streets, and other dogs, near yours, as millions of women do, is dangerous and disgusting to a Romany or any other decent person's idea. We think it better for the dog to get the dirt than for us. So we do it the hygienic way !

But then again you *gorgios* know so little about dogs, just enough to over-breed them till they get so expensive that they are mentally defective and hysterical. We Romanys never care for a true-bred dog. We find they are nowhere near so intelligent, useful, or reliable as a mongrel. They are too nervous for training and utterly unsuitable either for companionship or work. They are like the too rich and pampered as against some one alive and eager and having to use his own wits. And a Romany breeds for sense and stamina.

In Belgium, where they are so near to the true Romany in their passion for work and where they make their dogs work too, they breed their splendid animals from, say, a collie and a St. Bernard, or a great dane and a mastiff, for strength and brain. But never two collies or two St. Bernards, which would merely give them the defects of each and always less and less stamina. When we were in Belgium Mascka bred a litter out of which I had a pup and brought her to England. The Belgian dog-breeders who saw his dog, the things it could do, the way it could answer a command, were staggered. He told many of them the secret, sold many tips to the Belgian dog-fanciers, and even to-day on my last visit I saw the son of one dog-breeder who still used our methods.

If man would only follow nature! Millions of hysterical and feather-brained dogs, once of strong sporting breed, are cuddled all over the country in the name of fashion. In Japan they breed their waltzing mice in this way, from champion to champion, no doubt, and these *dindilo* mice which go round and round chasing their own tails are thought so clever and pretty, when they are merely epileptic through continuous inter-breeding. Our favourite dogs are lurchers, a dog always crossed in breed: a collie and a greyhound, or collie and airedale. The finest dog I ever had was a lurcher called Rufus, and never have I known such a beauty. He could do every trick of climbing trees and ladders. He knew every sign and every look and every language, and even had I used Chinese he would have known what I wanted. Hundreds of people, who knew Rufus well, have seen me throw my caravan keys into a wheatfield (I had such confidence in him!) and that dog would find them and would not come out till he did. He even got to estimate the strength of my throw and would land within a few yards of them with uncanny accuracy. If I went to a place and read a paper and walked on and scraped my foot, back he would go and take it! I once walked past a fishshop and touched the tail of a handsome haddock . . . that night I had haddock for my tea. But the most embarrassing situation I was ever in with Rufus I got into unintentionally. I had been examining some shoes strung up outside a local shoe shop as they do in the country towns to see whether they were my size and fit and had walked along and forgotten about it. Rufus evidently thought I looked down at heel for he kept looking up in my face for the signal, and went half a mile with me for the sound of the scraping of the foot which I never gave. But whether I accidentally gave it or whether Rufus took matters in his own hands I don't know, but he shot away like a bullet and the next I knew he was racing down the street and laying them at my feet with the bootmaker after him. Rufus had had difficulty in getting the pair I had touched off the hook and had marked the leather with his teeth, so I had to pay up to save further trouble. I needed no friend in the world while I had Rufus, he died at the age of nineteen, and I have never had the same feeling for a dog since.

Romany dogs never have distemper. We prevent it by giving them a piece of raw potato. But if you are unlucky enough to have a dog that already has it, ordinary brewers yeast is the finest thing. If a dog gets poisoned we give him emetic tartar to make him vomit and then a dose of castor oil. Dogs that run about a lot get cracked feet and a very painful complaint it is, equivalent to having the quick of your fingers open. We wash their feet in a solution of rock salt and paint them with arnica. If a dog is troubled with worms, a common complaint with dogs, we give him water in which carrots have boiled to drink and areca nut in a piece of butter in the morning before he has had his breakfast. All ladies like to make a dog's coat shine, so use an ordinary pepper box full of boracic powder and dust it well in. This not only makes his coat shine but it cures little pimples and stops itching.

LXXI

AGAIN, our power over horses is far-famed. The Romany *grye-kupers* have all the secrets of the Arabs and Berbers, at least they have on the continent, in England they perhaps still remember a few tricks. Like the Arabs they even sleep with their horses, certainly in Roumania we *chavis* slept beside them for warmth. Kindness is the only thing in dealing with a horse. It is not an intelligent animal like the dog. It is moody, hysterical, and suspicious. It needs much care and attention, and is a proper *kozac* for pampering. Once you make him know you will pat and pet him you can easily win his favours. As every one knows, a horse is a fussy animal, especially over his food, and he instinctively likes anybody who is careful over his food. You can feed a horse and he will eat with zest, another can do so and he will starve.

The old *grye-kupers* knew all the knacks of breaking down the ugly tempered ones. The worst are the kickers and biters. Where there is a biter force and cruelty has to be resorted to. There is no sense in letting a horse bite you because he likes it. Back go his ears, and the moment you see a horse do that you know you are in for it. For a biter the old Romany method was a sheet of hot tin. You armed yourself as you passed him with a hot tin from over the *yag*. He might try it a few times more but he was cured within a week.

The Romany has no illusions about the horse. He says that the eye of a horse magnifies three times and that that is the only reason man has power over him. But man has to have more power and intelligence than love. The kicker is another wicked devil. Another of the horses that the *gorgio* sells in despair and the Romany buys and hopes. A kicker is put in fixed shafts, the back part having been lined with hedge-hog skin. He soon learns kicking is no fun. The jibber is the temperamental one who stands dead in the middle of the road for no reason and will not go another pace. Everyone has heard of the miracle by which a Romany goes up to a horse and whispers in his ear and so makes a horse do anything he tells him on the instant. I cannot divulge the mystic word we utter, but it is perfectly true that however hysterical or stubborn a horse we have only to go and whisper in its ear to lead it away, docile as an old sheep. I cannot tell you what we whisper, and after all the *gorgio* is so sceptical and so clever, let him find out his own way of dealing with a jib-bing horse! Still, whatever the word and the obedience, the jibber must have his lesson. The best one is to tie him up all night to a gate or post, cold or warm. In the morning he will be cramped and penitent and only too glad to be on the road again, even without his evening meal or breakfast. Horses know what you are punishing them for and they know why they missed a night's sleep and the oats and hay. Of course, with the roarer it isn't his fault. He is like a man with a bad lung who breathes heavily. The old *kopers* trick was greasing them. An ordinary leaden shot in a lump of fat and put it down the horses throat. This was a temporary measure, as a roarer cannot be cured. This is a Romany trick for selling a roarer, and even a man who knows everything there is to know about a horse will buy it.

A thoroughly-trained *grye-koper* had and has one boast : that he can look at a horse, feel every muscle and sinew, and tell its age to a day up to seven years old. The secret of the dappled horse is also ours. None but Romanys have ever bred piebald horses as a speciality, at least none that I have ever heard of. The old gipsy *grye-kopers* bred the piebald horse and still does so to-day in a way known only to ourselves. Whenever I have told a *gorgio* how this is done, they have always mocked me and laughed incredulously. They say that science to-day has proved beyond a doubt that the living creature, human or animal, has no effect whatever in the being in its womb. Doctors and scientists to-day say that beyond the possibility of contradiction, the fears and shocks of a mother cannot influence the unborn child. That may be so to the learned, but I know a boy born with claws for hands because his father took a lobster claw and bit the mother's arm giving her a shock while she was pregnant. We Romanys breed our piebald horses from tricks just as ridiculous and unscientific. The same trick in fact which Jacob used on Laban's cattle with such splendid results to himself. But then Jacob had no scientists to tell him that his trick couldn't possibly work !

LXXII

I AM used to the scoffers by now, and indeed I wait for the laughter to begin at the first suggestion that I can do anything that science and the medical pundits say cannot be done, such as charming growths, warts, internal growths, and vesicas away.   I once gave the scoffer the fright of his life. Having come up to me and scoffed gratuitously and rolled off the latest authorities to refute my words, I entirely reversed the process by bringing some warts up on his nose.   He came back a week later begging me to take them off and I led him a pretty dance repeating his words and arguing that it could not be done !   It is a charm my mother told me, whose ancestors had charmed away many an internal growth from *gorgios* given up as hopeless by their doctors.   I remember my mother telling me that a Romany woman offered to take a wart off Oliver Cromwell's nose and was put to death as a witch.   Another gipsy woman then covered his face with them in revenge.

People have asked me why we Romanys do our spells and charms by the moon.   It is difficult to explain.   Briefly, gipsies believe in the sun as well as God.   The sun is life, the moon is water.   *Chun* is the *pala-parney,* the water-planet. We do our charms in the reflection of the sun.   The sun comes and brings life, the moon takes it . . . so it takes the ill.   At the rising and the full moon we get the reflection of the sun although we cannot see it.   We put our charms on at the full moon and the waning of the moon will see the waning of the wart or growth.

You may not believe in spells.   I do not believe in ghosts. I have never been able to see one, though I have laid many a one for nervous people.   My own sister has come shrieking out of a room having seen a ghost standing beside her bed.

I went straight in the room and slept in the bed yet it never appeared to me throughout the night, though many people had seen it before. The old religious method of exorcising evil spirits was by bell, book, and candle. We use garlic, fire and acid, and presumably with excellent results, for I have never heard any complaints after laying one. My zeal to see a ghost, just for once at least, led me to a place called Coldham Hall where every one including the maids testified that the ghost appeared regularly in the moat. It never appeared to me, and although it was an eerie sensation walking down the avenue of trees rustling in the cold October night, I still have never seen one. At such times of night I have always been more afraid of meeting a game-keeper than a ghost !

Modern science may also laugh at *dukkerin,* yet the Bible tells you that it is written in your hand, and every man put to death in Sing Sing has had the fatal star on the Line of Life. It may also laugh at charms. I have made tens of thousands of charms for people containing what we call their lucky birthday stones. If you laugh at us, then laugh at your Bible for you will find these stones set out in their correct order in Revelations, chapter xxi verse 18 and onward. King Saul put out of the land all those who had ' familiar spirits ' and all the wizards, yet how impatiently he besought his servants to find him a woman who had a familiar spirit to ask her advice and of the future. They found her and she foretold of the death of his two sons on the morrow, and as she prophesied it came to pass. Solomon, the wisest man who ever lived, believed in his astrologers and soothsayers. You have read of those who translated the writing on the wall and the strange dreams of uneasy kings. Read on and you will find it said that there are some who are given by God the gift of prophecy.

With us superstition, prophecy, magic, call it what you will, is bred in the bone. You breed a hen to lay a certain type of egg and that hen will lay that type of egg, and can lay no other. I have yet to hear that man is inferior to the hen. I have foretold the future and prophesied since my childhood days, in that I was greatly blessed in having a mother whose psychic powers were remarkable even for a Romany. I was on a journey to Sheffield and passing through the village of Cardington. The airship R.101 was preparing for a flight. The passengers in my compartment must have thought they had a lunatic among them when I suddenly said aloud but without thinking ' That will be burnt before a week is out ! ' That was on a Thursday, and on the following Sunday I read the news on the placards. I have often wondered what those passengers thought. They did not know who or what I was, and why I called out like that I myself cannot tell.

I sometimes wonder if there is a house in any village in Cornwall and Devon where I have not been called in to bless the witchball hanging in the window. Here, too, they still keep away the evil eye by a bottle of water up the chimney, an importation from the continent and much practised in Central Europe by the gipsies and prunellas. Then again there is the old charm of garlic, used not only in Wales and Cornwall but also in the Channel Isles. In all these places I have personally put in the charm of the garlic, with the ritual of the Romany for the driving out of evil. Incidentally, no Greek captain set sail whether in a fishing smack or cargo boat without nailing his head of garlic to the mast. We Romanys always have a head of garlic nailed up in the caravan, and always with the six partitions, the magic number six, the sign of VAU.

Times without number (townsfolk and the ' educated ' will smile I have no doubt) I have been called to the pagan or heathenish parts of the remote countryside to take away the spell from a house of a man. The Sign of the Stretcher is laid at a man's door far more frequently than you could believe to-day in modern England, in nice plain unmysterious daylight. This is the plaiting of four pieces of wood into a shape with six points and placing them on a man's doorstep being

sure death unless a Romany passes who can take off the spell.
I have known people break an exit through a back wall rather
than pass over that sign which an enemy has placed at their
door.

Even sceptics have heard and pondered the many stories
of death by wasting away which travellers tell of the East.
I have known them scores of times, and several cases in
England I have been called to for doctors are no use in such
cases and put up a lot of bluff saying the man is willing himself
to die. The Romany has the counter spell to this, and however
ill a man may be he can come to his aid. The spell is quite
simple to cast but they do not know that it is equally simple
to remove. In the practice of Ju-Ju the African witch-
doctor will use the same method, which I have known used
in England and have used myself to remove the Stretcher
spell. How is science and the medical world (the latter still
scoffing at osteopathy as though it were witchcraft and not
plain common sense and straightforward knowledge of the
bone and nerve structure of the human body !) to explain this
away ? I never argue with scoffers. If they know better,
let them know. I only know what I know. And what I
know I can at least put into practice. . . .

One or two of the Romany charms still in use to this day
may amuse readers. An ordinary field-mouse caught and
quartered and given to a child who has whooping cough,
is said to be a fine cure. Then there is the spider made into a
pill, for croup and rickets, or to charm any *chavi* ailments away.
Mothers have sworn by it and many a one has begged me
to catch her a spider. There is the old old charm of removing
scabs and sores from babies' faces by burning some of the
mother's milk and rubbing it on the sores. Mothers used
to come from miles around with their new-born babies,
their little faces a mass of scabs, to find the gipsies when I was
a boy. It is a method much used in Central Europe, but
how it travelled to England who can say ? Then there is the

maulo of the *mullah,* the hand of the dead, which must go back to the dawn of Time. This is a charm for the curing of malignant tumours. The dead hand must be newly dead and not mummified. It must belong to a person just about to be buried, the hand is laid on the affected part, always the hand of the opposite sex : if a man is suffering from the growth or cancer it must be the hand of a dead woman that is applied, to a woman sufferer the hand of a dead man. They say that when the hand rots so will the cancer vanish. Abroad the Romanys have a strange cure for jaundice. They take the inside of the barberry plant and then cut a piece of hair from every part of the patient's body and then put it in a piece of suet and give it to a dog. The jaundice always disappears. Many is the time I have been asked for dried weasel's liver, a superstition surviving to this day. It is said that when embalmed by a gipsy this preserves the owner from drowning, gives them gold, and the cunning and wisdom of the weasel with which to get the better of an enemy. I have also, in all parts of the country, been asked for burnt feathers to keep away the Devil. Preferably the feathers of a gull, a sure charm against the Evil Eye !

I will now surprise you by saying that I myself have carried only two things about with me in my life. The eye-tooth of my grandfather Zig given to me by my mother on her death-bed. And a golden sovereign which I have had mounted and wear on a watch chain, not as a charm but simply in memory of an interesting meeting, my first meeting with King Edward, then Prince of Wales.

I was camping as a young man on some ground near Sandringham, when a party of gentlemen came up to my *vardo,* began talking with me, and asking me questions. I had not the faintest idea who they were, but being used to ladies and gentlemen coming to the caravan for a talk and look round, did not find it unusual. We talked about horses, and the particular *boro-rye* who seemed most interested in me asked me for some racing tips which I gave him (I gave him a good many after that and he gave me some too!) and we talked on many things from fortune-telling to how the gipsies get their living. As he was leaving he asked me for a photograph of myself and asked me if I would sign it for him. I gave him one, and said: 'Now you give me yours!' He looked apologetic and said by way of explanation: 'Well, I can't give you one just now as I haven't got one on me. But I can give you a picture of my mother, if you like.' And he handed me a golden sovereign!

LXXIII

It was while I was demonstrating my wares at an exhibition that I was tempted to change my life of freedom for a life of slavery. A chance which took from me ten of the best years of my life, and on which I look back with bitterness and despair. I was tempted by the lure of money-making and I fell. I made money, sometimes taking hundreds of pounds in a week, and for every pound I made I paid with my heart's blood one hundred times its price.

I was demonstrating my patent rug-making device, when a buyer from a large store in Liverpool who had been watching me for some time, came up to my stand. 'If you brought your goods to our store,' he said, 'you would be able to sell all day and every day. We find you a "pitch" and you pay us a percentage of the takings.' I worked out that if I were selling an article costing sixpence for a shilling, I was to pay him thirty-three and a half per cent. I explained that he would be getting double what I should get. He was a business man and had the right answer to that: 'Double the

price of the article!' he said. The bait was tempting. I
wanted money and into the stores I went. But it took me
only the first two hours of captivity to realise that shop-life
is no life for the Romany. How that first day dragged on,
artificial light, stuffy heating apparatus, the breaths of the
crowds who surrounded me, the questions I was continually
being asked, sensible and otherwise! But I had given my
word and I would see it through. I worked hard at my new
life and soon won a reputation as a tip-top *grafter*, they
marvelled at my stamina, and the more money I took the
more they begged me to prolong my stay. I think it was
Faust who sold himself to the Devil. Well, I had done worse
than that. Hell may be a bad place to be in but a store of the
kind I was at was a close runner-up, and being 'requested'
to reply 'nice and politely' for eight hours to every daft
question asked by the hundreds of gaping nit-wits, was surely
a thousand times worse punishment than intelligent conversation with the Devil.

While in the provinces I heard from another worker that
the London stores were the ones to aim at for *bunce*. As I
had just got in a large stock of goods I decided to try my luck
at a West End store, and booked up for the Christmas season.
Before the week was out I was on the carpet. I had been
used to the freedom of speech of exhibition stands and fair-
ground pitches where it is one of the tricks of the trade to
get your crowd happy and laughing. I was feeling particularly happy on this morning in spite of the deadly monotony
of store life. It was Saturday, the half-holiday, and I was
going to the country where the rabbits and hares were waiting
for me. I was busy getting my table ready when a customer
came in—I was not looking up and did not see her face or
I should have known how to deal with her. She must have
wanted some fluffy little balls of wool for babies shoes but she
did not say so. She came up to me and in a voice that sounded
like a sergeant-major after a drinking bout rapped out ' POM-

POMS!' I didn't bother to look up and answered 'TIDD-LEY-OM POMS!' The lady went almost demented with rage and demanded to see the manager. She would get me 'sacked' as she called it. I have since seen many a hard-working man sacked through the whims of these vinegar-tempered old fossils who often walk through the stores simply looking for trouble. But with me it didn't matter a hoot whether I was 'sacked' or not, my *vardo* was parked twenty miles from London and I was going to it. However, the manager had me on the carpet. He weighed me up in a moment. This man should never have been a manager of a store, he should have been a judge and I've told him so many a time since. He could see the funny side of it although he did not want me to know it. But I had also weighed him up and I could see a wrinkle appear near his eye and a faint dimpling near his mouth. He told me I should use great discretion with customers and never offend them in the slightest way, always say they were right even when wrong, and lots of other 'good' advice as well. Then he questioned me as to who I was and where I came from, and unfortunately his kindness to me at that time led to my working so many moons in a store, his in particular. Three times in three days I was on the carpet, three times I was reprieved. To a lady who asked me peremptorily where she could 'find trunks!' and I replied just as peremptorily, 'On elephants, madam!' I owed the last visit to the manager. I must have beaten the record in the stair-climbing competition to the manager's office, and I have often wondered myself how he put up with me. I think he had himself in earlier days met with some of these 'meadow-ladies' as the shop assistants term them, so as to avoid insulting that placid giver of milk, the gentle cow, and so perhaps he understood that however right the customers can be they can also be deuced annoying.

It was bad enough to have to work under these conditions,

knowing that I could get away when I wanted, but it has made me understand how hard the real shopman and shop-girls' life can be. Had I ever married and had a daughter she would never be allowed to work in a shop. I would a thousand times rather she sold pegs at tuppence a dozen from door to door, in freedom, God's fresh air, and with good food before and after her work. My study of the average shop-girl has shown that they have to catch an early train or 'bus to work. A rush before their work even begins. In some cases I have known girls to travel eighteen to twenty miles to work with no time for a good meal before they leave, nor even did they know what a good meal meant. Ten minutes for a coffee and a bun in the morning ; a glass of milk with a piece of sodden toast and beans for lunch ; a cup of strong tea and a biscuit late in the afternoon, and the train or bus journey home, usually standing, too tired to eat. Can you wonder that these girls and women, earning a wage from fifteen to thirty-five shillings get a little bit irritable toward evening ? If only some of these whom they serve could take over the work for a week or two there would be a difference in the attitude the customer adopts toward the girl behind the counter. I have watched with sorrow and amazement these *gorgio* girls struggling on a pittance to keep parents or even husbands out of work, and the frightened shopmen bullying those below as they are bullied by those above, and have compared them with myself whose captivity was after all only recent and not life-long, happier and more care-free, even in my slave circumstances, than the head director could ever dare dream of being. Still, now and then one meets a woman who puts to shame the bad-tempered crabbed ones who make shop-life even more of a misery than it is. I have in mind one such lady living at Kingston Hill who has always a kind word for the gipsy and a hearty handshake when we meet, writing me letters even when away on holidays. Many a time her happy smile has made my day less dreary, and many a prayer I have said for her, thanking the *kooshti-duval* for giving us such people.

LXXIV

NOT only does one have to put up with the customer in shop-life, but there is another snag : the buyers. Some of these are admirable folk, good at their jobs, particularly in the provincial stores. But there are some, and these are the majority, who set me wondering how they got their jobs and still more extraordinary how they keep them. If some of them had to get their own living with their own brains and capital, they would be bankrupt in a day, and there would be several thousand more added to the moochers on the road. But my mother used to have a saying in Romany that God also provides for the lame and the lazy, and I think I have found the people to whom it most applies. The ' buyer ' is the head of the department in which you work, and as soon as they see you making money (of which, incidentally, they get the biggest share) they get nervous and afraid of being chided for not training their staff to sell properly. They put every obstruction in your way, such as wanting the pitch they have already given you, wanting a bit of your space to put some ' dud ' line on so that your customers shall be buying their goods. One such buyer, a female in the jewellery department of the store where I worked for some time, used to copy my line and deliberately put a ' barker ' near me to try and get off similar lines which I was demonstrating. I have always been copied in my stock by the *gorgios* who seem to have no originality of their own. If I had a new line in the stores the pitchers would gather around, listen to my patter, and in a week or two I would hear that such and such a store had a demonstration almost exactly like it. But I have had the satisfaction of getting one thing on the market, and selling it by the thousand, that I have never yet had a rival at. It was a little device for pleating dresses or cloth, an invention of my own, and it entailed a lot of talking and a lot of hard work using a hot flat-iron, making every known make of pleat and keeping up a rapid fire of patter from morn to night. I broke records wherever I went. I was busily engaged in breaking the record at a big Manchester store and was the envy of them all, when one dapper young man who had been hanging around the crowd for several days told me that I was getting too old to work and if I would teach him the patter and show him the tricks of the trade I could simply lie on the beach at New Brighton while he drew in the gold for us both, and to spare. I thought I would like to teach him a lesson regarding the stamina of the Romanys and I agreed to let him have a try. In three days he was having a rest cure and at the end of a fortnight the demonstration was closed and the firm was writing to me begging me to go back, as the space was mine. I had been taking very good money, he had taken a few pounds in three days, and then went to bed with a sore throat and done like a bad dinner.

My life in the shops has been a revelation to me of the stupidity of the *gorgio*. The lack of enterprise of most buyers is so shocking that I began to feel sorry for the directors and managers. Many a good line I have seen missed through the incivility of the buyers to the commercial travellers. I had one of the best deals of my life from a man who was snubbed by a buyer in a store where I worked for several years. A traveller had a parcel of real rock crystal, the usual price was something like seven and sixpence each wholesale, to be resold at from fifteen shillings to seventeen and sixpence each, in a good store. These were to be sold very cheaply and I learned afterwards that before he could even explain what he had got to sell to the buyers of at least three stores that

morning, he had got an answer with words to the curt effect :
' I don't want to see *your* face to-day ! ' I always feel sorry
for commercial travellers, I suppose because I had so many
snubs myself when I have been peddling my wares from door
to door as a boy, and also when I have been ' canvassing '
(which is what they call hawking when they've a thirty-five
shilling suit on !) and I saw that this particular traveller took
it sadly.

I smiled and said good morning in my usual good-tempered
manner, and asked him how trade was. His reply was short
and to the point : ' Like the temper of your buyer,' he said,
'ROTTEN ! ' Then he poured out his troubles to me.
' Honestly,' he said, ' I don't know how they get their jobs.
I've been running around with a parcel of stones which are
to be nearly given away and I can't get enough civility to
be able even to explain what I've got.' I suggested he should
show them to me, but he said they were not in my line, they
were real crystal sold usually for seven and sixpence and sold
now for two shillings. ' I have a hundred and twelve pounds'
worth of them,' he said mournfully. I looked at one and I
said : ' I'll have a deal with you and give you a level hundred
pounds for the lot.' He argued he couldn't take a penny
less as his firm was caught with a big bill and wanted cash,
otherwise these could not have been sold at such a price. He
gave me the name of the firm, I looked them up in the telephone book, called them up, and closed the deal. I sold
them to customers at five shillings each, half-a-crown less than
the wholesale price. The shop got a huge profit on this deal
of mine, and the only one who looked a fool was the buyer
who had missed the deal. But it made me ponder and I
thought what a pity the directors cannot fix up some real
Romany *chis* and *chals*. They would never let a deal go by.
At least we know the way to buy and what is better we
know how to sell what we have bought, a thing no ' buyer '
seems able to do.

In shop life I found petty restrictions vex one at every turn. Certain doors which one must come in by and other doors one must go out by. I have always used the one nearest to me, and told them to take it or leave it, and because of the money I was making for them—they left it. But not the hundreds of down-trodden people who smile brightly from behind the counter and have to walk half a mile through special doors for fear that by coming in logically by the door nearest their place customers would be offended and never return! In one big store in Manchester the staff was supposed to walk up six flights of stairs, morning and evening, to leave its hat on a hook. I put mine underneath the counter and for the first few weeks while the fight lasted you would have thought nothing so important in the world had ever taken place before as one Romany hat parked under a shop counter instead of six flights up on a peg. My 'eccentricities' as they called them, they had to stand, for the *gorgio* will stand any contretemps or humiliation for money. But who was I to scoff at humiliations? It seemed to me at times that I underwent them every minute of every hour, and the hour had ten thousand minutes and the day stretched into months. I knew in my heart that I had little excuse for myself. I knew why I was doing this thing, undergoing this voluntary imprisonment. I, a free-born Romany, was a thousand times more culpable than these people who were bred for humiliations and slavery and knew no other life.

Sometimes they put me down in underground bargain basements with the electric light burning all day, winter and summer, and with no air but what came thick and musty from the piles of cheap carpets, the foul chemical smell of mountains of bath-towelling and household linen and shoddy blankets, the surging of humanity in tight masses aimlessly wanting to be tempted into buying something it could as well do without. Through the thick grating above my head the feet of the people on the pavements were all I knew to remind me that there was light and air and space above me somewhere. At times I would break away, leave my stand vacant as it stood, and find a park or a green space somewhere and lie down on the grass, lie there for hours feeling I must not move or they would find me, thinking of my childhood days and of my mother with her bright shawl thrown with one deft movement about her head and shoulders like the earliest statues of Greek women, and her *kipsie* on her arm, and the way she would turn at the *vardo* door, look in my direction, and by the merest tilt of her head indicate that it was I who was to go with her to the village. Some seasons they gave me a pitch upstairs. There at least there was an effect of light, and one could see the sunshine streaking down through the windows and know that one was still on this earth and not in an electrically-lit inferno that had no seasons and no ending. The sunshine would stream down all the week and I would long for Saturday and plan to go herbing on Sunday morning and rabbiting in the evening, and lie out in the sun and smoke at my *vardo* door. And on Saturdays and Sundays the rain would pour down in torrents from black skies. Again and again this would happen and on the Monday morning the sun would come bright again. I used to think it was just for me that this happened. I thought the good God was angry with me for sacrificing for gold the brief time He had given me. It seemed to me that it was all a vengeance on me for shutting myself up in a *gorgio* prison when He had given me the key to freedom at my birth.

I used to think that soon I would become like the young man I met in a provincial store, where they made us all board-in. I used to think the episode excruciatingly funny and tell it to make people laugh, but I have grown wiser since and I think it is one of those very funny things that are so tragic that one laughs to keep from understanding the deeper significance. I had to share a cubby-hole of a room with an assistant from the drapery department. He was an anxious negative youth, a most harmless specimen by day, but a dreadful menace by night. He was obsessed by fear and anxiety for his job as by ten devils, and as far as I could see no charm of mine could exorcise this particular sort.

Night after night, hour after hour, he would make the night hideous by talking in his sleep. He would sit on the edge of his bed and he would begin in a bright smarmy salesman's voice : ' YES, modom, and what can I do for you to-day, modom ? O yes, modom, we have it plain *or* striped, modom. Yes, this is a very nice one, modom, a very nice one indeed. Quite one of the nicest we stock, in fact, modom. Yes, and quite new, modom. Absolutely the first season this pattern has been offered. Four yards, modom ? Not four yards and a quarter, to be on the safe side, modom ? O ! ONLY four, thank you, modom.' Crick—crick-crick—crick, here he would tear off four imaginary yards. ' FOUR yards at one and three, three-farthing, modom, yes (crick—crick)— that's five and threepence if you please, modom. Pay at the desk, will you please, while I wrap the parcel up."

Here there would be a slight pause while, I suppose, he kept his eye on the lady to see that she really did pay at the desk. But it didn't last. Immediately another urgent customer claimed his attention. ' Calico ? modom. Lovely calico, modom, an entirely new line ! Six yards, yes, modom, that is *quite* sufficient, modom. Yes—yes—I quite agree, modom. Six at one nine and a half, that will be ten and nine, modom. And it's *wonderful* material, modom, we can recommend it, modom. Never had a complaint yet, modom. Never ! ' That one would go off to pay at the desk too while he crick—crick—crick-d off and made up the parcel.

One night as I lay listening to his yes-modoms-four-yards-at-three-three-modom—CRICK—crick—C-R-I-C-K, the tearing sounded suspiciously real, and in the morning my suspicions proved only too well founded. He had crick—crick—cricked my shirt in three bits and I decided it was time to put an end to this night-shopping that was making me *bilaco*. I had to wait several nights for my chance, but one night sooner than I had dared hope it came. He was steaming away ' Yes, modom, very hard wearing material *indeed*, modom. *Very*, modom. Oh, but I assure you, modom, indeed, modom, yes, modom, just this plain poplin then, modom ? ' when he suddenly said, ' Three yards at two and eleven, modom, that comes to five and eight, modom.' I leapt up in bed and shouted : ' You're *wrong*! IT'S FIVE AND NINE ! YOU'RE SACKED !' He was so shocked by this terrible news that he fell off the bed with a bump, and he never sold another thing that night !

LXXV

Now in a little yard in Brighouse they are building for me the home which is to take me to freedom. From now on all I shall ask of the *kooshti duval* is to finish my days as I began them. I shall not envy those who earn their thousands ; I shall not again compete. My shining new *vardo* will take me on the road again far from the restless teeming life of London's melancholy streets, to where the eels abound in the ponds and rivers and where the rabbits and hares are waiting for me with my smoker and snare. Where the *hotchi-witchi* is still rolled in a ball in the *bouri* and where the cooking will be done on the embers of a gleaming *kash-yag* as my fore-bears cooked down the ages and as my mother taught me. No more stale water from the tap, but made crystal clear with a gipsy filter, water as it has come from the skies. I shall make my *kini* from the wild flowers and the meadows will supply my mushrooms and the hedgerows my tonics and medicines. If I get wet through I shall get dry again. At last I shall go back to the fields, to the streams, and the trees, and to the sea where I can gather samphire for my pickles, and shell-fish as I need them.   The birds shall have their share of my crumbs in return for their songs.   I think the birds sing sweetest to a gipsy.

Waiting to take me back on the road is my new *vardo*, designed by myself, finished in the wood my mother loved, the *kash* of the *akhor kopaci*, the walnut tree wood, though the rubber tyres and the springs are luxuries she would not recognise, for of these she never dreamed.   Mirrors line the walls engraved with her favourite design, the *lulagis*, and the colours of the upholstery are those she loved the best, lilac and straw.   There is a silver-plated stove and there is a bed, not too soft, but softer than the straw on which I was born. There is a little kneeling pad on which each night I can thank my Maker for giving me the mother I had, full of knowledge, power, and wisdom.

GLOSSARY

(Alb. Rom.) Albanian Romany.
(E.) English.
(K.) Kant or Slang Romany.

(R.) English Romany.
(S.) Slang used by market
    men and tramps.

Ake There is.

Akha Eye.

Akhas or *Argas* (Àlb. Rom.) Eyes.

Akhor (Alb. Rom.) Walnut.

Alev (R.) Name (title.)

Ande (R.) Into

Andre (R.) Inside.

Angar (R.) Coals.

Angar-yag Coal fire.

Ari (R.) Gold.

Auko (R.) Here

Avri (R.) Outside.

Baula-mull-engro (R.) Pork butcher.

Baulo-moosh (R.) Pig-keeper.

Beren (R.) Ship.

Beren-engro (R.) Sailor.

Bichadey-pawdel (R.) Banishment, prison.

Bilaco (R.) Soft, balmy (as village idiot.)

Bilovem (Alb. Rom.) Free, independent.

Blink-fencer (K.) Spectacle seller.

Boro (R.) Big or high.

Boro divvas (R.) Great day (such as feast or wedding.)

Boro-doriav (R.) Ocean.

Boro-drom (R.) Highway (or high road.)

Boro-gavaste (R.) Big town (or city.)

Boro-rani (R.) Big lady.

Boro-rye (R.) Big, man, Sir or Lord.

Bosa (Alb. Rom.) Fiddle.

Bosa-veno (Alb. Rom.) Fiddler.

Bosh (K.) Fiddle.

Bouri (R.) Hedge.

Bouri-cannie (R.) Pheasant (lit. hedgechicken.)

Bouri-pennen (R.) A gathering under the hedge (a conference.)

Bubbo (Negro) Baby

Bunce (K.) Profits.

Buskers (K.) Singers.

Busking (K.) Singing in the street or at the seaside.

Busni (R.) Those who are not Romany.

Cambri (R.) Enciente.

Cannie (R.) Chicken.

Cannie-moosh (R.) Bird-keeper or gamekeeper.

Caneegra (R.) Hare.

Chal (R.) Boy.

Chals (R.) Boys.

Chavi (R.) Child.

Chavis (R.) Children.

Chelav (Alb. Rom.) To play.

Chelav dur bosa (Alb. Rom.) To play the fiddle.

Cherinos (Alb. Rom.) Stars.

Chi (R.) Girl.

Chib (R.) Language.

Chis (R.) Girls.

Chiv (R.) Knife.

Chiv barrer (K.) Knife grinder.

Chockers (K.) Boots.

Choora (Alb. Rom.) Stop.

Choovahanees (R.) Witches.

Choovahani (R.) Wizard.

Chop to (K.) To change.

Chorar (*chorah*) (Alb. Rom.) Steal.

Chun (Alb. Rom.) One month.

Chuna (Alb. Rom.) Moon.

Coggies (K.) Turnips.

Coor (R.) To strike or fight.

Coor the drom (K.) Tramping (lit. striking the road.)

Coored (R.) Thrashed.

Corora (Alb. Rom.) Blind.

Covantza (R.) Anvil.

Crocus (K.) Quack doctor.

Dav (R.) Give.

Del (*della*) (R.) Hit.

Diddikai (R.) Half-bred Romany.

Dik (R.) Look (see.)

Dikked (R.) Looked.

Dickey (K.) Donkey.

Dindilo (Alb. Rom.) Idiot.

Dloova (R.) Money.

Doriav (R.) Sea.

Drom (R.) Road.

Dui-rommerin (R.) Double wedding (one at church, other by Romany ritual.)

Duk (R.) Hand.

Dukkerin (R.) Fortune-telling.

Dukkeripen (R.) Hand-reading.

Duvel (R.) God (or Christ.)

Duveleskoe (R.) Religious (God-fearing.)

Engala (R.) Cuddle.

Engro (R.) Maker.

Fakir (R.) Worker or mender.

Filisin (R.) Mansion.

Furo (Alb. Rom.) Oven.

Gavaste (R.) Town.

Gees (S.) Men who help grafter to force up bidding for sales.

Gillie (R.) Song.

Gils (R.) Sing.

Gojaver (R.) Clever.

Gorgio (R.) Non-Romany.

Grafter (S.) Worker.

Grouven (R.) Cow.

Grye (R.) Horse.

Grye-kuper (R.) Horse-dealers.

Guglo (R.) Sweet.

Gyas (R.) She.

Habben (R.) Food.

Hotchi-witchi (R.) Hedgehog.

Joskins(S.) Farm labourers.

Juggal (R.) Dog.

Juvval (R.) Flapper.

Kant (R.) Word for diddikai language.

Kash (R.) Wood.

Kash-yag (R.) Wood fire.

Kep (R.) Bed.

Kil (R.) Play.

Kil-i-bosh (K.) Play the fiddle.

Kini (Alb. Rom.) Wine.

Kip (K.) Bed.

Klizina (R.) Key.

Klizinen (R.) Locked.

Kooshti (R.) Good.

Kooshtichat (R.) The good thing.

Kooshti-Duval or *Duvel* (R.) The Good God or Duvee.

Kozac (R.) Pamper.

Kuster (R.) Ride.

Kustered (R.) Rode.

Lav (R.) Word.

Lekki (R.) His or her.

Lels (R.) Buys.

Len (R.) Had.

Levnerker (R.) Public-house.

Lil (R.) Book.

Lir (R.) Cheap.

Lulagis (R.) Flowers.

Mandi (R.) Me.

Manricli (R.) Cake.

Mastengro (R.) Butcher.

Mauleys (R.) Fists.

Maung (R.) To beg.

Merno (R.) Mine.

Moocher (K.) Beggar.

Mooch (K.) To beg.

Moosh (R.) Man.

Moosh-mulled-racklo (R.) Widow.

Mug-fakir (K.) Photographer.

Mullah (R.) Spirit, ghost.

Mulled (R.) Dead.

Mulled-moosh-engro (R.) Literally dead-man-maker (our name for Doctor.)

Mull-puv (R.) (lit. burying-field.) Graveyard

Mush (K.) Umbrella.

Mush-fakir (K.) Umbrella-mender.

Nanechib (R.) Dumb (mute.)
Nanti (R.) Never.
Nav (R.) Name.
Noki (R.) Either.

Odi (R.) All.
Opre (R.) Up.

Paddencan (K.) Tramps ' hotel.'
Patteran (R.) Design.
Parni (R.) Rain or water.
Patrin (R.) Leaf.
Ped (R.) Tramping.
Pellengro (R.) Grey or dappled.
Pennen (R.) Telling.
Phral (R.) Brother.
Plastramengros (R.) Policemen.
Plen (R.) Hill.
Poci (R). Pocket.
Pus (R.) Straw.
Puv (R.) Field.
Puvengra (R.) Potato.
Prunellas (E.) Descendants of Spaniards.

Racklers (R.) Women.
Racklo (R.) Woman.
Rat (R.) Night.
Rati (R.) Blood.
Rikkeni (R.) Beautiful.
Rig (R.) Carry.
Rokker (R.) Speak.
Rom (R.) Husband (also male.)
Rommered (R.) Married.

Rommerin (R.) Marriage (wedding.)
Rovel (R.) Wife.

San (R.) Are.
Santekash (R.) Health-wood (willow.)
Sapengros (R.) Snake-charmers.
Sasto (R.) Well.
Sastra (R.) Iron.
Scarper (S.) Run away.
Seal of the day (S.) Good morning or good afternoon, whichever time it is.
Shallow-runner (S.) Tramp who begs old clothes.
Sherengro (R.) Chief.
Shooshie (K.) Rabbit.
Sor (R.) Elderly.
Spiel (S.) Showman's patter.
Stiga (R.) Door.
Suv (R.) Needle.
Svegla (R.) Pipe.

Tadivvas (R.) To-day.
Tan (R.) Tent.
Tarni (R.) Young.
Tarno (R.) Little.
Tarno Roy (R.) Prince.
Tarots (R.) Fortune cards.
Tasaulor (R.) To-morrow.
Tatcho (R.) Genuine, true.
Tatting (S.) Collecting rags and bottles, etc.

GLOSSARY

Tele (R.) Down.
Tober (S.) Pitch for stall.
Toovla (R.) Tobacco.
Trin (R.) Three.
Trin chun (R.) Three months.
Truppo (R.) Body.
Tute or *Tutti* (R.) You.

Vardo (R.) Caravan.
Vek (R.) With.

Wafodi (R.) Bad.
Wendror (R.) Entrails.

Yag (R.) Fire.
Yagged (R.) Burnt.
Yagging (R.) Burning.
Yanaheim (R.) Lucky words.

Zingari (R.) Gipsy Romani.

Lightning Source UK Ltd.
Milton Keynes UK

176838UK00001B/40/P